Derivative Images

Edinburgh Studies in Film and Intermediality
Series editors: Martine Beugnet and Kriss Ravetto
Founding editor: John Orr

A series of scholarly research intended to challenge and expand on the various approaches to film studies, bringing together film theory and film aesthetics with the emerging intermedial aspects of the field. The volumes combine critical theoretical interventions with a consideration of specific contexts, aesthetic qualities, and a strong sense of the medium's ability to appropriate current technological developments in its practice and form as well as in its distribution.

Advisory board
Duncan Petrie (University of Auckland)
John Caughie (University of Glasgow)
Dina Iordanova (University of St Andrews)
Elizabeth Ezra (University of Stirling)
Gina Marchetti (University of Hong Kong)
Jolyon Mitchell (University of Edinburgh)
Judith Mayne (The Ohio State University)
Dominique Bluher (Harvard University)

Titles in the series include:

Romantics and Modernists in British Cinema
John Orr

Framing Pictures: Film and the Visual Arts
Steven Jacobs

The Sense of Film Narration
Ian Garwood

The Feel-Bad Film
Nikolaj Lübecker

American Independent Cinema: Rites of Passage and the Crisis Image
Anna Backman Rogers

The Incurable-Image: Curating Post-Mexican Film and Media Arts
Tarek Elhaik

Screen Presence: Cinema Culture and the Art of Warhol, Rauschenberg, Hatoum and Gordon
Stephen Monteiro

Indefinite Visions: Cinema and the Attractions of Uncertainty
Martine Beugnet, Allan Cameron and Arild Fetveit (eds)

Screening Statues: Sculpture and Cinema
Steven Jacobs, Susan Felleman, Vito Adriaensens and Lisa Colpaert

Drawn From Life: Issues and Themes in Animated Documentary Cinema
Jonathan Murray and Nea Ehrlich (eds)

Intermedial Dialogues: The French New Wave and the Other Arts
Marion Schmid

The Museum as a Cinematic Space: The Display of Moving Images in Exhibitions
Elisa Mandelli

Theatre Through the Camera Eye: The Poetics of an Intermedial Encounter
Laura Sava

Caught In-Between: Intermediality in Contemporary Eastern Europe and Russian Cinema
Ágnes Pethő

No Power Without an Image: Icons Between Photography and Film
Libby Saxton

Cinematic Intermediality: Theory and Practice
Kim Knowles and Marion Schmid (eds)

Animating Truth: Documentary and Visual Culture in the 21st Century
Nea Ehrlich

Derivative Images: Financial Derivatives in French Film, Literature and Thought
Calum Watt

Visit the Edinburgh Studies in Film website at www.edinburghuniversitypress.com/series/ESIF

Derivative Images
Financial Derivatives in French Film, Literature and Thought

Calum Watt

EDINBURGH
University Press

Edinburgh University Press is one of the leading university presses in the UK. We publish academic books and journals in our selected subject areas across the humanities and social sciences, combining cutting-edge scholarship with high editorial and production values to produce academic works of lasting importance. For more information visit our website: edinburghuniversitypress.com

© Calum Watt, 2022, 2024

This book is part of a project that has received funding from the European Union's Horizon 2020 research and innovation programme under grant agreement N°708042

Edinburgh University Press Ltd
The Tun – Holyrood Road
12(2f) Jackson's Entry
Edinburgh EH8 8PJ

First published in hardback by Edinburgh University Press 2022

Typeset in 11/13 Adobe Garamond Pro
IDSUK (DataConnection) Ltd,
Croydon, CR0 4YY

A CIP record for this book is available from the British Library

ISBN 978 1 4744 8645 3 (hardback)
ISBN 978 1 4744 8646 0 (paperback)
ISBN 978 1 4744 8647 7 (webready PDF)
ISBN 978 1 4744 8648 4 (epub)

The right of Calum Watt to be identified as the author of this work has been asserted in accordance with the Copyright, Designs and Patents Act 1988, and the Copyright and Related Rights Regulations 2003
(SI No. 2498).

Contents

List of Figures vii
Acknowledgements viii

Introduction: The 2008 Financial Crisis, Film and Literature 1

1. Lordon and the 2008 Crisis 15
   D'un retournement l'autre 15
   'Une image bien choisie qui fait bouillir les sangs':
      Images and Affects 22
   Lordon, Images and Committed Art 25
   The Anarchic Condition 28

2. The Saints of the Crisis: Larnaudie and Stiegler in the
   Oversight Committee Room 36
   Les Effondrés and the Collapse of Market Ideology 36
   Greenspan before Congress 41
   Prolétarisation and Transvaluation 49

3. The Derivative in Film and Literary Theory 59
   Derivatives and Nonknowledge 59
   Derivative Images 68
   Is the Psyche a Market? 77
   Derivative Creativity 81
   Conclusion 84

4. Trading in Images: The Case of Kerviel 96
   Screens within Screens 96
   Kerviel at Société Générale 97
   Trading as *métier*, the Trader as Functionary 106
   Suicide and Société Générale 109

5. Derivative Films 124
   Effacing the Visual Currency: *The Fountainhead* 124
   'L'argent est un bien public': *Film Socialisme* 134
   'The images are there for the taking': *Film Catastrophe* 143

6. Dreaming Futures 155
   Argent and Value 155
   'Fin de règne': *Rêver sous le capitalisme* 161
   'Ça imprime, ça imprime': *L'Époque, Escaparates* 166

Conclusion: Ambivalences of the Derivative 178

Select Bibliography 181
Select Filmography 186
Index 187

Figures

1.1	The banker explains structured finance. *Le Grand Retournement* (Gérard Mordillat, 2013)	20
1.2	Diagram of an asset-backed security (from *Jusqu'à quand?*, p. 61)	21
2.1	Henry Waxman, 23 October 2008	44
2.2	Alan Greenspan testifies before Congress, 23 October 2008	46
4.1	*L'Outsider* (Christophe Barratier, 2016)	96
4.2	*L'Outsider* (Christophe Barratier, 2016)	97
4.3	Screen-capture taken from 'Société générale: produits de bourse' advert (2006)	100
4.4	*L'Outsider* (Christophe Barratier, 2016)	110
4.5	*L'Outsider* (Christophe Barratier, 2016)	111
4.6	*L'Outsider* (Christophe Barratier, 2016)	111
5.1	*The Fountainhead* (King Vidor, 1949)	129
5.2	*The Fountainhead* (Société Réaliste, 2010)	129
5.3	*The Fountainhead* (King Vidor, 1949)	130
5.4	*The Fountainhead* (Société Réaliste, 2010)	130
5.5	Gross capital flows as a percentage of world GDP	131
5.6	The coin pusher. *Film Socialisme* (Jean-Luc Godard, 2010)	140
5.7	*Film Catastrophe* (Paul Grivas, 2018)	145
5.8	*Film Catastrophe* (Paul Grivas, 2018)	145
5.9	*Film Catastrophe* (Paul Grivas, 2018)	146
5.10	Script for *Film Socialisme* in *L'Incomparable du pas comparable* (Paul Grivas, 2018)	147
5.11	Maris and Maloubier in *L'Incomparable du pas comparable* (Paul Grivas, 2018)	147
6.1	French monthly net income distribution (from *Argent*, p. 7)	156
6.2	*Rêver sous le capitalisme* (Sophie Bruneau, 2018)	165
6.3	*L'Époque* (Matthieu Bareyre, 2018)	169

Acknowledgements

I wrote this book while enjoying a Marie Skłodowska-Curie Individual Fellowship (2016–18) and subsequently as a *chercheur associé* at l'Institut de recherche sur le cinéma et l'audiovisuel (IRCAV) at the Sorbonne Nouvelle. I am grateful to the European Commission/Horizon 2020 for the funding that made this research possible and to IRCAV for hosting me and providing such a stimulating environment while I researched and wrote this book.

For discussions on the subject of this book and various other forms of assistance in the course of its writing I would like to thank: Rabia Aok, François Athané, the staff of the Baron Rouge, Muriel Berthou Crestey, Jean-Pierre Bertin-Maghit, Alex Chester, Curtis Chomley, Laurent Creton, Martin Crowley, Marine Eyraud, Patrick ffrench, Evgenia Giannouri, Martin Goutte, Nigel Harkness, Christophe Henry, Alasdair King, Pierre Lautridou, Sebastien Layerle, Jacob McGuinn, Solange Manche, Richard Mason, Lisyane Mercadier, Juliana Park, Bruno Péquignot, Ewa Rakowska, Alain Sacrez, Guillaume Soulez and Beatriz Tadeo Fuica. For participating in the *journée d'étude* and film screening evening I organised in 2018, I thank Davide Abbatescianni, Lionel Bernardin, Jeanne Delafosse, Laura Kalba, Martin Le Chevallier, Anne Mulhall, Martin O'Shaughnessy, Constantin Parvulescu, Quentin Ravelli and Sarah Waters. For offering interviews drawn on in the book: Ferenc Gróf, Mathieu Larnaudie, Anna Malagrida and the late Bernard Stiegler. For permission to reproduce images: Archives Historiques Société Générale, Frédéric Lordon and Éditions Amsterdam. I also wish to thank Martine Beugnet, Kriss Ravetto-Biagioli, Gillian Leslie and the anonymous peer-reviewers for Edinburgh University Press, all of whose comments helped sharpen the book's focus at a critical stage. I am grateful to Christian Gosselin for allowing me to use his image 'Cosmos plus ou moins proche' (2018) for the book's cover.

Parts of this book have previously appeared as articles:

- 'L'image est-elle un produit dérivé? *Film Catastrophe*, la théorie du cinéma et la crise financière de 2008', *Théorème*, 'Crise, quelle crise? Cinéma, audiovisuel, nouveaux médias', 34 (2022).

- '"Une image bien choisie qui fait bouillir les sangs": Frédéric Lordon and the 2008 Financial Crisis', *Nottingham French Studies*, 60:1 (2021), 33–49.
- 'The Legend of Saint Alan: Larnaudie and Stiegler in the Oversight Committee Room', *French Cultural Studies*, 31:3 (Autumn 2020), 173–84.
- 'Iconomy of the Derivative Image: Effacing the visual currency in Société Réaliste's *The Fountainhead*', *NECSUS: European Journal of Media Studies*, 8:2 (Autumn 2019), 71–90.
- '"Money is a Public Good": Godard's *Film Socialisme* (2010) and Bernard Maris', *Studies in French Cinema*, 19:1 (2019), 40–54.

For Pierre

Introduction: The 2008 Financial Crisis, Film and Literature

The 2008 global financial crisis originated in the US subprime mortgage market in 2007 and reached a climax in September 2008. The US went into recession at the end of 2007, followed by several European countries in 2008–9, the crisis of eurozone public debt beginning in 2010. In his history of the financial crises, Adam Tooze argues that, despite popular beliefs in both Europe and the US, the eurozone crisis is the direct consequence of the 2008 financial crisis, 'a massive aftershock of the earthquake in the North Atlantic financial system of 2008, working its way out with a time lag through the labyrinthine political framework of the EU'.[1] The idea, then, that 2008 was an American or Anglo-Saxon crisis is 'deeply misleading'.[2]

This is a book about intellectual and artistic responses in France to a crisis that arose in the US but which implicated the world. The book develops a theoretical argument about the relation between images and finance in the post-crash period through an analysis of the representation of the financial crisis in a selection of contemporary French films and texts. The central hypothesis is that financial instruments and especially derivatives are taken up as a conceptual resource for thinking about creative practice and the circulation of media images in the post-crash world. This thinking of images through derivatives is the first and central sense that I give to the phrase 'derivative images'.[3] More generally, the book shows how the concepts at the heart of this crash – primarily derivatives, but also notions such as the market and exchange – have been creatively recuperated by theorists to think about images. Key moments of the history of the crisis and its fallout are sketched in the course of the book (the acute political fallout in Chapters 1 and 2, the nature of derivatives and their application in film and literary theory in Chapter 3, the Kerviel affair in Chapter 4, the transatlantic interbank lending seizure in Chapter 5, and the social consequences of the crisis in Chapter 6).

When one starts to think about the financial crisis, one must first address the word 'crisis', a word that several of the writers surveyed in this book dislike, dispute or seek to qualify.[4] For some writers, referring to 2008 as a crisis masks a chronic condition in which 'neoliberalism' has governed by means of 'crisis' since the 1970s.[5] For others, the financial crisis cannot be seen as a discrete event but must be considered as part of a wider systemic crisis, which has political, economic, ecological and other dimensions.[6] However, continual talk of some omnipresent and singular condition of *la crise* is potentially paralysing, giving the false impression that everything was previously fine and now one is stuck in crisis.[7] As the philosopher Myriam Revault D'Allonnes shows, while crisis at its Greek root signifies 'decision' or 'judgement' within an uncertain process, today it means a seemingly permanent state of indecision.[8]

As Edgar Morin suggests on the republication of his seminal 1976 essay 'Pour une crisologie' ('Towards a Science of Crises'), the notion of 'crisis' must be deployed prudently as it has become overused.[9] Crisis in his account refers to the growth of disorder in a given system (which could refer to everything from an individual through to a whole civilisation) caused by the blockage of regulatory functions and by the release of hitherto latent virtualities.[10] Crises are structural features of the complex systems through which human life develops, releasing intellectual and research activity, which may take the form of diagnosis, of corrections, of contestation of given orders, and of creation and innovation, or alternatively pathological solutions like scapegoating, messianism and other forms of magical thinking.[11] Crises are thus in essence marked by ambivalence: they may give rise to progressive or regressive solutions, or both at once to varying degrees.[12] More recently, Evelyne Grossman, in *La Créativité de la crise* (2020), has suggested Morin's account of crises releasing creative forces is a somewhat sterile dialectic that needs to be complicated. Informed by psychoanalysis and literature, Grossman thinks of crisis less dialectically in terms of psychic disequilibrium within the self or between the self and the world, which would be close to the source of creativity and which changes us; we may, for example, become interested in things that we hitherto had no interest in.[13]

In retrospect, it became clear rather soon that the 2008 financial crisis in the first instance gave way to regressive solutions in the form of economic austerity policies. Some ten years on from events, the sociologist Ève Chiapello remarks that while it looked during the acute period of the crisis as if it might be the occasion for a change in models of capitalist governance, in fact it was already clear by 2009 that 'critical forces were incapable of introducing a balance of power that would enable them to be taken into consideration'.[14] Revault D'Allonnes argues that crisis is not a concept but a metaphor with a long history.[15] This should not be taken as a deficiency, for metaphors tend to nourish reflection as 'antichambres de la formation des concepts' ('antechambers in the development of concepts').[16] In this sense, I will argue that one of the positive outcomes of the crisis has been the uptake of financial derivatives as a metaphor for thought, which in turn generates practical projects. This resulted from the fact that derivatives garnered a great deal of public attention due to their contribution to the 2008 debacle.

There is no doubt that 2008 feeds into a wider sense of crisis associated with the condition of work in postindustrial capitalism.[17] The philosopher Jean-Paul Dollé remarks that while the 2008 crisis seems to resemble the crisis of 1929 and others, it sets itself apart by its omnipresence, seemingly touching every field of human endeavour and every corner of the globe, and yet its spatial coordinates are difficult to fix.[18] Even what we call 'the financial crisis' is multiple: there is first the banking crisis (in which loans went bad), then the crisis of public finances (public debt and austerity), and then the crisis of the 'real economy' (stagnation and joblessness).[19] The second-order consequences of 2008 have included rising unemployment, identitarian retreat and anti-immigrant politics. The policy responses to the crisis also changed our understanding of the function of central banks and monetary creation. As the philosopher and economist Frédéric Lordon – a key figure in this study – suggests, it is typical of major crises to put everything in question.[20] Lordon remarks that in moments of crisis there is a need for a 'dé-division de travail' ('de-division or sharing of labour'), which, if it is not done in universities (likely being over-specialised), will be done outside.[21] By this he means that the economy has for too long been left to economists, and must be reshaped by involving people from all domains of life. All of this calls for an intermedial and interdisciplinary approach. As Leigh Claire La Berge puts it: 'At the moment, finance might be the interdisciplinary object par excellence, perhaps second only to digital humanities.'[22] It is in something of this spirit that this book is situated at the intersection of literary and film theory, French studies and critical studies of finance.

The 2008 financial crisis has catalysed study into the relation between culture (especially visual culture) and financial capital. Today the 'economic humanities' is an exciting area of research.[23] Within academic writing on 2008 and film and literature, we can roughly distinguish between, on the one hand, studies dealing more or less directly with the representation of the crisis and its fallout, and, on the other, more theoretical reflections on the relation between finance and culture.[24] This book aims to straddle this divide. Many of the works I discuss are only obliquely about the financial crisis, but I argue that the crisis forms a decisive context for them. Film and literature are sites within a wider contestation of the significance of the financial crisis; that is, they are sites within what sociologists, drawing on the work of the philosopher Cornelius Castoriadis, have called a 'struggle between different types of imagination' – a struggle between a 'rational' market imaginary and alternative, potentially social visions of the future.[25] What I call 'derivative images' is one particular – and a particularly ambivalent – constellation of the imagination arising from the financial crisis.

Why look at French work on this topic? Alice Béja argues that France has, in contrast to the Anglo-Saxon world, produced relatively few representations of the crisis.[26] Critics have suggested that the rare French films on the subject of the financial crash struggle to explain the economic complexity of the event.[27] This is not a new phenomenon. Discussing a number of French films from the 1970s and 1980s, Diane Gabrysiak writes that they contribute to the mystification of finance and fail to illuminate its mechanisms.[28] Noting that the crisis has had a bigger effect on cultural production and the humanities than on their own field, French sociologists of finance have generally found what they call 'finance-fiction' films (typically of the Hollywood variety) to be lacking, tending to rely on stereotypes.[29] Even in the realm of documentary, films tend to concentrate on the effects rather than the causes of financial crises.[30] However, the vibrancy of French-language film and cultural theory related to economic questions is suggested by the essays in the catalogue accompanying Peter Szendy's 2020 exhibition at Jeu de Paume, *Le Supermarché des images* (*The Supermarket of Images*).[31] Szendy's work exemplifies a French tradition of film theory which offers particularly rich resources for rethinking the nexus between finance and images in the shadow of the crash because of the facility – or better, sensibility – with which certain French thinkers treat 'images' on a single plane. Szendy's notion of *iconomy*, of a 'general economy of images', is one example of this, discussed in Chapter 3.

The problem of the representability of the financial crisis in general has been most clearly articulated by the cultural critics Alberto Toscano and Jeff Kinkle, who write:

> In a period when images of social and environmental collapse are ubiquitous in all spheres of culture [. . .] cinematic depictions of the ongoing economic crisis have been comparatively sparse, and rarely compelling. [. . .] Filmmakers have struggled to incorporate economic turmoil into their works without reverting to some long-standing and ultimately comforting tropes: families reuniting to overcome economic hardship, the machismo and malevolence of stockbrokers, the corrosive power of greed. Whether in fiction or documentary, the temptation has been not so much to dramatise as to *personify* systemic and impersonal phenomena, resolving widespread anxiety and hardship either into the simplistic identification of culprits or into the backdrop for the trials and tribulations of the nuclear family and the aspirational individual. [. . .] [I]t is the centrality of finance to the current crisis that poses representational problems of its own, namely the forbidding mathematical and legal complexity of the financial instruments (derivatives, CDOs, CDSs, etc.) at the heart of the crisis.[32]

In this book I respond to Toscano and Kinkle's valuable and influential argument – that more representations of 2008 and finance in general are needed which better 'map' the flows of contemporary finance capitalism – by proposing that the works in my study generally tend to displace the issue of the representability of the 2008 crisis by thinking the derivative at the level of form. The question, then, becomes less how images can be used to map derivative finance than the effects of the derivative on images and our relation to them. In this sense, throughout this book one should see the notion of 'derivative images' as an implicit alternative to Toscano and Kinkle's argument. The risk throughout will be of falling into an 'aesthetic of capital'.[33]

Film, it goes without saying, has a long and deep historical connection to finance,[34] while the generative interaction more broadly between images and money goes back even further.[35] The derivative as an aesthetic concept should thus be situated within a longer history of economic conceptions of the literary or artistic work. For Jean-Michel Rey, for example, the modern condition of the work of art, which begins with a gesture of simultaneously crediting and unworking itself, mirrors that of an economic system based on credit and its immediate failure, a situation stretching back paradigmatically to the John Law scandal and the collapse of the French banking system in 1720.[36] In this book I am indebted to the sociologist Randy Martin's notion of a 'social logic of the derivative' (discussed in Chapter 3), characterised by the bundling of dispersed elements and the attachment of the future to the present within a context of volatility.[37] In this way, Martin gives us a clue to how we can break down the various protocols that make up derivative finance in order to identify them within a wider social or, I would argue, aesthetic logic. In other words, what would it mean to conceive of a literary or filmic work *as* a derivative or other financial instrument; that is, to think or imagine the financial derivative as, so to speak, superimposed over the work of art? Throughout we will be particularly interested in such metaphors which construct images *as* derivatives or currencies. This is one of the core senses of 'derivative images'.

Theoretical reflection on the questions evoked above is pursued through detailed close readings of a constellation of post-2008 French and francophone literary, filmic and theoretical texts. My corpus is typified (with the notable exception of the Kerviel material mentioned below) by relatively low-budget films and experimental literary texts which are also in some sense theoretical or speculative interventions tending to transgress generic and medial boundaries. The parameters for this corpus of study – at once relatively broad across media and narrow in temporal and linguistic specificity – are a function, firstly, of the hypothesis that 2008 marks a significant growth in awareness of derivatives generally, and, secondly, of the fact that the derivative – a vector for all kinds of convertibility – is inherently interdisciplinary and intermedial. These terms, like the derivative, are a matter of operating through in-between spaces, like an arbitrage within a spread.

'Doubtless the derivative is another way of thinking interdisciplinarity, one that draws attention to the epistemic arbitrage undertaken by those who operate between fields.'[38] The chosen texts offer a way of thinking the derivative in such a way that it might be empowering or productive for individuals and their creative practices, without negating the inherent ambivalence of the derivative. We are dealing partly with cases of conscious appropriation (see Chapter 3) and partly with a more general speculative argument whereby the works evince what we might think of as an aesthetic logic of the derivative (see Chapters 5 and 6). In that sense, I argue that an important dimension of what we think of as the financialisation of culture is the creative appropriation of financial concepts by writers, artists and theoreticians as a schema for thinking both the circulation of images as well as their own practice. Here the financialisation of culture is not so much something culture passively undergoes, but also reveals the potential of culture to repurpose financial concepts and protocols.[39]

While broadly sketching the impact of the financial crisis in France, noting how the French bank BNP Paribas saw one of its early flash points in August 2007, Chapter 1 analyses the way Frédéric Lordon engages with this history. The main focus is on Lordon's satirical play written in Alexandrine verse and loosely based on the Sarkozy government's response to the financial crisis, *D'un retournement l'autre: Comédie sérieuse sur la crise financière. En quatre actes, et en alexandrins* ('From One Turnaround to Another: Serious Comedy about the Financial Crisis', 2011), and its film adaptation by the prolific left-wing director and writer Gérard Mordillat, *Le Grand Retournement* ('The Great Reversal', 2013). The chapter contextualises Lordon's play, its style and its conceptual aims within his wider intellectual project, which draws on Marx and Spinoza to provide a theory of how affects underpin social and political structures, and also reads the play in relation to his more recent activism and engagement with documentary filmmaking. Lordon has long been interested in crises of capitalism and he argues that what is distinct about 2008 is the centrality of financial derivatives. After drawing out Lordon's understanding of crucial terms such as 'crisis', 'image' and 'affect', I compare the ways Lordon demystifies derivative finance and its often translingual vocabulary in both his play and his economic writings. Through a comparison between a diagram explaining the anatomy of a derivative financial product found in Lordon's economic writings and a moment in *Le Grand Retournement* in which a banker scribbles on a whiteboard in a bid to 'explain' structured finance to the president, I argue that there is a tension between how Lordon wants to explain the crisis and at the same time inspire the desire for radical political change in his audience, which he suggests is possible through the use of affective images (broadly conceived) 'which make one's blood boil'. Surveying Lordon's subsequent turn away from theatre and his increasingly visible activism in various protest movements and critique of established media outlets in the decade since he wrote the play, as well as the relative lack of success for his brand of politics in this period, the chapter concludes by asking critically how useful Lordon's play – and the concepts of image and affect through which he theorises it – are in a time of crisis.

Continuing the examination of different strategies for putting the financial crisis in images (another sense of 'derivative images'), this chapter shows how two writers – the novelist Mathieu Larnaudie and the late philosopher Bernard Stiegler – understand the financial crash as marking the collapse of faith in a certain ideological fiction: that of the self-regulating free market. The primary focus is on the place of images in Larnaudie's novel *Les Effondrés* ('The Collapsed', 2010), which consists of short chapters (but long sentences) recounting in a stream-of-consciousness style the fates of the principal actors of the crisis. *Les Effondrés* offers a series of tableaux in which many of these figures – politicians such as Sarkozy as well as American, French and Swiss financiers implicated in the crisis – undergo a kind of transvaluation in which a habitual relation to the market passing through images (via trading terminals or stock indices, for example) is broken. I examine not only how Larnaudie relates the manner in which the crisis manifests itself as a mediatised event, but also how Larnaudie derives a literary text across media from the images of the crisis (official government speeches and inquiries, press cuttings and other images) and thus shows how we live in a world of 'derivative images'. My core example is Larnaudie's use of a video recording of a famous US Congressional hearing which took place at the acute moment of the crisis. Here I offer a detailed close reading of the image of Alan Greenspan – the former Chairman of the US Federal Reserve, whose reputation was damaged by the subprime mortgage bubble which developed under his watch – in what I propose is an ekphrasis of the hearing video (widely shared online at the time) in which Larnaudie describes Greenspan's cross-examination by senators in surreal micro-detail. I compare this with how the example of Greenspan is deployed in the elaboration of the concept of *prolétarisation* ('proletarianisation') in interventions by Bernard Stiegler, who prescribes precisely such a transvaluation as undergone by Greenspan and others in Larnaudie's text. I set out Stiegler's understanding of the crisis, which he says is 'not a *financial* crisis', but one of generalised economic insolvency. I conclude the chapter by developing the counter-intuitive notion common to the two writers that Greenspan is a 'saint' of the crisis.

In these first two chapters I draw out how dealing with 2008 in literary texts entails an engagement with its mediatisation and the contemporaneous emerging new media culture. Chapter 3 is the book's core theoretical chapter in which I develop the phrase 'derivative images' to name the way this culture has been thought in relation to financial derivatives. The chapter shows how the concepts associated with the financial crash – primarily financial derivatives, but also, for example, the market and exchange – have been creatively refashioned by theorists to conceptualise media images. The chapter begins by fleshing out exactly what is meant by 'derivative' in this context, tracing its etymology and technical usage by financial professionals before discussing its application in a rich emerging seam of film theory concerned with finance. I suggest, drawing on an idea from the poet and theorist Christophe Hanna, that the derivative can be seen as a *calque* ('tracing') for thinking the audiovisual image today: in other words, we can think of images in terms of derivatives, tracing one on top of the other. The American film and media theorist Jonathan Beller, for example, has recently put this most explicitly, arguing that films and digital images should be seen *as* derivatives: that is, they are acts of composition in which we are forced to bundle together (or 'securitise') semiotic elements derived from life or pre-existing images as a hedge against the volatility and risk of contemporary social and economic conditions. Like Beller, Peter Szendy has developed a theory of images as a form of currency circulating within an economy reaching down to the viewer's psyche; I here also discuss how Szendy developed these ideas in the major 2020 exhibition he curated at the Jeu de Paume gallery in Paris. While for Beller our 'derivative condition' is a state of existential alienation and exploitation, for the theorists Randy Martin and Yves Citton it presents possibilities for new modes of sociality. Coming down on the side of Szendy and Citton while maintaining Beller's notion of a 'derivative condition', I hypothesise and set out some of the stakes of a silent kinship between artists, writers, critics and financial traders, based on shared gestures of cutting, recombination, the search for gaps between fields, the exploitation of 'nonknowledge' and putting images into circulation with a view to a future profit. I also suggest in this chapter that while practices of securitisation and derivation have been maligned in the post-2008 world as symptoms of a hypertrophic financial system, such practices long predate the era of financialisation and in fact resemble creative and critical protocols which, like their financial counterparts, are designed to manage forms of radical uncertainty and ambiguity. One of the most original commentators on derivatives, Elie Ayache, a former trader who uses literary theory to describe derivatives markets and, inversely, derivatives to think creativity, is the final figure discussed. In the chapter I trace the influence of conceptions from previous French thought on these contemporary ideas: notably Georges Bataille's 'nonknowledge', Raymond Bellour's notion of 'between-the-images', Gilles Deleuze's 'dividuals' and other notions from poststructuralist thought. I also discuss Beller's hypothesis that cryptocurrencies and blockchain technology may enable a 'decolonisation of finance' and compare this with the current projects of French financial professionals and French banks to put blockchain in the service of film financing and to create derivatives thereof.[40] We shall see just how productive the derivative as a metaphor is at generating various works (and not merely for analysing them): Beller is involved in projects to engineer a 'socially just' derivative (with the Economic Space Agency), Citton refers to derivatives in his rationale for a graduate school, and Szendy curates his exhibition exploring the relations between images and economy and finance. Readers most interested in the book's theoretical argument about derivatives may wish to begin with this chapter.

The focus of Chapter 4 is on the memoir of Jérôme Kerviel, its film adaptation, *L'Outsider* (Christophe Barratier, 2016), and the brand identity of the French bank where he worked, Société Générale. As is well known, Kerviel was a young man who worked as a derivatives trader until January 2008 when he became the object of a major scandal as he was accused by the bank of having taken huge unauthorised speculative positions on futures contracts which the bank unwound, incurring a record loss of €4.9 billion. I argue that the film and the source text can be taken together as an instructive comparative case study of the complexities of representing derivative financial culture in France in the run-up to 2008. Through a close reading of Kerviel's memoir and analyses of sequences from the film as well as of a contemporaneous advert for the financial products Kerviel was selling, and by drawing on research into the communication strategies of Société Générale, my discussion centres on the way Kerviel shows derivative trading to be a fundamentally screen-based activity entailing an iconomy which insinuates itself in Kerviel's experience outside the trading hall and which is then remediated in the cinematic adaptation. The chapter also examines Kerviel's decidedly ambivalent experience of trading as at times a *métier* or vocation and at other times as entailing the sense of being a 'functionary' or a cog in a machine. As with *Les Effondrés*, the horizon for this reflection becomes the way the 2008 crisis disrupts a habitual or automatic relation to the market which takes place across media images, opening a space for a potential rediscovery of a mode of freedom. In this chapter I situate *L'Outsider* within a nexus of post-crash French films featuring traders, arguing that what is distinctive about this film is the recurring (and unauthorised) presence of Société Générale's brand logo, which serves to bring forth the sense of the film as itself a derivative product and Kerviel's experience as exemplifying the 'derivative condition'.

Developing the notion of the filmic derivation broached in the previous chapters, Chapter 5 analyses three experimental films relating to the financial crash: *The Fountainhead* (2010) by Société Réaliste, who were a Paris-based artist cooperative, now dissolved; *Film Socialisme* (2010) by Jean-Luc Godard; and *Film Catastrophe* (2018) by Paul Grivas. *The Fountainhead* is, like *Film Catastrophe*, clearly a 'derivative film': Société Réaliste's film reworks the 1949 Hollywood film of the same name by King Vidor (itself based on a novel by the influential libertarian writer Ayn Rand) by digitally erasing the actors and soundtrack. This leaves a stark, silent film in which we are left to contemplate the sets and props of this film which, reflecting Rand's philosophy, originally served as a paean to architecture and the cult of the entrepreneurial individual. Société Réaliste's film was inspired by the 2008 crisis and was originally shown at Jeu de Paume in Paris as part of a broader exhibition on the ideological interplay between art and economy. My discussion of *Film Socialisme* focuses on the first part of the film, which takes place on a luxury cruise liner sailing the Mediterranean Sea and which, among many other things, reflects on the then-ongoing Greek debt crisis, notably featuring the presence of the French economist Bernard Maris, who chronicled the financial crisis for the satirical magazine *Charlie Hebdo*. My reading shows how Godard's highly fragmentary style constructs meaning, notably in relation to Maris's statement which opens the film: 'money is a public good'. I suggest that the film proposes images as a 'public good'; that is, available to be used by anyone for derivative operations and themselves derived from a variety of sources. This logic is extended in *Film Catastrophe*, which is at first glance a kind of 'making of' *Film Socialisme*. Grivas is Godard's nephew and was an assistant on *Film Socialisme*. He assembles *Film Catastrophe* from unused footage from *Film Socialisme*, his own footage of the shoot, showing Godard and his small team's working methods on board the famous cruise liner which would later shipwreck, as well as mobile phone footage taken by passengers. Through a sequence analysis, I demonstrate the way in which Grivas's film underscores the deep relation between the crisis and the contemporary condition of technical images, showing the capacity of the tourists' and other cameras to yield innumerable derivative images and, indeed, implicitly encouraging the viewer to produce their own. These three films are in contextual terms films of the 2008 crash and are in stylistic terms 'derivative films'; that is, films which are in large part derived from and which reconfigure other films and media, collapsing the relation between original and derivative into one of a general iconomy. While Société Réaliste show the critical potential of filmic derivation (that is, to suggest the ideological wipe-out brought about by the 2008 crash), Godard and Grivas gesture to the creative possibilities for artists and amateurs opened by derivative image technologies.

Carrying forward the idea of a creative use of derivative procedures, the final chapter analyses a group of literary and visual works which refashion the derivative in socially productive ways, even if they do not explicitly conceive of these procedures in derivative terms. One of the key examples is Christophe Hanna's book *Argent* ('Money', 2018), whose organising principle is an econometric which divides the French population into slices of net monthly income. The book – somewhere between a sociological report and a work of poetry – recounts Hanna's discussions on the subject of money with one hundred (real) individuals, each individual corresponding to a percentile of income distribution and identified by their income amount. At the same time as offering an image of a community of artists and poets in Paris, Lyon and Marseille and the material conditions of possibility of their work, through its structure Hanna's book practises what, I contend, is a derivative operation of disassembling people by attribute before then ordering, profiling and pricing them in tranches, like a securitised derivative product. Something comparable takes place in the experimental, poetic documentaries *Rêver sous le capitalisme* ('Dreaming Under Capitalism', Sophie Bruneau, 2017) and *L'Époque* (*Young and Alive*, Matthieu Bareyre, 2018). In Bruneau's film, twelve individuals recount a dream or experience relating to their working life. These recitations are given in most cases in voiceover over still, crepuscular shots of glass office windows, workplaces being cleaned at night, transport hubs and other locations in Brussels. The speakers vividly describe how their lives are overburdened with work. Sharing with *Rêver sous le capitalisme* a concern with dreams and the night, Bareyre's film follows a number of young people in nocturnal Paris in the period 2015–17 as they discuss, in the street or in cafés, their concerns, aspirations and dreams. Through an associative, oneiric logic, these short monologues are visually connected to street life, omnipresent media forms and screens as well as contemporary political events (notably the Nuit debout protests of 2016). Like Bruneau's film, it looks through the glass into office buildings at night to show the after-hours economy while also lingering on broken glass displays, high-street signs and adverts, smashed ATM screens and other cracks in the halting contemporary iconomy. Inviting many ordinary people to reflect on the nature of work and money in the post-crisis period, all these works play on an intermedial spread opened between word (as text or speech) and image (of sites and phenomena relating to the contemporary economy) such as to write possible new meanings over these images. Finally, I discuss a 2008–9 series of photographs by the Paris-based photographer Anna Malagrida showing the windows of Parisian businesses which closed in the wake of the crisis and were boarded up and painted over, strangely evoking abstract art and opening a space for speculation on possible futures for these buildings. The various literary and visual works discussed in this chapter all respond at the ground level to the crises and collapses described in Chapters 1, 2 and 4 while taking forward the creative potential of the derivative outlined in Chapters 3 and 5. I argue that all of these works package together 'derivative images' along with the social residue of non-knowledge (in the form of the monologues and dreams, for example) needed to glimpse alternative possible futures.

Notes

1. Adam Tooze, *Crashed: How a Decade of Financial Crises Changed the World* (London: Allen Lane, 2018), p. 14.
2. Ibid. p. 5. Among other histories of the crash, see Marc Roche, *Histoire secrète d'un krach qui dure* (Paris: Albin Michel, 2016) and Gillian Tett, *Fool's Gold: The Inside Story of J.P. Morgan and How Wall St. Greed Corrupted Its Bold Dream and Created a Financial Catastrophe* (London: Free Press, 2010).
3. The American film theorist Jonathan Beller uses the phrase 'the derivative image' in the title of a 2019 interview – see Jonathan Beller, *The World Computer: Derivative Conditions of Racial Capitalism* (Durham, NC; London: Duke University Press, 2021), p. 267. While my book is indeed indebted to Beller's work, in what follows I develop the phrase in my own way.
4. In his analysis of the film *Margin Call* (J. C. Chandor, 2011), Bruno Péquignot argues that 2008 should be seen not as a 'crisis *of* capitalism' but a 'crisis *within* capitalism': 'De ce point de vue, la crise boursière dans le capitalisme, loin de l'affaiblir, le renforce et est même une condition nécessaire à son existence, c'est-à-dire à son développement. Le capitalisme ne peut survivre que dans la crise, elle n'est pas conjoncturelle, comme l'écrivent les journalistes et les politiques et certains économistes, elle est structurelle, c'est-à-dire, pour être bref, que la crise est l'essence même du capitalisme.' Bruno Péquignot, 'Un récit pour faire peur: la crise du capitalisme', in Christiana Constantopoulou (ed.), *Récits de la crise: Mythes et réalités de la société contemporaine* (Paris: L'Harmattan, 2017), pp. 39–50 (p. 44, pp. 47–8).
5. For example Maurizio Lazzarato, *Gouverner par la dette* (Paris: Les Prairies ordinaires, 2014), pp. 8–9.
6. For example Razmig Keucheyan, 'Anatomie d'une triple crise', *Le Monde diplomatique*, August 2017, p. 3.
7. Yves Citton, *Renverser l'insoutenable* (Paris: Seuil, 2012), pp. 11–12.
8. Myriam Revault D'Allonnes, *La Crise sans fin: Essai sur l'expérience moderne du temps* (Paris: Seuil, 2012), p. 10.
9. Edgar Morin, *Pour une crisologie* (Paris: L'Herne, 2016), pp. 7–8.
10. Ibid. p. 17.
11. Ibid. pp. 51–2.
12. Ibid. pp. 58–9.
13. Evelyne Grossman, *La Créativité de la crise* (Paris: Les Éditions de Minuit, 2020), p. 86.
14. Luc Boltanski and Ève Chiapello, 'Preface (2017)', in *The New Spirit of Capitalism*, trans. Gregory Elliott (London: Verso, [1999] 2018), pp. xviii–xix.

15. Revault D'Allonnes, *La Crise sans fin*, pp. 15–16. In the ancient world, crisis had medical, juridical and political meanings. With modernity, it becomes constitutive of the modern experience of time and history as marked by ruptures. Ibid. p. 111.
16. Ibid. pp. 172–3.
17. See Jeremy Lane and Sarah Waters (eds), 'Work in Crisis', *Modern & Contemporary France*, 26: 3 (2018).
18. Jean-Paul Dollé, *L'Inhabitable Capital: Crise mondiale et expropriation* (Paris: Éditions Lignes, 2010), p. 11.
19. Wolfgang Streeck, *Buying Time: The Delayed Crisis of Democratic Capitalism*, 2nd edn, trans. Patrick Camiller and David Fernbach (London: Verso, [2014] 2017), pp. 6–10.
20. Frédéric Lordon, *La Malfaçon: Monnaie européenne et souveraineté démocratique* (Paris: Les Liens qui libèrent, 2014), p. 7.
21. Remark made by Frédéric Lordon, 'Des intellectuels et des GJs [Gilets Jaunes], lundisoir #4', dialogue with *Lundimatin*, Théâtre de l'Échangeur de Bagnolet, 9 May 2019.
22. Leigh Claire La Berge, 'The Rules of Abstraction: Methods and Discourses of Finance', *Radical History Review*, 118 (Winter 2014), 93–112 (p. 94).
23. For some recent perspectives, see the podcasts of the 'Cultural Life of Money and Finance' project at the University of Leeds, https://culturallifeofmoney.leeds.ac.uk/podcast-2/ (last accessed 16 August 2021).
24. On the representation of the crisis, see for example Miriam Meissner, *Narrating the Global Financial Crisis: Urban Imaginaries and the Politics of Myth* (Basingstoke; New York: Palgrave Macmillan, 2017); Michelle Gales and Claudie Jouandon (eds), 'Crises en thème: Filmer l'économie', *La Revue Documentaires*, 25 (2014); Constantin Parvulescu (ed.), *Global Finance on Screen: From Wall Street to Side Street* (London: Routledge, 2017); Joël Augros (ed.), 'CinémArgent', special number of *CinémAction*, 171 (2019). On the longer history of the representation of money in French cinema, see Diane Gabrysiak and Phil Powrie (eds), 'Money: now you see it now you don't', special issue of *Studies in French Cinema*, 15: 3 (2015).
25. Aris Komporozos-Athanasiou and Marianna Fotaki, 'The Imaginary Constitution of Financial Crises', *The Sociological Review*, 68: 5 (2020), 932–47. For another perspective on the place of imagination in struggles over the future, see Kara Keeling, *Queer Times, Black Futures* (New York: New York University Press, 2019).
26. Alice Béja, 'Les crises en mal de représentations esthétique et politique', *Esprit* (June 2012), 19–21 (p. 20). In another piece, she writes: 'Plus généralement, le problème est que, quand on pense à la crise en France, on est encore attaché à des images vieillottes d'usines, de syndicats, à un traitement du sujet dans la frontalité. Ou bien on tombe dans des films de genre (par exemple le polar) situés dans un "contexte" de crise, souvent de manière un peu artificielle.' Alice Béja, 'La lente mue de la fiction télévisuelle: Entretien avec Dominique Jubin et Bruno Nahon', *Esprit* (June 2012), 59–67 (p. 63).
27. Louis Andrieu, 'Le capitalisme au cinéma', *Esprit* (April 2018), 149–52 (p. 151).
28. Diane Gabrysiak, 'L'argent à l'écran', in Joël Augros (ed.), 'CinémArgent', special number of *CinémAction*, 171 (2019), 144–51 (p. 150).

29. See Jacques-Olivier Charron, 'Finance-fiction: De la mythologie au dévoilement', *Cahiers de la SSFA*, 3 (2016), 2–5 and Olivier Godechot, 'Une finance-fiction est-elle possible? À propos de trois films récents sur la finance', *Contretemps* (November 2011), contretemps.eu/une-finance-fiction-est-elle-possible-a-propos-de-trois-films-recents-sur-la-finance/ (last accessed 16 August 2021). For an introduction to French social studies of finance, see Isabelle Chambost, Marc Lenglet and Yamina Tadjeddine (eds), *The Making of Finance: Perspectives from the Social Sciences* (Abingdon: Routledge, 2019).
30. Bruno Tinel, 'Rendre visible', in Michelle Gales and Claudie Jouandon (eds), 'Crises en thème: Filmer l'économie', *La Revue Documentaires*, 25 (2014), 9–14 (p. 9).
31. Peter Szendy, Emmanuel Alloa and Marta Ponsa (eds), *The Supermarket of Images* (Paris: Gallimard/Jeu de Paume, 2020).
32. Alberto Toscano and Jeff Kinkle, *Cartographies of the Absolute* (Alresford: Zero Books, 2015), p. 158–60.
33. As Toscano and Kinkle remark critically of Isaac Julien's *Playtime* (2013): 'The more we are bewitched by "the" crisis and financialisation, the more we risk treating a capitalist aesthetic as an aesthetic of capital, mistaking the redundancy of re-presentation for the complex seeing that our times demand.' Ibid. p. 182.
34. See for example Lee Grieveson, *Cinema and the Wealth of Nations: Media, Capital, and the Liberal World System* (Oakland: University of California Press, 2018). On risk and finance in filmmaking more generally, see indicatively J. D. Connor, *Hollywood Math and Aftermath: The Economic Image and the Digital Recession* (London; New York: Bloomsbury, 2018). For studies of the representation of stock markets going back to the silent era, see Christina von Braun and Dorothea Dornhof (eds), *Spekulantenwahn: Zwischen ökonomischer Realität und medialer Imagination* (Berlin: Neofelis Verlag, 2015).
35. See for example Yves Citton, Martial Poirson and Christian Biet (eds), *Les Frontières littéraires de l'économie: XVIIe–XIXe siècles* (Paris: Desjonquères, 2008) and Marie-José Mondzain, *Image, icône, économie: Les Sources byzantines de l'imaginaire contemporain* (Paris: Seuil, 1996).
36. Jean-Michel Rey, *Le Temps du crédit* (Paris: Desclée de Brouwer, 2002).
37. Randy Martin, *Knowledge LTD: Toward a Social Logic of the Derivative* (Philadelphia: Temple University Press, 2015).
38. Ibid. p. 223.
39. On financialisation, see Randy Martin, *Financialization of Daily Life* (Philadelphia: Temple University Press, 2002).
40. One minor consequence of the financial crisis was to put paid to a nascent US project to establish a derivative futures exchange dedicated to the Hollywood film industry; for a journalistic account, see Shaun Raviv, 'Box Office Bomb: The Short Life of Popcorn Prediction Markets', *The Ringer*, 15 November 2018, theringer.com/movies/2018/11/15/18091620/box-office-futures-dodd-frank-mpaa-recession (last accessed 16 August 2021).

CHAPTER ONE

Lordon and the 2008 Crisis

D'UN RETOURNEMENT L'AUTRE

At the end of August 2008, just weeks before the collapse of the US investment bank Lehman Brothers on 15 September, which was the most acute moment of the crisis, provoking real fears that the entire global banking system was on the brink of collapse, the philosopher and economist Frédéric Lordon was finishing the manuscript of *Jusqu'à quand? Pour en finir avec les crises financières* ('For How Much Longer? Let's Finish With Financial Crises'). This text should be read alongside his satirical play about the crisis, *D'un retournement l'autre: Comédie sérieuse sur la crise financière. En quatre actes, et en alexandrins* ('From One Turnaround to Another: Serious Comedy about the Financial Crisis', 2011). Explaining the financial turmoil, Lordon refers to autumn 2007 as 'le grand retournement' ('the great reversal').[1] Referring to the closure of investment funds at Bear Stearns on 22 June 2007 as a key point in the brewing crisis, but also events in France, such as the closure of funds by the management company Oddo on 26 July 2007, Lordon remarks with typical wit: 'On y voit, comme à l'endoscopie, l'intérieur de la machine en train de convulser' ('Here we see, as in an endoscopy, the convulsions inside the machine').[2] However, more serious alarm was sounded on 9 August 2007, when funds were frozen at France's biggest bank, and the second biggest bank in the eurozone, BNP Paribas.[3] For Marc Roche, a former journalist at *Le Monde*, this should be taken as the real start date of the crisis.[4] At 7 a.m. the bank published a laconic communiqué announcing the freeze:

> La disparition de toute transaction sur certains segments du marché de la titrisation aux Etats-Unis conduit à une absence de prix de référence et à une illiquidité quasi-totale des actifs figurant dans les portefeuilles des fonds quelle que soit leur qualité ou leur rating. Cette situation ne permet plus d'établir une juste valorisation des actifs sous-jacents et donc de calculer une valeur liquidative pour ces 3 fonds.[5]
>
> [The complete evaporation of liquidity in certain market segments of the US securitisation market has made it impossible to value certain assets fairly regardless of their quality or credit rating. The situation is such that it is no longer possible to value fairly the underlying US ABS assets in the three above-mentioned funds.][6]

The word jumped on by the financial press, Roche notes, was liquidity: the ready availability of funds. If an institution lacks liquidity, it may not be able to make payments, even though it may be solvent. In other words, it was impossible to calculate the value of the funds that had been invested in sub-primes. Unable to value their assets, this limited the ability of already highly over-leveraged banks to borrow. This cast in doubt the state of not just BNP Paribas, but of Europe's banks in general.[7] All major French banks suffered that day losses of between 3 and 6 per cent.[8] The leaders at BNP were perplexed that such an apparently insignificant action had set off concern. The director general Baudouin Prot had only a week earlier given assurances about its liquidity, saying that it had not been affected by the growing concerns about subprimes, 'grâce à sa politique de risque prudente' ('thanks to its prudent risk policy').[9] The European Central Bank under Jean-Claude Trichet, like the Federal Reserve in the USA, was at this point lending large sums to refinance the banks.[10] Adam Tooze agrees that this was 'the really decisive break in market confidence [. . .] the equivalent of a giant bank run'.[11] It was only a few weeks later that the British bank Northern Rock would fail. This date is alluded to rather elliptically in *D'un retournement l'autre*, when the fourth banker says to the third, implying he is a BNP Paribas banker: 'Vous avez eu, dit-on, des craintes assez fortes, / Pour que trois de vos fonds mettent clé sous la porte' ('It is said you must have had serious concerns / To close three of your funds').[12]

Lordon is a prominent public intellectual who makes regular appearances in the French media, was a key figure in the Nuit debout movement of 2016 and is active in support of the *gilets jaunes* and various other protest movements.[13] He also comments on political and economic developments on his blog and in *Le Monde diplomatique*.[14] His play is loosely based on the Sarkozy government's reaction to the financial crash and shows the interaction between a group of bankers and the office of the president as the crisis unfolds. The play gave rise to several stage productions and was filmed by the prolific left-wing director and writer Gérard Mordillat as *Le Grand Retournement* ('The Great Reversal', 2013).[15] In this chapter I briefly outline the conceptual aims of the play, situating it in respect of Lordon's more recent activism before asking critically how effective Lordon's play – and the concepts of image and affect through which he theorises it – are in a time of crisis.[16]

Lordon's play opens with a group of bankers discovering their exposure to the subprime mortgage crisis: the property market is collapsing, everyone is up to their neck in debt and nobody can pay. The new financial products, it is said, are so complex that no one understands how they work. It is decided that they will collude with journalists and blackmail the state to save themselves.

In the second act we move to the Élysée Palace where the president is thinking about his re-election with his two advisors. He is shown to be extremely self-centred and infantile. The bankers arrive and use a drawing board to 'explain' the problem. (I discuss this moment in detail below.) The governor of the central bank announces that he has already provided liquidity to the banks as the lender of last resort. The president harrumphs and says that if someone is going to save the day, it should be him. The advisors and the governor discuss the measures needed to recapitalise the banks. In contrast, the 'second advisor' (*deuxième conseiller*) urges that the state take action and nationalise the banks, both to ensure the situation does not recur and so the banks are not simply seen to be bailed out gratis. This is greeted with stupefaction by the president and his entourage. The president says this is 'du pur communisme', and the advisor – who can be seen as the voice of Lordon – is summarily dismissed.[17]

The third act takes place six months later. While liquidity from the central bank seems to have temporarily resolved the immediate economic side of the issue, it becomes clear that a popular revolt is growing. The bankers arrive at the Élysée to urge the president not to be influenced by the public unrest: there must be no regulation imposed on the banks. One of the president's advisors warns that this situation will recur endlessly, while the president is concerned only with his own stature. At the end of the third act, the president says he will resolve the situation by making a great speech at Toulon. This is of course a reference to Sarkozy's speech at the height of the crisis, on 25 September 2008, in which he famously pronounced the end of laissez-faire capitalism.[18] Here and throughout, what Lordon wants to communicate about the crisis in his play is 'la crise en ses passions' ('the passions of the crisis'): in other words, the avarice of the bankers, the imbecility of those in charge politically and their cynical, incestuous relationships. He is thus more unforgiving than some commentators, for whom French banking elites cooperated closely with the Sarkozy government to provide an effective response, which took the form of the government offering, on 16 October 2008, and as part of a series of parallel actions by other European heads of government, €360 billion to support and recapitalise the banks.[19] In December 2008 Sarkozy presented the recovery programme for France. As Bruno Amable has argued, the crisis and its aftermath led to a reappraisal of the merits of the French economic model, with the superiority of deregulation as a paradigm for modern economies no longer seeming so clear.[20] This sentiment did not, however, last very long: by 2010 Sarkozy followed Angela Merkel in imposing a degree of austerity (although not as severe as in other European countries).[21] Fiscal austerity policies stunted the recovery as French unemployment increased following the crisis.[22] According to one estimate, up to 5 million people in France lost their jobs between July 2008 and January 2016.[23]

The final act takes place one year later. The new second advisor – replacing the one who was dismissed – explains to the president that, by absorbing the banks' losses, the state is now bust and the deficit and the debt are rising. The *premier ministre* evokes a well-known line uttered by François Fillon when he was in this role in 2007, as the crisis approached: 'Je suis à la tête d'un État en faillite' ('I am at the head of a bankrupt state').[24] The new second advisor explains that the state is soon going to get the blame for what was a private banking crisis, now turning into a recession in the wider economy: 'La crise financière se fait donc oublier, / Et de crise privée se fait crise publique . . .' ('The financial crisis is now forgotten / And private crisis now becomes public crisis').[25] The bankers then return and claim that now it is the public debt that is upsetting the markets:

> Vos déficits s'amassent, ils sont pyramidaux,
> Et mettent en péril la solvabilité
> De titres nationaux autrefois réputés.[26]
>
> [Your deficits are growing like pyramids and jeopardising the solvency of hitherto reputable national bonds.]

What is needed is 'la rigueur', even if that means layoffs and factory closures.[27] The final scene takes place six months later, where we see the president complain that his powers of rhetoric are no longer working. An advisor argues that the programme of cutting the budget makes no economic sense. All of Europe is doing the same thing, led by the European Commission, and all are headed towards recession: 'L'Europe, unie mais pour le pire, / Semble avoir décidé de s'auto-estourbir' ('Europe, united but for the worst, / Seems to have decided to take itself out').[28] Everyone begins to fall out, while the president shrugs comically and says at least he made a good speech. The play ends with an assistant entering to say that riots are breaking out and the people are taking over the banks. At the end of the film adaptation, this is made visible through archive footage of demonstrations and rioting. In the final lines of the play, the new second advisor remarks: 'D'un retournement l'autre, l'histoire a ses relèves. / Fuyez quand il est temps, le goudron se soulève . . .' ('From one reversal to the next, history is turning. / Run while there's still time, the tarmac is rising').[29]

Let us return to the second act of the play when the bankers offer to the president what is in effect a summary of the financial mechanics that triggered the subprime crash. This offers a good example of Lordon's marriage of the alexandrine and financial jargon. The following is what is said to the president:

Ne les écoutez pas [the other bankers], c'est incompréhensible,
Je vais dire les choses en termes accessibles.
Tout vient de ce qu'on nomme 'finance structurée':
Elle enfante des monstres et des dégénérés.
Ces tranches de crédit avaient si bonne mine,
Attirant si bien l'œil – surtout la mezzanine.
Le bout de l'*equity* allait aux plus joueurs,
Et la tranche senior aux plus conservateurs.
Elle était réputée magnifiquement sûre,
Notée d'un triple A, c'était comme une armure . . .
Mais ce sont les agences, chargées de notation,
Privées de tout bon sens, et de circonspection:
Tout était certifié mériter les trois A,
Les bonnes notes étaient données à tour de bras.
Transfigurant les déchets en tranches seniors,
Immunes de défaut, aussi franches que l'or,
Elles n'ont point cessé de nous en assurer:
Nous pouvions y aller, presque les yeux fermés.
Mais tout était pourri, et l'or était en toc,
Croyant à des bijoux, nous n'avions que breloques.[30]

[Don't listen to them, it's incomprehensible. I'll explain things in accessible terms. Everything comes from 'structured finance'. It gives rise to monsters and degenerates. These credit tranches looked great and drew the eye, especially the mezzanine. The equity went to those who wanted most risk and the tranche senior to the most conservative types. It was supposedly perfectly safe, noted triple-A, strong as armour. But it was the ratings agencies who lacked good sense and circumspection: everything was certified with three As, good scores were given out left, right and centre. Turning garbage into senior tranches, immune from default, as safe as gold, they never stopped assuring us that we could snap them all up with our eyes closed. But it was all rotten: we thought we had gems, but it was all fool's gold.]

Securitisation (French: *la titrisation*) refers to the transformation of income streams from loans into securities. In theory, this allows banks to mitigate against risk by recycling risky loans (prototypically mortgages) as securities which can be made into blocks and sold to investors according to the level of risk desired, thus creating liquidity for the bank.[31] The asset-backed security (ABS) is split into tranches, and the top ones (*tranches senior*) were supposed to be risk-proof investments and the lower ones (*tranches mezzanine* and *equity*) for risk-taking hedge funds. (It is worth noting in passing that 'tranche', from the French *trancher* meaning 'to slice', is one example among many translingual financial terms – including 'finance' and 'derivative' – whose etymologies are French.) However, as the scandal turned out, the triple-A-rated securities were often worthless and the rating agencies were compromised as they too were selling derivatives.[32] From 2007, the value of subprime derivatives became a systemic problem as banks across the world, already extremely over-leveraged, had huge numbers of them on their balance sheets. Towards the end of the first act of Lordon's play, the bankers become unwilling to lend to each other because of fears that other banks are compromised by subprimes. Lordon here dramatises the seizure of interbank lending, a key driver of the systemic spread of the crisis.[33] As one banker says to another, all the banks were implicated in this: 'Tous nous en avons pris, tous nous avons baffré / Vous, tout comme les autres, vous en êtes gavé' ('We all stuffed ourselves with them – and you too').[34] The long quotation above also demonstrates how Lordon demystifies loaded language to expose underlying exploitative practices.[35] In *Jusqu'à quand?* he explains how the chimera of gaining more by risking less with derivatives is masked under the name of 'innovation', a word which 'soutient le déni imaginaire des risques . . . et leur accumulation réelle' ('underpins the imaginary denial of risks . . . and their real accumulation').[36] The problem is partly that risk is fundamentally incalculable when dealing with collective movements in markets.[37] 'Innovation' is thus like calling a tranche 'equity' while those who sell it call it 'toxic waste'.[38]

This passage where the banker explains subprimes to the president 'en termes accessibles' is an example of Lordon's political-aesthetic strategy (which I discuss below), in particular the idea that his play should both 'faire entendre' the crisis and also 'faire bouillir les sangs'. In *Le Grand Retournement*, the banker (played by Jacques Weber) brings forth a whiteboard and draws while delivering his suave explanation (Figure 1.1). But what he draws are scribbles, and this makes the president's head spin in confusion.

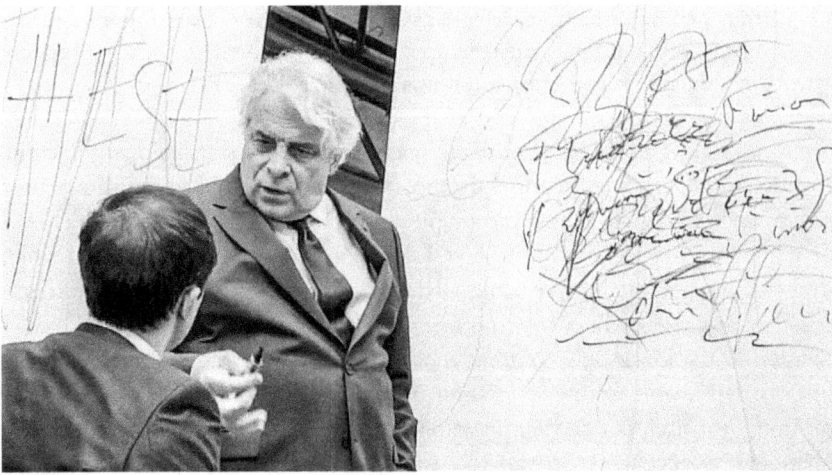

Figure 1.1 The banker explains structured finance. *Le Grand Retournement* (Gérard Mordillat, 2013) © Solaris Distribution.

This image dramatises a key concern in the secondary literature on the crisis and the arts: how to 'explain' the mathematics involved in derivatives. We could think through what Lordon is doing here with the notion of the 'contre-fiction politique', a term put forward by the journal *Multitudes* and of which *D'un retournement l'autre* is named as an example.[39] This term identifies a particular kind of intersection between narrative art and political activism (but which could include everything from graffiti to video games) where a work short-circuits a real fiction operating in the world while offering another fiction to show how the world might be otherwise.[40] So, in this passage, the banker frankly demonstrates how financial innovation (such as triple-A-rated derivatives) is often based on fictions, while at the end of his play Lordon offers a counter-factual vision of protestors taking over the banks. However, this is a telling moment as the banker, through his scribbles, foregrounds how a play is not the place for an analytical exposition, and in this sense – as we will see throughout this book – what I call 'derivative images' do not 'explain' derivatives. This moment thus contrasts with the correlative passage in *Jusqu'à quand?* where Lordon sets out a simple diagram showing how debts are ordered into tranches in an asset-backed security (Figure 1.2).

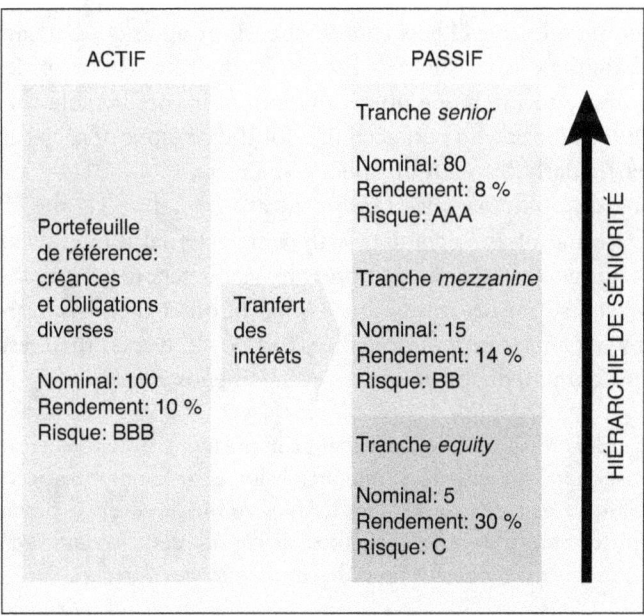

Figure 1.2 Diagram of an asset-backed security (from *Jusqu'à quand?*, p. 61) © Frédéric Lordon/Raisons d'agir.

Before discussing these images, it is necessary to briefly explain Lordon's theory behind the play.

'Une image bien choisie qui fait bouillir les sangs': Images and Affects

Lordon sets out the conceptual underpinnings of the play in two companion essays. In the first of these, 'La crise économique en ses passions', first published in *Critique* in 2012 and collected in *La Société des affects* (2013), Lordon explains how he understands capitalism as a sequence of regimes of accumulation, and a crisis as the transition from one regime to another.[41] Given that under any particular set of institutional arrangements there are various social contradictions that can only be temporarily 'regulated' (hence the 'Regulation school' that influences him), '*il y a nécessairement crise*' ('there will always be crises').[42] Since 2007 the regime has gone into crisis: 'Mais il n'y est qu'entré. Que faut-il donc de plus pour qu'il y soit tout à fait? Il y faut les forces motrices effectivement productrices de changement – c'est-à-dire de transformations institutionnelles susceptibles d'accoucher d'une nouvelle "cohérence" d'ensemble de l'accumulation capitaliste' ('But only just. What needs to be done for it to be really in crisis? There need to be driving forces which really produce change – that is, institutional changes which would bring in a new "coherence" in capitalist accumulation as a whole').[43] Strikingly, the appeal to 'une science sociale spinoziste' and the notion of collective affects comes when Lordon asks what can be done to exacerbate the crisis.[44] Here as elsewhere, the recourse to Spinoza comes from the desire to intervene politically among unpredictable forces.[45] For Lordon, it is Spinoza who best accounts for the passions of social and political life, particularly through his theory of affects.

Drawing on Spinoza, what Lordon means by 'affects' is the effect on a body and a mind of an encounter with some external thing (an 'affection'). Lordon is always thinking of Spinoza when he refers to affects, and his use of the term must not be confused with that of other theorists. Lordon gives a sense of what affects mean in practice, and how the crisis manifests itself in visible signs both mediated and in everyday phenomena:

> Regarder un journal télévisé rendant compte d'une fermeture d'usine, lire des statistiques économiques d'emploi en baisse et de bonus financiers en hausse, remarquer plus de pauvres dans les rues ou bien recevoir sa propre lettre de licenciement: ce sont des rencontres de choses, des affections – et même en tout premier lieu des affections du corps: voir, entendre, lire.[46]
>
> [Watching a TV report about the closure of a factory, reading economic statistics of falling job numbers and rising financial bonuses, seeing more poor

people in the street or indeed receiving one's own redundancy letter: these are encounters of things, affections – and first of all bodily affections: seeing, hearing, reading.]

In the second companion essay, 'La surréalisation de la crise' ('The Crisis Turns Surreal'), published together with the play, Lordon begins by quoting Spinoza to argue that ideas have no effect in themselves but only have force through affects.[47] Affects then lead to a change in the movement of forces or what Spinoza calls *conatus*; in practical terms, changes in people's behaviour.[48] So, affects are what comes between affections in the real world (encounters with social and economic phenomena, for example) and the resulting actions of bodies. Art can create affects, Lordon writes, because it generates movements of the body: increased heart rates, increased blood pressure, getting legs moving, legs carrying bodies on to the street.[49] As Lordon makes explicit in terms of the crisis in a crucial passage:

> On pourra analyser la crise financière sous toutes ses coutures, raffiner l'argument autant qu'on veut, démonter les systèmes, exposer les rouages, *tout ça ne vaudra jamais une image bien choisie qui fait bouillir les sangs* ou, comme le dit fort à propos une expression commune, qu'on prend en pleine gueule – la gueule: le corps. *Il ne faut plus seulement dire la crise capitaliste, il faut la montrer, ou bien la faire entendre.*[50]

> [One can analyse the financial crisis from all angles, refine the argument all you want, take the systems apart and expose its inner workings, but none of this will ever be worth one well-chosen image which makes the blood boil, or as we say in French, which hits you full in the gob. The gob: the body. It is no longer enough just to talk about the capitalist crisis: it must be shown, you must make people understand it.]

Lordon here cuts to the quick of one of this study's core concerns: the stakes of putting the crisis in images. Here the relation that we have with an image is one particular form of affection: an encounter with some external thing in the world that addresses itself to our bodies and which creates affects (and different affects for different individuals). For Lordon, its principal value is as a vector for political mobilisation.[51]

Looking for an image within the play that might make one's blood boil, we could consider for example the moment in which the bankers work out how best to rip off the state to maintain their positions, or when one of their number eulogises the (rather clichéd) trappings of the trader life, or when another dismisses 'le peuple' as 'sot' ('thick').[52] The crucial point is that, with the play, 'des corps affectent d'autres corps et ajoutent à un certain discours la force extrinsèque des affects' ('bodies affect other bodies and add to a certain discourse the extrinsic force of affects').[53] For Lordon, the play should make visible – as an image – the causal connections of the crisis that get lost in the day-to-day coverage or that are obscured by a euphemistic official discourse.[54] In doing this, and in charging the play with affects, the theatre of the crisis 'renders the crisis surreal'. His characters are intentionally generic and identified solely by their professional position within the network of power: 'Tout ces gens ventriloquent des positions et n'ont pas d'autre caractère que celui de leur genre' ('These people ventriloquise positions and have no other character than their type').[55] He sees his play as concerned with social structures and forces, not individuals or individual psychology, referring to it as a theatre '*sans profondeur*' ('without depth'): 'Un théâtre donc de la surface, des forces et de l'extériorité: si l'on veut, un théâtre matérialiste' ('A theatre, then, of the surface, of forces and of exteriority; if you like, a materialist theatre').[56] This programmatic statement comes from Lordon's belief that it is structures that determine people's interests and denouncing individuals is simply a deflection from the real issues.[57]

While the allusion to 'un théâtre matérialiste' signals an implicit debt to Brecht (to whom he does not refer by name) and may seem difficult to reconcile with the notion of a theatre of the 'surface', Lordon explicitly relates his work to French classical theatre through his use of alexandrine verse. This theatre plays on a tension between the elevated connotations of the seventeenth-century verse style and 'l'absolue vulgarité du capitalisme contemporain' ('the absolute vulgarity of contemporary capitalism'); that is, the esoteric jargon from the world of derivative finance.[58] He explains how the form allows him to mix humour with critique when dealing with material liable to induce despair:

> On sait l'alexandrin propre à la pompe bossuétienne ou à la tragédie, mais on le sait également capable de faire rire, peut-être plus encore s'il est un peu trafiqué – et l'avantage n'est pas mince quand par ailleurs tout donne envie de pleurer. Appliquer une forme, connue pour accompagner les grands sentiments moraux, aux plus misérables manœuvres de la finance en capilotade est peut-être ainsi l'un des moyens de ne pas céder complètement au désespoir quand, précisément, on voit dans la réalité ces manœuvres outrageusement triompher.[59]
>
> [We know the alexandrine associated with Bossuetian pomp or with tragedy, but we know it is also capable of eliciting laughter, perhaps all the more so when it is a bit adulterated – and the advantage shouldn't be underestimated when everything makes you want to cry. Applying a form associated with great moral sentiments to the wretched manoeuvres of finance in a mess is perhaps thus one of the ways of not giving in to despair when, in reality, it is precisely these manoeuvres that we see scandalously triumph.]

The moral charge given to language by the poetic form is thus theorised as a means of mobilising an affective force. The ambivalence or tension between high and low register is doubled in the film adaptation, which, while showing events taking place in the Élysée Palace, was shot in the disused Babcock factory in Aubervilliers.[60] The film thus contains throughout in the same image the loftiness of the great offices of state and a backdrop of industrial ruin.

Lordon was clearly already thinking about finance in relation to literary style before the crash reached its climax, noting sardonically that: 'La finance a une langue. Et ce n'est pas celle de Molière. Contrairement à ce qu'on pourrait croire, ce n'est pas celle de Shakespeare non plus . . .' ('Finance has a language, and it isn't the language of Molière. Despite what we might think, it isn't that of Shakespeare either . . .').[61] On one level, Lordon plays for laughs, and several jokes in the play turn on how much of the 'babillage' ('baby talk') and 'globish' language of the traders consists of 'quelques mots d'anglais, francisés à la main [. . .] Ça n'est plus une langue mais une soupe horrible' ('a few gallicised English words . . . It is not a language but a horrible soup').[62] One example is when a trader explains, 'J'ai mal *pricé* mon *swap* et mon *spiel* a *losé* / J'ai été un peu *long* et j'aurais dû *shorter*' ('I badly *priced* my *swap* and I *lost* my *spiel* / I went *long* when I should have *shorted*').[63] However, *D'un retournement l'autre* also does in verse what *Jusqu'à quand?* does in prose; that is, it offers an admirably clear demystification of derivative finance and its vocabulary. Lordon argues that the jargon of derivatives exists primarily to help finance keep its practices obscure and thus away from democratic scrutiny. If no one understands what the traders are talking about, it is very difficult to put controls on them.[64] Lordon's use of financial vocabulary thus has an explicatory purpose at the same time as the alexandrine is a motor for affect. Together with the other theatrical strategies, it is thus that Lordon aims to affect his audience, to 'faire bouillir les sangs'.

Lordon, Images and Committed Art

In the theory of affects discussed above, we saw that, for Lordon, the purpose of the play is to *add* affects to 'un certain discours'. However, going back to the two images introduced above, it might be argued that 'adding affects' in Figure 1.1 through the gestures of the banker tends to negate the explanatory power of the 'discours'. When we move from the diagram to the scribbles, all of the content about the makeup of derivatives is evacuated. The scribbles on the whiteboard thus appear to represent something like the limit of the capacity of the film adaptation of Lordon's play to 'faire entendre' the technical origins of the crisis, which are nested in the diagram. Instead, the shot foregrounds the implicit power relation of the banker looming over the president like a schoolmaster – which may constitute its own form of 'faire entendre', but it is quite different from the explanation of derivative finance that

Lordon performs in *Jusqu'à quand?*. This image thus exposes the tensions at the core of his strategic use of images. It is as if it were inherent in the logic of 'faire bouillir les sangs' – and therefore in the theory of affects *tout court* – that the whiteboard as metonym for expert exposition must be dispensed with.

In this sense, Lordon's decision to write the play perhaps bespeaks a frustration with the lack of effect of his earlier texts and an increasing sense of the imperative of political activism.[65] By the time he wrote the play, he had in fact already published two detailed books on the crisis as it was unfolding, books which explain how derivatives work and also include quite practical policy proposals for structural change to deleverage the banks and protect Europe from some of the dangers of financial capitalism. By structures, Lordon means institutions such as the International Monetary Fund, the European Central Bank, national laws, and so on. He proposes banning all transactions between European financial institutions and offshore entities, and more radically suggests breaking the dependence on British and American financial zones, which he says will never accept regulation.[66] Lordon, who is well known in France as a left-wing critic of the euro and the EU, here suggests nationalising (at the European level) the stock market and ending the independence of the European Central Bank in order to have an anti-speculative monetary policy.[67] In *La Crise de trop* (2009), he develops further proposals for socialised credit and a SLAM (Shareholder Limited Authorised Margin) tax, which would set a maximum shareholder return.[68] As regards financial regulation, Lordon is surely right that the problem is not the want of policy options but rather in creating the popular political will for their implementation – and this is part of the purpose of a theory of collective affects.

In seeking to create this political will, at several points in his recent work Lordon accords a privileged position to images and, I would argue, increasingly comes down on the side of 'faire bouillir les sangs' over 'faire entendre' (even if he does not entirely resolve this opposition and does not dispense with such an approach). Thinking of Jean-Robert Viallet's documentary series *La Mise à mort du travail* (France 3, 2009), in which he appears, Lordon writes that only images can shock us into understanding the construction of what he sees as a totalitarian neoliberal subjectivity.[69] In *Les Affects de la politique* (2016), he argues that campaigns for action on climate change will continue to make no difference until the ideas are given 'figurations vivaces' ('representations which cut through').[70] He is a stinging critic of the media and the role of their favoured 'expert' economists in inculcating orthodox ideas, as evidenced by his appearance in the documentary *Les Nouveaux Chiens de garde* (Gilles Balbastre and Yannick Kergoat, 2012). Most recently he writes that in our culture the media are 'instruments de servitude, de conformisme et d'abêtissement' ('instruments of servitude, conformism and dumbing-down') which, in a hypothetical post-capitalist society, must be put in the service of human development.[71] This opposition to established media outlets and also to the Macron administration comes sharply into focus as he provides web links to grisly videos of police brutality, taken by protestors during the *gilets jaunes* demonstrations. He argues that such graphic images are concealed by major television channels such as BFM and TF1, but must be seen and must generate anger.[72] In contrast to the attempts to 'faire entendre' the mechanics of the financial crisis in his play, it is rather more obvious how this kind of image might 'faire bouillir les sangs'. The history of the decade following the 2008 crisis is also the history of the increasing centrality of new media in politics. The move to 'faire bouillir les sangs' is thus the corollary of a general adoption, since the time of *D'un retournement l'autre*, of new media methods for the activist use and dissemination of images.

Lordon's reflections clearly fit within a long history of debate in France on the idea of 'committed' cinema and literature.[73] However, he has not returned to theatre. Rather, his activism in recent years has involved increasing engagement with documentary cinema and deploying his rhetorical skills in protest movements. In addition to the examples given above, he appears in Mariana Otero's documentary about Nuit debout, *L'Assemblée* (2017), where we can see how he retrains his undoubted eloquence from alexandrine verse to rousing public speaking at the Place de la République. While Otero's film shows the difficulties of the Nuit debout movement in developing collective means of organisation and decision-making, Lordon finds in François Ruffin's hit comedy documentary *Merci Patron!* (2016) something like a model of the kind of political art that he thinks is needed. He remarks that, in contrast to many other films dealing with the contemporary condition of workers, the film 'n'a aucune visée analytique ou pédagogique. C'est un film d'un autre genre [. . .] Le plus juste serait sans doute d'en dire qu'il est un film d'action directe' ('has no analytic or pedagogical aim. It is a completely different kind of film. Most accurate would probably be to say that that it is a direct action film').[74] This is a remarkable statement as it advances on the theorisation of *D'un retournement* which, as shown above, seeks both to explain the crisis and to incite anger about it. What films of direct action do is give viewers the desire to take action and they give them the sense that action is possible: *Merci Patron!* 'nous sort de l'impuissance et nous rebranche directement sur la force. Ça n'est pas un film, c'est un clairon, une possible levée en masse, un phénomène à l'état latent' ('relieves us of our impotence and reconnects us directly with forces. It is not a film, it is a bugle, a possible mass rising, a phenomenon in a latent state').[75] While one might question the extent to which the film really has 'aucune visée analytique', what is important is that this appears to signal an increasing desire for political agitation on Lordon's part and a clearer sense that political art should generate energising, angry affects. (He has also stated that while art can have political effects, it of course cannot be an alternative solution to real politics.[76]) Lordon has continued to engage with Ruffin (a *député* for La France insoumise) by taking part in debates following screenings of the latter's second film, *J'veux du soleil* (co-directed with Gilles Perret, 2019), a road movie which follows *gilets jaunes* protesting on the outskirts of cities. In a forceful letter to Macron rejecting his invitation to debate with intellectuals at the Élysée, read out in a speech at a rally at the Bourse de travail on 14 March 2019, Lordon again alludes briefly to this film.[77] While *D'un retournement* sought to generate affects by showing the mechanisms of the financial crisis in small theatres, his increasingly insurrectionary rhetoric is now redeployed, aimed directly at power, pronounced before crowds of activists and circulated in activist documentary and in online videos.

THE ANARCHIC CONDITION

It was still relatively soon after the crisis that Lordon asked:

> Quels affects collectifs l'état de *credit crunch*, de récession économique et de politiques d'austérité va-t-il produire? C'est à cette question que demeure suspendu le devenir-crise de cet état, c'est-à-dire la naissance contingente de dynamiques passionnelles collectives suffisamment puissantes pour aboutir à une transformation (politique) des institutions du capitalisme – et à un changement du régime d'accumulation.[78]

> [What affects will be produced by the credit crunch, economic recession and austerity policies? This is the question that remains in suspense in the becoming-crisis of this state of affairs, that is, the contingent birth of collective passional dynamics which are sufficiently powerful to bring about a political transformation of capitalist institutions and a change in the regime of accumulation.]

Writing on 22 September 2008, just after the collapse of Lehman Brothers, Lordon called for a serious political response to the crisis: 'Arraisonner la finance n'est plus une option' ('Simply checking up on finance is no longer an option').[79] He thought 2008 was going to be a 'crise de trop' ('a crisis too far') that would go beyond the limits of public tolerance and lead to a popular uprising. At the close of the play, one of the advisors observes the revolutionary violence taking place outside the Élysée and the forcible public takeover of the banks and notes, 'C'est l'insurrection qui vient' ('The insurrection is coming').[80] More than ten years on from the crash, this allusion to le Comité invisible cannot but evoke how this kind of insurrection has not in fact come.

This is not to say that there have not been popular or 'populist' revolts in which outrage about the financial crisis was one among other factors. Lordon considers the 2018–19 demonstrations of the *gilets jaunes* as a 'soulèvement' of ordinary people, angry at having been pushed too far by a Macron administration after thirty years of 'neoliberal' policy.[81] But what is striking is how often the sentiments animated in revolts over the last decade were mobilised more successfully by the forces of reaction, such as the political upheavals in the US and UK in 2016 and Le Pen's relative success in 2017, forces which, through their campaigns, clearly did understand and put to work the power of affects in the service of anger (and without requiring a lengthy exegesis of Spinoza).[82] Lordon describes how, despite material conditions supposedly being favourable to the left, it is the right and radical right that profit as they are better able to appeal to people's 'imaginations'.[83] Why is this? He meditates on the way people respond differently to the same affection (each person's *ingenium* or affectability is different), but his political theory would be more persuasive if he engaged more with the fundamental ambivalence of the affective responses – and, indeed, the images – elicited by recent crises and by attempts by different political quarters to mobilise them.[84] In a text critiquing what he sees as the Panglossian outlook of pro-Europeans during the 2019 European elections, he writes that the fading of the 2008 crisis into memory gives us a false sense of security. European banks remain fragile while public and private debt are higher than ever. The underlying conditions of 2008 remain unchanged, meaning that we will soon see another crisis: as he put it, writing before the Covid-19 pandemic, 'la prochaine crise financière nous pend au nez comme un sifflet de deux ronds' ('the next crisis is just around the corner').[85]

Lordon wrote in 2008 that a financial crisis is first of all the collapse of a collective belief.[86] By this he means that finance is about faith in a system and stock values sustained by opinion and should be studied in the framework of social anthropology rather than as a mathematical science. But the crisis undermined belief more widely in free markets and liberal democracy, the cornerstones of contemporary Western society.[87] The collapse of faith in a system leads to what he has theorised as 'la condition anarchique' ('the anarchic condition').[88] It is collective opinion that founds society in general. Financial markets in this sense are merely exemplary of a general rule: institutions are held together by collective belief and affects *invested* in them, and uncertainty leads to *disinvestment* in them. The anarchic condition is one of potential new orders as well as chaos. His analysis of the crisis and his policy ideas are very compelling, and it is indisputable that human beings are driven by what could be called affects, but it is less clear how far Lordon's theory of affects and images 'to make our blood boil' gets us in terms of inspiring or programming productive political action as a result of the financial crisis. Part of Lordon's usefulness for his activist readers is – as in his reading of Stéphane Brizé's film *En guerre* (2018), and as we saw in relation to alexandrine verse – to help them ward off despair.[89] But in this deeply uncertain context – in this anarchic condition – it is imperative that we ask the more profound question of whether we really do understand the affects and passions that govern us.

Notes

1. Frédéric Lordon, *Jusqu'à quand? Pour en finir avec les crises financières* (Paris: Raisons d'agir, 2008), p. 45.
2. Ibid. p. 104.
3. For a recent history of the bank, see the documentary *BNP Paribas: Dans les eaux troublés da la plus grande banque européenne* (Thomas Lafarge and Xavier Harel, France 3, 2018).
4. Roche, *Histoire secrète*, p. 9.
5. BNP Paribas press release, 'BNP Paribas Investment Partners suspend temporairement le calcul de la valeur liquidative des fonds Parvest Dynamic ABS, BNP Paribas ABS EURIBOR et BNP Paribas ABS EONIA', 9 August 2007, group.bnpparibas/communique-de-presse/bnp-paribas-investment-partners-suspend-temporairement-calcul-liquidative-fonds-parvest-dynamic-abs-bnp-paribas-abs-euribor-bnp-paribas-abs-eonia (last accessed 16 August 2021).
6. BNP Paribas press release, 'BNP Paribas Investment Partners temporaly [sic] suspends the calculation of the Net Asset Value of the following funds: Parvest Dynamic ABS, BNP Paribas ABS EURIBOR and BNP Paribas ABS EONIA', 9 August 2007, group.bnpparibas/en/press-release/bnp-paribas-investment-partners-temporaly-suspends-calculation-net-asset-funds-parvest-dynamic-abs-bnp-paribas-abs-euribor-bnp-paribas-abs-eonia (last accessed 16 August 2021).
7. Roche, *Histoire secrète*, p. 70. As an indication of how Europe was even more heavily 'overbanked' than the US, Tooze notes that at this point BNP Paribas's balance sheet was close to France's GDP – see Tooze, *Crashed*, p. 110.
8. Elsa Conesa, 'Les banques françaises sanctionnées sur les crédits immobiliers à haut risque', *Les Echos*, 10–11 August 2007, p. 26.
9. 'Ombre et lumière', *Les Echos*, 10–11 August 2007, p. 36.
10. On central banks and monetary creation during the crisis, see Thomas Piketty, *Capital and Ideology*, trans. Arthur Goldhammer (Cambridge, MA: Harvard University Press, [2019] 2020), pp. 696–700.
11. Tooze, *Crashed*, p. 144.
12. Frédéric Lordon, *D'un retournement l'autre: Comédie sérieuse sur la crise financière. En quatre actes, et en alexandrins* (Paris: Seuil, 2011), p. 31.
13. For an introduction to Lordon's work in English, see Alberto Toscano, 'A Structuralism of Feeling?', *New Left Review*, 97 (2016), 73–93.
14. Lordon's blog, 'La pompe à phynance', is hosted on the *Le Monde diplomatique* website, blog.mondediplo.net/-La-pompe-a-phynance- (last accessed 16 August 2021).

15. Excerpts from the play also feature in Jeanne Delafosse's *Et que ça saute!* (France: Come and See, 2013), a low-budget short film in which three young women draw diagrams showing, for example, the falling wage share of French GDP between 1983 and 2006, and interrogate cardboard cut-outs of various French chief executives.
16. For French intellectual responses to the crisis more generally, see Sarah Waters, *Between Republic and Market: Globalization and Identity in Contemporary France* (London: Continuum, 2012), pp. 107–16 and Adrian May, *From Bataille to Badiou:* Lignes*: The Preservation of Radical French Thought, 1987–2017* (Liverpool: Liverpool University Press, 2018), pp. 159–84.
17. Lordon, *D'un retournement*, p. 74; *Le Grand Retournement* Dossier de presse, solaris-distribution.com/le-grand-retournement/ (last accessed 16 August 2021).
18. 'L'autorégulation pour régler tous les problèmes, c'est fini. Le laissez-faire, c'est fini. Le marché qui a toujours raison, c'est fini. Il faut tirer les leçons de la crise pour qu'elle ne se reproduise pas. Nous venons de passer à deux doigts de la catastrophe, on ne peut pas prendre le risque de recommencer. Si l'on veut reconstruire un système financier viable, la moralisation du capitalisme financier demeure la priorité.' Nicolas Sarkozy, 'Le discours de Nicolas Sarkozy à Toulon', *Le Monde*, 25 September 2008, lemonde.fr/politique/article/2008/09/25/le-discours-de-nicolas-sarkozy-a-toulon_1099795_823448.html (last accessed 16 August 2021).
19. Cornelia Woll, *The Power of Inaction: Bank Bailouts in Comparison* (New York: Cornell University Press, 2014), pp. 112–38. On Sarkozy's interventionism at this point, see Liêm Hoang-Ngoc, 'La *Sarkonomics* entre promesses électorales et crise économique. Bilan d'étape fin 2008', *Modern & Contemporary France*, 17: 4 (2009), 423–34. See also Sarkozy's reflections on the anniversary of the crisis: 'Sarkozy: "Les coups pleuvaient de tous les côtés"', *Le Monde*, 5 July 2017, pullout supplement, p. 4.
20. Bruno Amable, *Structural Crisis and Institutional Change in Modern Capitalism: French Capitalism in Transition* (Oxford: Oxford University Press, 2017), p. 33.
21. Ibid. p. 145. The Treaty on Stability, Coordination and Governance was signed on 2 March 2012. During the 2012 presidential election, François Hollande promised to renegotiate this treaty; in the event, he accepted it. As presidential candidate, he promised to separate investment from retail banking, to regulate stock options and bonuses and to tax financial transactions. In the famous speech at Le Bourget, 22 January 2012, he had claimed his enemy was finance: an enemy with neither name, nor face, nor party. Such measures were eventually given up. On this, see ibid. pp. 217–18.
22. Ibid. pp. 33–4, p. 15.
23. Pierre Larrouturou and Dominique Méda, *Einstein avait raison. Il faut réduire le temps de travail* (Ivry-sur-Seine: Les Éditions de l'Atelier, 2016), p. 23.
24. Lordon, *D'un retournement*, p. 97. For Fillon's exact words, see ina.fr/video/I09082525 (last accessed 16 August 2021).
25. Lordon, *D'un retournement*, p. 102.
26. Ibid. p. 105.

27. The 'exceptional' or 'emergency' decision-making process that Vogl describes in relation to the US government's response is also what is portrayed in Lordon's play: 'What happened needs to be understood as an exemplary endgame, as an illustration of the creation, development and logic of policy-making processes in the financial-economic regime. The consortium of public and private actors, the improvised meetings, the secret deals, the urgency dictated by the movements of the financial markets – the events of 2008 demonstrate how all this determines the actions of government and the fate of contemporary economies and societies. [. . .] [I]t is possible to observe an informalization of policy-making in the grey zone between economies and politics, a deregulation of its procedures and authorities.' Joseph Vogl, *The Ascendancy of Finance*, trans. Simon Garnett (Cambridge, UK; Malden, MA: Polity, [2015] 2017), p. 4.
28. Lordon, *D'un retournement*, p. 113.
29. Ibid. p. 127.
30. Ibid. pp. 52–3.
31. André Orléan, *De l'euphorie à la panique: Penser la crise financière* (Paris: Éditions Rue d'Ulm, 2009), p. 104. For more detail on securitisation, see John C. Hull, *Options, Futures, and Other Derivatives*, 9th edn (Harlow: Pearson, 2015), pp. 185–99; on its history, see Gerald F. Davis, *Managed by the Markets: How Finance Re-shaped America* (Oxford: Oxford University Press, 2009), pp. 102–53. In the USA in the 2000s, there was an explosion of predatory mortgage lending to meet subprime demand, as detailed for example in Jean-Stéphane Bron's film *Cleveland contre Wall Street* (France: Les Films du Losange, 2010).
32. See Tooze, *Crashed*, pp. 42–71. On the significance of the rating agencies within a wider logic of evaluation or 'notation', see Michel Feher, *Le Temps des investis: Essai sur la nouvelle question sociale* (Paris: La Découverte, 2017), pp. 64–70.
33. Lordon, *D'un retournement*, pp. 29–32.
34. Ibid. p. 29.
35. The idea that speculation was inherent in trading was already identified by Pierre-Joseph Proudhon in his famous *Manuel du spéculateur à la Bourse* (1854) – see Christophe Reffait, 'La Crise financière actuelle, selon les écrivains du XIXe siècle', *Esprit* (January 2010), 57–72.
36. Lordon, *Jusqu'à quand?*, p. 12, p. 21.
37. Ibid. p. 22.
38. Ibid. p. 63.
39. Multitudes, 'Entre storytelling et contre-fictions: L'activisme mystificateur', *Multitudes*, 48 (2012), 79–80 (p. 80).
40. Multitudes, 'Réalités, fictions, contre-fictions . . .', *Multitudes*, 48 (2012), 70–1.
41. Frédéric Lordon, *La Société des affects* (Paris: Seuil, 2013), pp. 110–14.
42. Ibid. p. 111. My emphasis.
43. Lordon, *La Société des affects*, p. 113.
44. Ibid. p. 114.
45. While Lordon started out his career as an economist with a Bourdieusian sociological emphasis, as a philosopher at the CNRS his major intellectual project

over the last decade has been to conjugate an understanding of economic and political institutions with the philosophy of Spinoza. For the Spinozist project, see Yves Citton and Frédéric Lordon (eds), *Spinoza et les sciences sociales: De la puissance de la multitude à l'économie politique des affects* (Paris: Éditions Amsterdam, 2008) and Frédéric Lordon, *Capitalisme, désir et servitude: Marx et Spinoza* (Paris: La Fabrique éditions, 2010).
46. Lordon, *La Société des affects*, p. 115.
47. Lordon, *D'un retournement*, pp. 129–30.
48. Conatus means the impulse or striving of life itself; Lordon, *Capitalisme, désir et servitude*, p. 17.
49. Lordon, *D'un retournement*, pp. 130–1.
50. Ibid. pp. 131–2. My emphasis.
51. Lordon's use of 'image' is capacious and somewhat ambiguous: while it is associated with art (for example a piece of theatre), the same category would include documentary and, as the previous quotation suggests, such things as TV news reports. Lordon's use of 'image' is sufficiently elastic to allow us to consider as an 'image' both the play as a whole and moments within it. Reading the two quotations in the main text together, images appear indistinguishable from affective moments in a quotidian phenomenology (seeing poor people in the street, for example).
52. Lordon, *D'un retournement*, pp. 34–7, p. 26, p. 84.
53. Ibid. pp. 132–3.
54. Ibid. p. 133: 'Le temps ramassé de la représentation reconcentre ce que le temps social réel avait dilué et démembré, il rétablit dans leur intégrité les consécutions brisées, les liaisons perdues, il remet bien ensemble les enchaînements du scandale et leur donne une nouvelle densité: tout s'ensuit *visiblement*, tout est représenté d'un seul tenant, et alors ressaisi dans l'unité d'une idée affectante.' For a discussion of how other plays represent the economy in crisis, see Martial Poirson, 'La crise du change dans le théâtre contemporain: Affabulations théâtrales et allégorisation de l'économie', in Geneviève Sicotte, Martial Poirson, Stéphanie Loncle and Christian Biet (eds), *Fiction et économie: Représentations de l'économie dans la littérature et les arts du spectacle, XIXe–XXIe siècles* (Québec City: Les Presses de l'Université Laval, 2013), pp. 183–215.
55. Lordon, *D'un retournement*, p. 134.
56. Ibid. p. 134.
57. Lordon, *Jusqu'à quand?*, p. 48.
58. Lordon, *D'un retournement*, p. 134. The classical alexandrine is associated with Corneille, Molière and Racine. See 'Alexandrin', in Jacques Charpentreau, *Dictionnaire de la poésie française* (Paris: Fayard, 2006), pp. 23–30.
59. Lordon, *D'un retournement*, pp. 134–5.
60. Exhibiting a nostalgia for a lost industrial past, Mordillat explains his choice of setting for the film: 'L'idée de la ruine industrielle s'est très rapidement imposée. Elle renvoie métaphoriquement à la destruction absolue provoquée par la crise financière et bancaire. C'est un décor de désolation. Les lieux gardent la trace de leur splendeur passée dont il ne reste que des vestiges, ferrailles, gravats, effondrements;

la banque centrale n'est plus qu'un trou et l'Élysée un pan de mur ... Dans cet espace, dans ce désastre architectural si photogénique, je pouvais à la fois faire du cinéma et laisser du champ aux acteurs sans les contraindre à l'excès' – *Le Grand Retournement* Dossier de presse. Babcock is also where the interviews take place in the documentary film *Après la gauche* (Jérémy Forni, 2010), another film about 'crisis', in which various French thinkers appear.

61. Lordon, *Jusqu'à quand?*, p. 23.
62. Lordon, *D'un retournement*, p. 22.
63. Ibid. p. 21.
64. As he writes, 'la finance prospère à l'abri de cet ésotérisme qui tient les profanes éloignés et détruit *ab initio* les conditions de possibilité d'un débat démocratique qui la prendrait pour objet' ('finance prospers under this veil of esotericism which excludes the uninitiated, thus destroying from the outset the conditions of possibility of a democratic debate about it'). Lordon, *Jusqu'à quand?*, p. 24.
65. Generally, Lordon has been critical of the political ineffectiveness of intellectuals – see Frédéric Lordon, *Les Affects de la politique* (Paris: Seuil, 2016), pp. 166–70 and *D'un retournement l'autre*, p. 130. He also sees universities in general as compromised, having long ago succumbed to 'l'esthétique de la finance'. Lordon, *Jusqu'à quand?*, p. 54.
66. Lordon, *Jusqu'à quand?*, p. 176, p. 179.
67. Ibid. pp. 178–81. For Lordon's critique of the euro, see Lordon, *La Malfaçon*.
68. Frédéric Lordon, *La Crise de trop: Reconstruction d'un monde failli* (Paris: Fayard, 2009).
69. Lordon, *Capitalisme, désir et servitude*, p. 108.
70. Lordon, *Les Affects de la politique*, pp. 56–8, p. 60.
71. Frédéric Lordon, *Figures du communisme* (Paris: La Fabrique éditions, 2021), pp. 10–11.
72. Frédéric Lordon, 'Fin de monde?', 5 December 2018, blog.mondediplo.net/fin-de-monde (last accessed 16 August 2021).
73. See for example Benoît Denis, *Littérature et engagement: De Pascal à Sartre* (Paris: Seuil, 2000) and Martin O'Shaughnessy, 'Fiction, Documentary and the Political', in Michael Temple and Michael Witt (eds), *The French Cinema Book*, 2nd edn (London: Palgrave, 2018), pp. 297–303.
74. Frédéric Lordon, 'Un film d'action directe', *Le Monde diplomatique*, February 2016, p. 28, monde-diplomatique.fr/2016/02/LORDON/54740 (last accessed 16 August 2021).
75. Ibid.
76. Frédéric Lordon, *Vivre sans?: Institutions, police, travail, argent* ... (Paris: La Fabrique éditions, 2019), p. 45.
77. Frédéric Lordon, '65 Intellectuels invités à débattre à l'Élysée', lundi.am/65-intellectuels-invites-a-debattre-a-l-Elysee (last accessed 16 August 2021).
78. Lordon, *La Société des affects*, p. 119.
79. Lordon, *Jusqu'à quand?*, p. 6.
80. Le Comité invisible, *L'Insurrection qui vient* (Paris: La Fabrique éditions, 2007). Lordon's relation with this current of the insurrectionist left is complex. While

sympathetic to anti-capitalist movements, Lordon is critical of the idea that (through local autonomous communes, for example) people will ever be free of the state, of institutions, of police and vertical power structures in general. These structures are inherent in the social as such. Which is not to say he opposes the overthrow of these structures in their current form. He develops this critique in *Imperium: Structures et affects des corps politiques* (Paris: La Fabrique éditions, 2015) and *Vivre sans?*. Nevertheless, Lordon has collaborated with the revue *Lundimatin*, associated with le Comité invisible. Situating le Comité in relation to Lordon and other factions on the radical left, see Ugo Palheta, 'L'insurrection qui revient: Les influences visibles sur le Comité invisible', *Revue de crieur*, 4 (2016), 58–73.
81. Lordon, 'Fin de monde?'.
82. With the caveat that affects are not the same as feelings, see William Davies, *Nervous States: How Feeling Took Over the World* (London: Jonathan Cape, 2018).
83. Lordon, *Les Affects de la politique*, pp. 52–4.
84. Ibid. pp. 23–7.
85. Frédéric Lordon, 'Après "l'Europe sociale", "l'Europe démocratique" . . . (ou l'art de regarder ailleurs)', 17 May 2019, blog.mondediplo.net/apres-l-europe-sociale-l-europe-democratique-ou-l (last accessed 16 August 2021). For a more sceptical argument about the imminence of another crisis, see Christian Chavagneux, 'Une nouvelle crise financière?', *Esprit* (July–August 2019), 103–8.
86. Lordon, *Jusqu'à quand?*, p. 101.
87. See Tooze, *Crashed* and Wolfgang Streeck, *How Will Capitalism End? Essays on a Failing System* (London: Verso, 2016).
88. Frédéric Lordon, *La Condition anarchique: Affects et institutions de la valeur* (Paris: Seuil, 2018).
89. Frédéric Lordon, 'En guerre – pour la préemption salariale!', 21 May 2018, blog.mondediplo.net/en-guerre-pour-la-preemption-salariale (last accessed 16 August 2021).

CHAPTER TWO

The Saints of the Crisis: Larnaudie and Stiegler in the Oversight Committee Room

LES EFFONDRÉS AND THE COLLAPSE OF MARKET IDEOLOGY

Like Lordon, the literary writer Mathieu Larnaudie was also watching events closely in 2008.[1] Larnaudie's novel about the 2008 global financial crisis, *Les Effondrés* ('The Collapsed', 2010) provides a series of scenes or tableaux in which his characters stop working and undergo a transvaluation. A *récit* spanning twenty-four chapters, *Les Effondrés* recounts the fate of the key players involved in the crisis. Although not directly named, they are identifiable by descriptors and clues in the text. They are principally: Angela Merkel; Nicolas Sarkozy; Richard Fuld, Chairman of Lehman Brothers; Bernard Madoff, the financier whose Ponzi scheme was the biggest financial fraud in US history and who was serving a 150-year prison sentence until his recent death in April 2021; Thierry Magon de La Villehuchet, a French businessman who took his own life after losing his fortune in Madoff's scheme; and Adolf Merckle, a German entrepreneur who also took his own life following losses during the crisis. In this chapter I will analyse how Larnaudie uses media images in his literary text, and how these images play a role in the crisis. In particular, I will focus on Alan Greenspan, former Chairman of the US Federal Reserve (1987–2006) and generally considered an extremely influential figure in post-war US economic history, whose reputation was damaged by the crisis, when he was criticised for the unchecked growth of the subprime mortgage bubble occurring under his watch which contributed to the crash. As the title suggests, Greenspan and the other figures in the book were all in some sense 'ruined' by the crisis; they are, as Larnaudie remarks in an apparently throwaway comment to which I will return, the 'saints' of the crisis.[2]

Les Effondrés is made up of relatively short chapters that are often comprised of a single very long sentence, typically running to several pages. Larnaudie's prose is relentless in the manner in which it relates the very moment of the *effondrement* or collapse.[3] As one critic argues: 'Par la démesure de la phrase, le texte signifie la crise dans l'écriture même, mimant en quelque sorte cette économie dématérialisée' ('Through the excess of the sentence, the text communicates the crisis in the writing itself, in a way mimicking the dematerialised economy').[4] The work is highly quotable at the level of vivid individual phrases, but the rhythm of the sentences cannot be evoked without quoting *in extenso* (as I will do below).

What is typical of the style of the book is given in the syntax of the opening chapter, 'Effondrement'. The first sentence runs to eight pages in length. The sentence opens by evoking how, after the end of the Cold War, it was supposed that history had ended: 'ce grand récit maintenant passé, relégué, frappé d'obsolescence, qu'ils continueraient d'appeler l'Histoire' ('this great story now over, relegated, obsolete, that they would continue to call History').[5] The 'triomphateurs' ('triumphant ones') were those who 'se félicitaient de concert d'avoir su échapper à (débarrasser la planète de) ce fléau nommé "idéologie"' ('together congratulated themselves for having known how to escape from (to rid the world of) the scourge named "ideology"').[6] But now, 'soudain, tout s'est effondré' ('suddenly, everything collapsed').[7] The evocation of the end of history follows only after the book's opening words: 'Et puis un jour, alors même que' ('And then one day, even though').[8] This syntactical structure thus sets the putative 'fin de l'Histoire' ('end of History') retrospectively as something merely held in suspension, a sentence waiting to be resumed; the 'fin de l'Histoire' is constructed as the anomaly, rather than the crisis. The first 'alors même que' ('even though') is followed by three further instances of 'alors que' ('even though') and then an 'alors même, enfin, que' ('even though, finally'), each opening a clause of about half a page which only closes with a semi-colon before the next 'alors même que'. In addition, each clause is packed with parentheses, giving the text a tumbling rhythm. Only at the end of this elaborate grammatical construction do we arrive at the 'soudain, tout s'est effondré', which is followed by a colon opening the next part of the sentence.

But what is it that collapsed? This is the subject of the next part of the sentence, whose activating word is the 'tout' ('everything') of 'tout s'est effondré' ('everything collapsed'). What collapsed was 'tout ce en quoi ils avaient fait profession de croire, ou plutôt dont ils avaient fait profession d'exploiter, de justifier et de propager partout' ('everything that they had professed to believe in, or rather everything they had professed to manage, justify and propagate').[9] It is 'cette étrange foi devenue injonction, devenue horizon providentiel' ('this strange faith become injunction, become providential horizon') that is the free market outlook.[10] Everything had worked, or seemed to work thanks to an 'acte de foi continu' ('a continuous act of faith').[11] In short, then, what collapsed were the ideological underpinnings of the economic system. Thus, most pithily, Larnaudie writes: 'la fin de l'Histoire était finie' ('the end of History was at an end').[12] For Larnaudie, the financial crisis represents fundamentally an ideological collapse because it required the elite proponents of the free market making the biggest state intervention in the market in the history of the US (the bank 'bailout' packages of 2008). It is not the financial loss for those involved that is most crushing, but the more profound sense that their worldview was flawed: what crashed was the idea that markets were naturally capable of self-regulation. The quotations above show how the text employs frequent religious metaphors to construct ideology as a secular faith. In a similar vein, we might say that what was shaken was the core of what Joseph Vogl calls liberal *oikodicy*, 'a theodicy of the economic universe': that is, 'the fiction of self-balancing market forces provides a privileged source of images from which modern societies draw their self-representations'.[13]

The final part of the long first sentence is a series of sketches, each introduced in the third person with 'l'on vit' ('one saw'), describing traders reacting to the crash, despairing about their presumed imminent dismissal and cursing within the privacy of a toilet cubicle. The primary responses of those actors most directly affected by the crisis are of course firstly either incredulity or rage at having been 'betrayed' by the system. And yet, here as elsewhere in Larnaudie's book, this incredulity of those who are ruined by the crisis gives way to a state of fascination:

> Et de même, sur les écrans qui propageaient les multiples représentations de leur décontenancement, les images et les preuves de leur faillite, ou dans les lieux où ils évoluaient et qui avaient été à travers les âges récents exclusivement consacrés à l'édification de leur gloire, l'on put voir (tous, nous pûmes, unanimes, voir) une torpeur incrédule se saisir de leurs gestes et de leurs corps, s'inscrire sur des visages éberlués aux yeux mangés par le désarroi, hagards, ébahis de s'être à ce point trompés, ou bien consternés d'avoir été trahis par le système auquel ils s'étaient voués, auquel ils avaient juré cette fidélité implicite qui est celle de la certitude, floués dans leurs plus intimes convictions et, dans le même temps, fascinés devant le désastre qu'ils avaient suscité [. . .][14]

> [And likewise, on the screens which spread the various representations of their discombobulation, the images and the very proof of their failure, or in the places in which they had performed and which had been throughout recent times exclusively dedicated to their glory, one could see (all of us, everyone could see) an incredulous torpor take hold of their gestures and bodies, write itself on their dumbfounded faces, their eyes eaten by the confusion, distressed and dumbfounded to have been so mistaken, or else dismayed at having been betrayed by the system to which they had been devoted, to which they had sworn the implicit loyalty of certitude, conned in their most intimate convictions and, at the same time, fascinated before the disaster that they had brought about [. . .]]

Here it becomes clear that the crisis is bound up with its audiovisual image: the crisis was among other things a screen event. What Larnaudie shows is how in a culture of the image, crises appear like cracks on the surface of screens: trading screens, news footage, ATMs. The cracked images are 'proofs' of the failure of the bankers. Similarly, Larnaudie will describe the reaction of the only fictional character in the book, a man known as 'le boiteux' ('the man with the limp') who lives in Geneva, who is resigned:

> à contempler, presque enclin, par moments, à une forme de désintéressement, comme si le sens de ce qui s'affichait en fût venu à lui échapper et qu'il n'y eût plus vu qu'un pur jeu de formes abstraites, sur son écran d'ordinateur, cliquant pour les agrandir l'un après l'autre sur de multiples diagrammes et graphiques, les lignes brisées ou sinusoïdales, toutes ou presque, avec quelques rebonds et accidents, quelques cassures, tendanciellement inclinées en diagonale vers le bas et la droite, voyant s'évaporer, partir en fumée les sommes considérables d'argent qu'il avait amassées, le fruit du labeur (pensait-il) de toute une vie et l'objet de sa fierté [. . .][15]
>
> [to contemplate, almost prone, every now and then, to a kind of disinterestedness, as if the meaning of that which was shown had just escaped him and he could no longer see anything but a pure game of abstract forms, on his computer screen, clicking to enlarge one after the other the various diagrams and charts the broken and wavy lines, nearly all of them, save for a few rebounds, accidents and breaks, trending diagonally down and right, seeing the considerable sums of money that he had amassed, the fruit of his whole life's labour (he thought) and the object of his pride, evaporate and go up in smoke [. . .]]

It is not just that the scales fall from his eyes, but he dissociates. A little before this passage, he is described as watching the collapse of his stocks 'à la manière du spectateur impuissant d'une course hippique' ('like a powerless spectator at a horse race'), watching in a slow agony as the animal that has already lost completes the track.[16] (The chapter continues with a flashback describing how he made his fortune; the character is said to be handicapped from a horse-riding accident.) This scene describes at the moment of the crash the (dis)functioning of what Yves Citton calls *plout-éido-scopes*: media which fascinate us with images or ideas of wealth, of which the classic example is the slot machine in a casino.[17] If such machines entice us into fascinated fusion with the machine, tending to blur the boundary between production and consumption – and it seems that watching the movement of stocks, like the advance of a horse in a race, would fit this category – then, as Citton suggests, within an economy in which our attention is an exploitable financial asset it would be possible to see many or most of our interactions with media as increasingly resembling *ploutéidoscopes*.[18] The crisis marks a change in the nature of engagement with such media: the crisis is a moment of stunned passivity. Here as elsewhere, the temporality of the financial crisis is figured as a 'sorte d'absence du temps' ('kind of absence of time').[19] One of the trope images of the media coverage of the crisis was that of traders staring in disbelief at trading monitors whose information and graphs no longer made sense. What they were watching was something like the unworking or erasure of the world financial system. The crisis has revelatory power in that it breaks a habitual, functional relation to the image, thus allowing the Swiss character to undergo a kind of transvaluation and discover a kind of freedom.[20] What should be clear already, then, is that while Lordon approaches the crisis in terms of its politics and financial mechanisms, Larnaudie approaches it in and through its images. What Larnaudie shows in a literary text is what successive chapters will demonstrate in relation to film and film theory: the financial crisis is indissociable from an imaginary of derivative images.

With the sequence on the traders, the first sentence of the first chapter ends and is followed by just two more sentences, each about a quarter of a page in length. Thus, in this final part of the chapter we have a slowing and fragmentation of the rhythm. This slowing rhythm is like the rhythm of the *effondrement*, as if to evoke the final falling pieces of debris of a demolished building, a metaphor Larnaudie will use later.[21] Just looking at the first sentence of *Les Effondrés*, we can thus see why the prodigious French translator Claro – known for his work translating such American authors as Thomas Pynchon – has noted the Proustian quality to Larnaudie's sentences.[22]

The phrase 'l'on vit' and variations thereof are found in other parts of the book. In one instance, Larnaudie describes how 'l'on put lire, un matin, dans la presse généraliste' ('one could read, one morning, in the daily news') a report about a study into the relation between the length of the fingers of forty-four City of London traders and their financial success, which found that those with a ring-finger longer than their index were likely to be better traders than those without (a ratio supposedly related to increased exposure to testosterone in the womb).[23] Studying the French press of the period, it is likely that the specific article Larnaudie has in mind is from an edition of *Le Figaro* from January 2009.[24] Larnaudie writes that in the same edition one could find news of the crisis under way:

> si, pour les mettre en regard, on les eût agencées en vis-à-vis de cette colonne orpheline et risible, aberrante, égarée dans les pages 'Sciences' (en rejouant, par exemple, une formule de la technique du cut-up [. . .]), l'on eût pu s'étonner de la continuité incongrue et pourtant significative des fragments de texte ainsi obtenus, de leur cohérence [. . .][25]

[if, to compare them, one had arranged them side by side with this lost, aberrant, laughable orphan column in the science pages (playing, for example, with an up-to-date cut-up technique [. . .]), one might have been stunned by the incongruous yet meaningful continuity, the coherence, of the text fragments [. . .]]

It is as if in the midst of the crisis, *homo economicus* was grasping at straws for new evidence of his ordained nature. Closing the second chapter on an absurd note, we read that the blame should perhaps have fallen not on those running the system, but on those whose index fingers were longer than their ring-fingers.[26] With this reference to the cut-up technique, associated notably with William S. Burroughs, Larnaudie inscribes in the text its origins in the press reporting of the crisis. *Les Effondrés* plays frequently on the tension between recounted fact and imagined psychological detail. Larnaudie has described the thrill of writing the piece 'sur le vif' ('in real time') as the events were unfolding (he wrote the book in Berlin in 2008–9 and it was published in spring 2010). The choice of long sentences allowed him to capture the flow of the story as it emerged, offering a 'grande plasticité' in which the sentence develops organically.[27] As I will show in the next chapter, this gesture of cutting and recombination is central to derivative procedures.

Greenspan before Congress

The section on Greenspan, 'Les Reniements du Maestro' ('The Renunciations of the Maestro'), is the core of Larnaudie's book and the Congressional hearing it describes was the inspiration for the book. This hearing took place on 23 October 2008, when Greenspan was summoned to the United States House of Representatives Committee on Oversight and Government Reform to 'expliciter sa pensée dans un langage limpide' ('explain his thinking in a clear language') – his thought, that is, about the work of risk management supposedly done in part by financial derivatives.[28] 'I would like to provide my views on the source of the crisis', Greenspan said as he read out his opening statement, and 'discuss how my thinking has evolved and what I have learned this past year'.[29] It is clear that Greenspan's thinking did change in this period. In April 2008, Greenspan was still firm in his position that regulation was not the answer to the developing crisis.[30] By September, however, Greenspan was calling for Lehman Brothers to be rescued. The US Treasury chose not to do this, allowing the bank to declare bankruptcy on 15 September 2008.[31] This immediately caused widespread panic, marking the acute moment of the crisis.

Before Congress, Greenspan appears like a mythical figure: the committee members are conscious of 'la légendaire fresque de son existence et de son œuvre' ('the legendary saga of his life and work'), themselves involved in 'le culte des valeurs et des idées dont il était la plus brillante incarnation' ('the cult of values and ideas of which he was the most brilliant incarnation').[32] Greenspan is referred to by his soubriquet 'le Maestro', a moniker which is increasingly put under strain as the text goes on.[33] With an ironically hagiographical rhetoric, Larnaudie sketches Greenspan's career:

> en sa qualité d'apôtre parfait et de prosélyte convaincant de l'évangélisme libéral, propulsé à la tête de la Réserve fédérale, y mener une politique opiniâtre et réputée pragmatique, ainsi qu'il s'en était lui-même toujours targué [. . .], couronnée d'un succès amplement célébré, encensée pour la manière dont elle avait su contrer les conjonctures défavorables et accompagner la prospérité spectaculaire que l'avènement de la révolution industrielle des nouvelles technologies avait suscitée; cet homme, enfin, qui avait quitté sa place tandis que commençaient de poindre les frémissements annonciateurs de la catastrophe qu'il avait largement contribué à provoquer: et c'était cela, précisément, sa contribution, la part qui lui incombait, son désastreux héritage, ou plutôt son legs devenu l'envers désastreux de sa légende dorée [. . .] qu'il était du devoir de ses auditeurs, tous plus jeunes que lui, incrédules, désemparés non moins que lui sans doute, et investis d'une haute mission de justice, d'évaluer et de juger là.[34]

> [in his capacity as a perfect apostle and compelling proselyte of liberal evangelism, propelled to the head of the Federal Reserve, there to lead an unrelenting and supposedly pragmatic policy, just as he himself always boasted [. . .], rewarded with fabulous success, acclaimed for the manner in which it had overcome unfavourable conditions and accompanied the spectacular prosperity brought about by the advent of the industrial revolution of new technologies; this man, finally, who had left his position while the portentous murmurs were starting to be heard of the catastrophe that he had to a great extent contributed to; and it was precisely this, his contribution, his part in it all, his disastrous heritage, or rather legacy become the underside of his golden legend [. . .] that it was the duty of his listeners, all of them younger than him, incredulous, doubtless no less disconcerted than he was, and invested with a great mission of justice, to evaluate and judge.]

A sequence of semi-colons then separates various adumbrations of the man, introduced by 'lui qui' ('he who . . .'), for example 'lui qui s'était, depuis toujours, fait l'apologiste ardent de la main invisible' ('he who had forever acted as the ardent apologist of the invisible hand').[35] Here we see how the humbling of Greenspan is essentially bound up with the fact that he is regarded as the incarnation of the ideology, couched in religious terms as a kind of failed saint (later this 'sorte de pape pour notre temps' ['sort of pope for our times'] will be described as apostasised and as 'défroqué' ['defrocked']).³⁶ As head of the Federal Reserve, his success was the success of the whole American economy. Yet he is also the one partly responsible for the crisis – his is a 'désastreux héritage'.

The whole eight-page chapter dealing with Greenspan consists of only three very long sentences, each of which contains very long parentheses. The scene is described in surreal detail. In one parenthesis we are treated to a microscopic description of the face of the committee Chairman (Figure 2.1), who:

> se penchait sur son pupitre chaque fois qu'il prenait la parole, qu'il posait une question ou demandait une précision, jusqu'à presque coller ses lèvres à la petite boule de mousse noire de son micro, [. . .] en fronçant, sous les plis attentifs, concentrés, de son grand front dégarni, ses sourcils broussailleux, lourds, ou en avançant, dans une mimique nerveuse, sous la barre de moustaches grises en surplomb de sa bouche, les grandes dents écartées de rongeur qui conféraient l'aspect outré et élastique d'une caricature de presse ou d'un personnage de cartoon à ce sénateur affublé par ailleurs d'un nom saugrenu, résultant de l'apposition des mots anglais qui signifient 'cire' et 'homme', et que l'on eût donc pu traduire par 'l'homme-cire', ou 'l'homme de cire', nom qui avec la laideur exceptionnelle et la grande malléabilité de ses expressions contrastait résolument, à moins qu'on ne pût penser que l'ensemble de sa tête était effectivement taillé dans une boule de cire qui, en fonction des variations de température, se déformait, se liquéfiait ou durcissait [. . .]³⁷

> [leaned on his desk each time he spoke, each time he asked a question or requested a clarification, almost to the point of pressing his lips to the little black foam ball on his microphone [. . .], frowning under the attentive, focused wrinkles of his large balding brow, his bushy eyebrows, heavy, or advancing, in a nervous grimacing, under the line of his grey moustache which hung over his mouth, the large, rodent-like, gapped teeth which gave this senator the astonished and exaggerated aspect of a press caricature or cartoon character, who moreover was saddled with an absurd surname resulting from the apposition of the English words for 'wax' and 'man', and which one could translate by 'the wax man' or 'the man of wax', a name which contrasted resolutely with its exceptional ugliness and the great malleability of its expressions; one could even imagine that the whole of his head was indeed sculpted from a ball of wax which, according to changes in temperature, would become deformed, liquify or harden [. . .]]

This is Henry A. Waxman, a Democrat Representative from California. Here the diminutive descriptions of the senator's features point to the impotence of the 'oversight' functions of Congress in contrast to the power of the 'Maestro' on whose every word the assembled company hangs. As well as showing how Larnaudie gives crossword-like clues as to his real-life references, the humorous

Figure 2.1 Henry Waxman, 23 October 2008. Source: https://archive.org/details/gov.house.ogr.20081023_hrs15REF2154.

wordplay on the senator's name dissolves the reality of the proceedings in an oneiric fashion, much as does the reverie of the melting of his waxen head. Larnaudie's text zooms in on hallucinatory, hyperreal details to evoke a real-life figure, the prose underscoring the unreality of the situation. As we see in this quotation, then, Larnaudie, like Lordon, insists on the surreal nature of the crisis – which is to say, the febrility of the atmosphere it engendered and the sense that the established order was, like Waxman's head, dissolving. Larnaudie's text is not animated by the same political commitment as Lordon's play, but both works expressly crystallise the sequences of events that made up the financial crisis in images of the collapse of faith (here, we shall see, faith invested in the authority of the former Chairman of the Fed), showing how such collapses consist in their being visible as an image.

Larnaudie's text was composed from repeated viewings of the hearing video and from adapting press reports. I want to suggest that what is particularly important here is how the writer treats the footage and transcript of the hearing – documentary legal evidence given under oath – as raw materials for a literary text. The media is generally a key subject and resource for Larnaudie's fiction: the main character of his 2012 novel *Acharnement* is a political speech writer, while another novel is loosely inspired by the life of the actress Frances Farmer.[38] When put to him that the chapter constitutes an ekphrasis of the hearing and press documents, Larnaudie comments:

> Oui, exactement. Mais en plus le mot est juste parce que quand je travaillais sur ces documents [. . .] j'ai fait une sorte d'ekphrasis d'image et de représentation contemporaine. Ce n'est pas un tableau classique, ce n'est pas une sculpture antique, c'est du vidéo d'un dirigeant de la Fed devant le congrès [. . .] L'idée c'était comme dans une ekphrasis, la description rigoureuse doit déployer, déplier les significations contenues dans l'image. Là c'est un peu ce que j'ai fait.[39]
>
> [Yes, exactly. But also it's the right word because when I was working on these documents [. . .] I made a sort of ekphrasis of the image and contemporary representation. It's not a classical painting, it's not an ancient sculpture, it's some video of a director of the Fed before Congress [. . .] The idea was like an ekphrasis, the rigorous description must unfold and stretch out the meanings contained in the image. That's a little bit what I did.]

Larnaudie's work thus offers one example of the way an American media-political event at the heart of the global financial crisis finds its way into a French cultural representation of that crisis, the literary text becoming an intermedial reflection on the way the crisis crystallised as image. While this operation could be considered ekphrastic – that is, the literary aspect here consists partly in the (slightly parodic) rendering in words of an image – the close description of the footage and the unpacking of the image might also suggest a film sequence analysis, an analysis of an image from which Larnaudie derives a literary text.[40] The significance of this practice of describing images in writing is that it allows us to grasp the experience of an age submerged in images and, seemingly for that reason, marked by a 'deficit of description'.[41] Thus in another context, Larnaudie remarks: 'La crise était pour moi le nom de l'apparition des corps, des gestes, des fragments de discours, qui composaient une nouvelle scène où j'ai eu envie de faire circuler un récit' ('For me the crisis was the name for the appearance of bodies, of gestures, and of fragments of speech which composed a new scene where I wanted to circulate a récit'); what he was seeking was the 'l'expérience sensible' ('perceptible experience') of events.[42] The apparently incidental details, then, are precisely the point of these long quotations: it is the surface of the visible that comes to the fore as an image when the scaffolding of sense in the world collapses behind it. These figural elements of the real image serve as a base from which come further imagined or derived details, that is, what Emmanuel Siety calls *fictions d'images* or 'fictions of the image'.[43]

Like Waxman, Greenspan is also described in close detail:

> aussi, tandis que son visage aux lèvres épaisses et, lorsqu'il parlait, humides, presque retroussées, aux larges lunettes rondes grossissant de petits yeux myopes et mobiles rétractés dans leurs cavités et animés par des paupières papillonnantes, marquait sa volonté de se rendre parfaitement intelligible, s'efforçait de revêtir la juste formule intermédiaire entre le sourire affable et la gravité circonstanciée – entre la stupeur et la sérénité –, l'entendit-on reconnaître, médusé

lui-même par les paroles qu'il articulait, que les institutions économiques et celle qu'il avait dirigée en premier lieu avaient traversé 'une période de sous-estimation des risques' [. . .]⁴⁴

[also, while his face with his thick and, when he spoke, humid, almost puckered lips, with his large round glasses magnifying his little mobile and myopic eyes, retracted in their cavities and animated by fluttering eyelids, marked his desire to make himself perfectly intelligible, struggling to find the correct middle-way between affable smile and calm seriousness – between stupor and serenity –, he was heard to acknowledge, himself astonished by the words he was pronouncing, that the economic institutions, including the one which he had led in the first place, had gone through a 'period of underpricing of risk [. . .]']

Again, part of what is striking is how the older religious language of saints and legends is contained in the description of details of a modern media image. More importantly in this quotation, however, there is an effect of bathos in the switch of register from surreal micro-detail to euphemistic economic jargon of 'risques'. Coming at the end of this meandering sentence, the mention of underpricing of 'risk' sets up a parodic contrast between the all-too-human Greenspan and the pretensions of the 'risk management' industry, one of whose forms were the subprime financial derivatives involved in the crisis. 'Risk', then, stands as a metonymy for the whole arcane infrastructure of derivatives. Against this backdrop Greenspan is 'effondré' – he is almost in a stupor, fallen from his legendary status and revealed to be a mortal 'myopic' man.

Figure 2.2 Alan Greenspan testifies before Congress, 23 October 2008. Source: https://archive.org/details/gov.house.ogr.20081023_hrs15REF2154.

In terms of the wider significance of this hearing within the context of the crisis, the crucial concession from Greenspan's testimony is quoted in Larnaudie's text (in French), that he had 'made a mistake in presuming that the self-interests of organizations, specifically banks, were such that they were best capable of protecting their own shareholders and their equity in the firms'.[45] Larnaudie recounts the moment when Waxman asks whether there was a flaw in Greenspan's ideology. Quoted below is the key exchange from the official transcript:

> Chairman WAXMAN. You feel that your ideology pushed you to make decisions that you wish you had not made?
> Mr. GREENSPAN. Well, remember, though, whether or not ideology is, [sic] is a conceptual framework with the way people deal with reality. Everyone has one. You have to. To exist, you need an ideology. The question is, whether it exists [sic] is accurate or not. What I am saying to you is, yes, I found a flaw, I don't know how significant or permanent it is, but I have been very distressed by that fact. But if I may, may I just finish an answer to the question –
> Chairman WAXMAN. You found a flaw?
> Mr. GREENSPAN. I found a flaw in the model that I perceived is the critical functioning structure that defines how the world works, so to speak.
> Chairman WAXMAN. In other words, you found that your view of the world, your ideology, was not right, it was not working.
> Mr. GREENSPAN. Precisely. That's precisely the reason I was shocked, because I had been going for 40 years or more with very considerable evidence that it was working exceptionally well.[46]

Recounting this exchange, Larnaudie adds imagined details absent from the transcript to describe the feelings of those in the hall as the master responds:

> sans doute furent-ils, à l'instant précis où ces mots franchirent ses lèvres, nombreux ceux dont le sang se glaça, nombreux ceux qui guettèrent autour d'eux, sur d'autres visages, les réactions les assurant qu'ils n'avaient pas été les victimes d'un problème acoustique, que la scène pour ainsi dire surréaliste, impensable à laquelle ils assistaient avait bel et bien lieu [. . .][47]

> [doubtless they were, at the moment gripped when these words passed his lips, numerous those whose blood froze, many were those who looked around themselves, at others' faces, those other reactions assuring them that they hadn't been the victim of a problem with the acoustics, that the unthinkable, as it were surrealist scene they had attended had indeed taken place [. . .]]

Larnaudie underlines the importance of the word 'idéologie' in the exchange:

> le fait qu'à ce moment il n'eût pas reculé devant le mot 'idéologie' [. . .] équivalait rigoureusement à confesser soudain que sa foi béate dans le libre marché avait été anéantie, que sa confiance inconditionnelle en l'invincibilité du système était désormais caduque, que ses conceptions de la vie des hommes et

de la nature, de l'ordre leur convenant, se révélaient tout simplement fausses, erronées, inadéquates au réel [. . .].[48]

[the fact that at this moment he had not recoiled before the word 'ideology' [. . .] was exactly tantamount to suddenly confessing that his blessed faith in the free market had been destroyed, that his unconditional confidence in the invincibility of the system was henceforth obsolete, that his conceptions of the life of men and of nature, of the order that suited them, had revealed themselves to be quite simply false, erroneous, and inadequate to reality [. . .]]

While the moment when he agreed to discuss the meaning of the word 'ideology' has been read by some as a serious error by Greenspan, his biographer defends him on this point: 'It was an unremarkable observation. Of course, all ideologies had flaws; the fact that Greenspan had acknowledged his went only to show his pragmatism [. . .] In Greenspan's understanding, the statement that his ideology was flawed was almost a statement of the obvious.'[49] Furthermore, he disputes the idea that Greenspan was an ideologue: 'He was not simply an ideologue who believed in deregulation as a matter of faith. He was a pragmatist who had surveyed the evidence and concluded that private risk managers, however fallible, might be better than regulators.'[50] Yet it is as if merely acknowledging the relevance of the concept of ideology itself constitutes a 'confession' that Greenspan was ideologically driven. Ideology is not to be directly referred to, for that is to step outside of it, whose purpose is to encompass and regulate discourse. It wants to set the limits on the speech of others, rather than be revealed as itself a limit. What is inventive about Larnaudie's technique of description or ekphrasis of the media image is that it allows him to pinpoint, replay, dilate and textually analyse the precise moment when the shock occurs, when ideology is revealed as a limit.

Larnaudie remarks that Greenspan was 'sincère dans son effarement' ('sincere in his disbelief'). He was 'accusé' ('accused'), even though he was not on trial as such. The result was that 'il a plaidé sa cause et il a plaidé coupable' ('he pleaded his case and he pleaded guilty'). Given that in subsequent interventions Greenspan would return to a pro-market position, for Larnaudie:

Ça prouve qu'il est effectivement allé sans doute un peu trop loin par rapport à ce qu'il aurait pu se contenter de dire. Peut-être qu'il l'a regretté. Mais justement c'est ça qui est intéressant. C'est que parce qu'il est allé trop loin qu'il est sans doute allé dans le vrai. [. . .] Sans trop le dissimuler, sans trop le déguiser, sans trop atténuer les choses.[51]

[That proves that he doubtless went too far in relation to what he perhaps wanted to say. Perhaps he regretted it. But that is precisely what is interesting. It is because he went too far that he was doubtless speaking the truth. [. . .] Without especially hiding, disguising or qualifying things.]

Towards the close of the chapter, Larnaudie writes that:

> lorsqu'il se tut [. . .] dans les effluves de transpiration, d'eaux de toilette et de bois suintant qui circulaient dans la salle, au lieu du tumulte usuel et immédiat par quoi les auditeurs reviennent à eux-mêmes et à leurs préoccupations, un silence gêné continua de planer pendant quelques minutes, et le Maestro repenti se retourna pour parcourir l'assemblée du regard, adresser quelques signes de tête à l'intention de certains, peut-être pour évaluer les effets de la soudaine et désarçonnante transvaluation qui venait de s'opérer [. . .]⁵²

> [when he [Greenspan] fell silent [. . .] in the rivers of sweat, of aftershave and oozing wood which circulated in the hall, instead of the usual and immediate tumult in which the listeners went home or back to their business, an embarrassed silence continued to linger for several minutes, and the redeemed Maestro turned around to cast a glance at the assembly, to make a few signs with his head at particular individuals, perhaps to evaluate the effects of the sudden and disconcerting transvaluation that had just taken place [. . .]]

Amidst the imagined olfactory details, crucial here is the notion that what took place was a 'transvaluation', a notion I will develop in the next section. The sweat of the journalists and other attendees, like the hallucinatory details of the Waxman quotation, points to the physical effects brought on for those present at this seemingly arcane discussion about the oversight of the financial system. Zooming out from Greenspan, Larnaudie reinscribes his French position in relation to this event by alluding to the immediate radio reaction of the economist Alain Minc (not directly named) as one of those who failed to grasp the amplitude of what had taken place, and to deny its significance.⁵³ The final lines of the chapter lay bare the material, digital source of the text, evoking how the words of Greenspan instantly became a viral media event in 2008 as people – including, presumably, Larnaudie – received derivatives of this video, 'transférés par e-mail, les liens vers les vidéos mises en ligne présentant les séquences les plus significatives du témoignage du Maestro' ('forwarded by email, the links to uploaded videos showing the key sequences of the Master's testimony'), the event thus rippling out into the wider cultural circulation.⁵⁴ Ending on this note inscribes the *récit* in a quite specific moment of media history: in a time when media events become cut into video clips and shared online but before the massive generalisation of this practice with the uptake of social media. In other words, the text testifies to its provenance in an emergent media culture of derivative images.⁵⁵

Prolétarisation and Transvaluation

Like Larnaudie, the philosopher Bernard Stiegler argues that we have to be careful when interpreting Greenspan's remarks because at the same time as they constitute a 'un aveu' ('a confession'), they are also a 'un système de défense' ('a defence mechanism'): 'il est obligé d'avouer pour pouvoir se défendre' ('he has to confess in order to defend himself').[56] Like Larnaudie, Stiegler was quick to recognise the significance of the Greenspan hearing, it becoming for Stiegler a resource for the development of a philosophical concept. Stiegler has alluded frequently to Greenspan's appearance on Capitol Hill as a privileged example of what he theorises as *'prolétarisation'* ('proletarianisation'), a concept distinct from, but which nonetheless resonates with, Larnaudie's description of a collapsing ideology.[57] According to Stiegler, in this moment in the Oversight Committee Room Greenspan had lost all economic 'savoir'. Of course, he still had a salary of millions of dollars, Stiegler says, but he had no more knowledge:

> ce salarié avait lui aussi perdu son travail, car un travail est toujours un savoir, et réciproquement, mettre en œuvre un savoir, c'est toujours travailler [. . .] Greenspan, désœuvré, n'avait plus qu'un emploi: c'était un employé de la bureaucratie financière mondiale, prolétarisé comme le sont tous les employés.[58]

> [this salaried worker had also lost his work, because work is always a knowledge, and reciprocally, developing a knowledge is always to work [. . .] Greenspan, out of work, now had only a job: that of being an employee of a globalised financial bureaucracy, proletarianised like all employees.]

Stiegler's play on the meanings of work and unworking offers a different sense from Larnaudie's of Greenspan's fall, of how he appeared 'comme un prolétaire d'un nouveau genre' ('like a new kind of proletarian'), yet like Larnaudie he sees this as an almost surreal moment in which a world came undone.[59]

What is *prolétarisation*? Ars Industrialis, the activist group with which Stiegler is associated, offers a definition: 'Proletarianisation is, generally, that which consists in depriving a subject (producer, consumer or creator) of all their forms of knowledge (*ses savoirs*): know-how, life skills, theoretical and conceptual knowledge (*savoir-faire, savoir-vivre, savoir concevoir et théoriser*).'[60] Classically, this is due to technology. Here Stiegler's reading of the Greenspan testimony plugs into his broader philosophical project, notably as articulated in the series *La Technique et le temps*, according to which the exteriorisation of memory in writing constitutes a loss of memory and knowledge. For Stiegler, this is now our experience in every aspect of our existence, especially our feeling of powerlessness in the face of the vastness of human memory made available by digital networks. While we may have been accustomed to think of the proletariat as those rendered the appendage of a machine and who have lost their savoir-faire, now it is consumers who are deprived of knowledge by service industries. What the 2008 crisis brought to light was that now it is those like

Greenspan who run the system – 'les concepteurs et les décideurs' – who are proletarianised as a result of their reliance on trading software.[61] Stiegler thus refers to Greenspan as this 'new kind of proletarian' because he is 'un symptôme particulièrement symbolique de cette situation' ('a particularly symbolic symptom of this situation').[62] As Stiegler puts it in a key statement of his outlook:

> La situation contemporaine de prolétarisation généralisée s'est planétairement avérée constituer en 2008 une *économie de l'incurie*, une *déséconomie généralisée*, installant une dissociété intrinsèquement irresponsable parce que *systématiquement fondée sur la dilution de responsabilité*, c'est-à-dire sur une bêtise systématique, anti-noétique, qui est aussi une *infidélité systémique* du consommateur aussi bien que du spéculateur, qui jettent leurs objets, et qui est en cela génératrice d'une défiance structurelle, destructrice de ses propres conditions de possibilité: elle mène au gaspillage énergétique et à l'épuisement de toutes les formes d'énergie – énergies de combustion, c'est-à-dire de subsistance, et énergies libidinales, c'est-à-dire d'existence.[63]

> [In 2008, the contemporary situation of generalized proletarianization revealed itself to be a global *economy of carelessness and negligence*, a *generalized dis-economy*. This installs an inherently irresponsible 'dis-society', because it is systematically founded on the dilution of responsibility – that is, on a systemic, anti-noetic stupidity, which is also a systemic infidelity and faithlessness of the consumer and the speculator, who jettison their objects. This generates a structural distrust in a manner destructive of its own conditions of possibility: it leads to the waste of energy and the depletion of all forms of energy, both the combustion energies of subsistence and the libidinal energies of existence.[64]]

In the above quotation, we can see how Stiegler is unusual even among severe critics of the financial crisis in seeing the profundity of its causes and consequences. This is why Stiegler disarmingly avers that 'la crise n'est pas financière' ('it's not a *financial* crisis').[65] What we call the financial crisis is really the symptom or forewarning of a more serious crisis of '*l'insolvabilité économique générale*' ('general economic insolvency'), an economic crisis in the widest sense of the word 'economic', thus having social, moral and even existential ramifications and which will become more dangerous as automation in the world of work continues.[66] In 2015, Stiegler was already predicting a drastic increase in unemployment, in France as well as globally, which would contribute to the increasing entropy or disorder in the world.[67] Within this context Stiegler asks whether another future is possible. For him, the increased free time created by automation must be used to rethink the meaning of work and value in general. Stiegler considers policy ideas such as the universal basic income, but his prescription is for a broader metaphysical change, a '*transvaluation*' of economic and moral values whereby we try to reverse the chaos and toxic elements in the world.[68] We should thus cultivate knowledge and the individual through practices of *déprolétarisation* by which we learn new techniques, recover lost skills, take up our responsibilities toward others, and generally put things back in order.[69]

Stiegler attributes the failure to respond adequately to the crisis by states and institutions like the European Central Bank to the complete disappearance of critical political-economic thought, in France and globally, in the face of the prevailing ideology, which is now in comprehensive crisis.[70] Here Stiegler's analysis connects with Larnaudie's: *prolétarisation* is both a cause and consequence of submersion in ideology. This conditions the 'immense régression' of recent decades, intensified by rapid technological change and the rise of digital media, and whose culmination is the election of Donald Trump and the so-called post-truth era.[71] While Larnaudie offers us an extreme close-up of the moment of Greenspan's ideological *effondrement*, in many stark formulations Stiegler situates the financial crisis against a vast and catastrophic horizon, within a contemporary moment marked by an 'accumulation des calamités' ('an accumulation of calamities'), 'une *démoralisation généralisée*' ('generalised demoralisation') and '*un devenir fou planétaire*' ('a planet-wide descent into madness').[72]

The Greenspan hearing nonetheless does offer for Stiegler a symbol of the transvaluation of values and the new political economy of *déprolétarisation* that remains to be accomplished. As Larnaudie shows in *Les Effondrés*, it is precisely in conceding the word 'idéologie' as a term of argument that the terrain of ideology is itself revealed, and this is the first step in transvaluation. For Stiegler, ideology must be understood in the sense of that which surrounds us and that we do not see, in the sense that a fish does not see the water.[73] Specifically, it should be understood as the way the human mind and body are produced by technology. Ideology is an illusion which inverses cause and effect, Stiegler says, allowing us to think it is the mind that creates technology, rather than the other way around. Thus what Greenspan 'confesses' is that he had not seen, until the crisis, that he had inverted cause and effect: he thought he was in control of the algorithms underpinning the system of financial derivatives, but in fact it was the other way around.[74] While the concept of *prolétarisation* may at first glance lead us to think that Stiegler constructs the financial crisis as a question of technology rather than ideology, in fact the Greenspan testimony illustrates how these are mutually implicated: it is ideology that both causes the loss of *savoir* in technology and blinds one to this state of affairs. Thus Greenspan's transvaluation is to have stepped outside of his ideology and recognised himself as proletarianised. Stiegler claims it must have been an ordeal for Greenspan to see the whole system that he had created collapse. Exactly like Larnaudie, Stiegler comments that while

Greenspan was not on trial as such during his hearing, he was 'mis en cause' ('put into question'). This, says Stiegler, gave him a new and lucid perspective.

Larnaudie's quasi-religious reading of Greenspan as a 'saint of the crisis' finds an unexpected parallel when Stiegler compares Greenspan to the legend of Saint Julien l'Hospitalier, best known in the dreamlike retelling by Gustave Flaubert in his *Trois Contes* (1877).[75] A brief recap: when Julien is born, his parents receive visions telling them that their son will become a saint. He grows to be a bloodthirsty hunter of animals. One day, however, Julien encounters a deer which prophesies that he will kill his parents. Thenceforth, Julien abandons hunting and leaves his castle, for fear of accomplishing the prophecy. He becomes a famous soldier and takes an emperor's daughter for a wife. He lives in a palace and no longer wages war. Yet, one night temptation takes him, and he goes out to hunt. At the same time, two elderly beggars arrive, who are in fact Julien's parents, who have been travelling the world for years looking for their son. Julien's wife puts them in the marital bed. Out on the hunt, Julien finds himself thwarted at every turn, can no longer kill and returns home in a rage. Finding the couple in bed, he believes he sees a man in bed with his wife and murders them both – thus realising the prophecy. Julien becomes a wandering outcast. The tale ends when a leper calls to Julien, and Julien cares for and embraces him before ascending into heaven.

For Stiegler, the saint's life is about a conversion. He believes that Greenspan experienced a conversion: not a religious conversion, but a phenomenological one. As in Larnaudie's text, it was a transvaluation by which Greenspan saw beyond his ideology. He was forced to shed his illusions and, for Stiegler, we must generalise this process and make others too lose their illusions and recognise themselves as *prolétarisés*. For Stiegler, the way out of the present impasse will be through not Christianity but a new critique of political economy. Although Greenspan has not become a wandering mendicant, and even if he later downplayed his 'conversion', it is in the sense common to both Larnaudie and Stiegler that, as the one who before the world's media underwent an ideological transvaluation, he is a 'saint' of the crisis.[76]

Larnaudie remarks that what he tried to make palpable in *Les Effondrés* was 'la naissance d'une incertitude' ('the birth of an uncertainty').[77] It was ideology that constructed the putative certainty of the 'end of history'. Larnaudie and Stiegler represent two French interpretations within a much wider debate in the West on the significance and impact of the 2008 global financial crisis for the post-war geopolitical order. Reflecting on Covid-19 in a text written shortly before his death, Stiegler called for a new form of credit to found human society. Human social groups accord themselves a kind of credit or primordial certitude, without which no exchange is possible. In modern societies, it is called reason, and has become market individualism, the data economy and proletarianisation.[78] Stiegler writes that it is only now, after the event, that we can see the 2008 crisis as 'un signe annonciateur d'une vulnérabilité systémique beaucoup plus grave et beaucoup plus profonde' ('a forewarning of a much more profound and serious systemic vulnerability'), just as the Covid crisis foreshadows even worse disasters if nothing changes. While economists came out of the 2008 crisis discredited, 'le crédit discréditant' ('the credit which discredits') of speculative finance came out stronger. After the discredit into which things fell at the beginning of the twenty-first century, he writes, anyone who wishes to hope for the future must begin by investigating the conditions for the possibility of a reconstruction of a credit based around the public good.[79] This rethinking of credit and currency will find its echoes in the coming chapters. The religious rhetoric deployed by the two writers when describing Greenspan, whose hearing was framed in the most modern, digital conditions, points to the untimely or anachronistic nature of that ideology or faith that collapsed in 2008. The value of Larnaudie's and Stiegler's texts is their return to the critical moment – this transvaluation – when the new uncertainty was born under the sign of Saint Alan. Both texts, recounting the crisis in their different ways, force us, like Greenspan, to shed our illusions.

Notes

1. Larnaudie is the author of several novels and a director of Éditions Inculte, which specialises in cutting-edge fiction.
2. Interview with the author, Café de l'Industrie, 75011 Paris, 20 October 2017.
3. 'Effondrement' has in recent years in France been a term associated with a particular discourse which envisages the collapse of civilisation, sometimes called 'collapsologie' or 'effondrisme'. On this topic and its connection with the notion of crisis, see Laurence Allard, Alexandre Monnin and Cyprien Tasset, 'Est-il trop tard pour l'effondrement?', *Multitudes*, 76 (Autumn 2019), 53–67.
4. Guillaume Paugam, 'Mathieu Larnaudie: Une écriture de (la) crise', *Contemporary French and Francophone Studies*, 19: 5 (2015), 593–601 (p. 597).
5. Mathieu Larnaudie, *Les Effondrés* (Arles: Actes Sud, 2010), p. 8.
6. Ibid. p. 9.
7. Ibid. p. 9.
8. Ibid. p. 7.
9. Ibid. p. 9.
10. Ibid. p. 10. On global free market capitalism as a utopian, faith-based ideology, see John Gray, *False Dawn: The Delusions of Global Capitalism* (London: Granta, [1998] 2009).
11. Larnaudie, *Les Effondrés*, p. 11.
12. Ibid. p. 11.

13. Joseph Vogl, *The Specter of Capital*, trans. Joachim Redner and Robert Savage (Stanford, CA: Stanford University Press, [2010] 2015), p. 16, p. 36.
14. Larnaudie, *Les Effondrés*, p. 17.
15. Ibid. p. 25.
16. Ibid. p. 23.
17. Yves Citton, *Médiarchie* (Paris: Seuil, 2017), p. 372.
18. Ibid. p. 375.
19. Larnaudie, *Les Effondrés*, p. 33. See also the chapter 'Chronométrie des temps suspendus' ('Chronometry of Suspended Times'), in which we are given a description of a deserted New York apartment in which a copy of *Forbes* magazine lies open at an advert for a luxury watch. The watch seems to offer 'une représentation stylisée de l'instant soudain où (de l'heure à laquelle) s'était constituée cette scène globale, nébuleuse et simultanée, cet accident planétaire dont le mot "crise" était le nom, ce moment où étaient apparus les visages et les corps l'incarnant, avec eux les rumeurs et les lambeaux de phrases, les instantanés, les extraits vidéo, les audits, les proclamations et les récits, les titres de journaux, les commentaires consignés et à leur tour commentés sur la Toile, dans la multiplicité infinie des sites d'information, des tribunes, des pages personnelles, des blogs, toute cette vaste et incessante circulation parcourant le monde à la vitesse de la lumière et dont ils semblaient émaner, qui les portaient à l'existence publique, qui les manifestaient pour ainsi dire à nos yeux, eux, les anciens triomphateurs effondrés, gorilles, maestros et autres' ('a stylised representation of the very instant (of the time at which) this troubled, global and simultaneous scene, this planetary accident named by the word "crisis", this moment when the faces and bodies forming it appeared, and with them the rumours and fragments of phrases, the snapshots, the video extracts, the audits, the proclamations and the stories, the newspaper titles, the comments recorded and in turn commented upon online, in the infinite multiplicity of news sites, columns, personal pages, blogs, this whole vast and incessant circulation traversing the world at the speed of light and from which they seemed to emanate, making them public, bringing them as it were before our eyes, them, the collapsed erstwhile victors, gorillas, maestros and the rest') (pp. 73–4). In the next sentence, the watch is transported onto Sarkozy's wrist as he delivers the 'Discours de Toulon' (p. 75).
20. At the end of *Les Effondrés*, Larnaudie describes his Swiss character going outsider to take in the fresh mountain air, but in some sense he is still watching the market: 'paupières closes, il massa ses yeux, encore fatigués, emplis de l'intensité lumineuse de l'écran devant lequel il avait passé trop de temps, comme si le défilement des chiffres et de dépêches, l'indexation des pages eussent continué à innerver sa rétine, comme un calque ou un filtre en mouvement, en perpétuelle transformation, persistants, en surimpression à la réalité, et ne disparaissant que petit à petit, ne cessant vraiment que lorsque son regard se porta au loin, parcourant le cirque immense des berges du lac, observant le jeu de reflets du soleil sur l'eau et l'infime tache blanche des rares yachts qui croisaient au large' ('eyelids closed, he massaged his eyes, still tired, full of the intense light of the

screen in front of which he had spent too much time, as if the passage of figures and news and the indexing of pages had continued to innervate this retina, like a tracing or a filter in movement, in continual transformation, persisting, superimposed on reality, only disappearing little by little, only really stopping when he held his gaze at a distance, skimming over the immense scene of the banks of the lake, observing the play of reflections of the sun on the water and the tiny white yachts crossing far off') (p. 30). As I will develop in the next chapter, the notion of the *calque* helps understand the relation to the market that almost all the characters of this book have.

21. Ibid. pp. 31–2.
22. Claro, 'A la recherche du tant perdu' (2010), towardgrace.blogspot.fr/2010/04/la-recherche-du-tant-perdu.html (last accessed 16 August 2021).
23. Larnaudie, *Les Effondrés*, p. 19.
24. Yves Miserey, 'L'annulaire long, signe distinctif du trader', *Le Figaro*, 13 January 2009, p. 11.
25. Larnaudie, *Les Effondrés*, pp. 20–1.
26. Ibid. p. 21.
27. Interview with the author.
28. Larnaudie, *Les Effondrés*, p. 37.
29. Committee on Oversight and Government Reform, 'The Financial Crisis and the Role of Federal Regulators', Government Publishing Office, U.S. Congress House of Representatives, 23 October 2008, p. 11 of transcript, gpo.gov/fdsys/pkg/CHRG-110hhrg55764/pdf/CHRG-110hhrg55764.pdf (last accessed 16 August 2021).
30. Alan Greenspan, 'The Fed is Blameless on the Property Bubble', *Financial Times*, 6 April 2008, ft.com/content/81c05200-03f2-11dd-b28b-000077b07658 (last accessed 16 August 2021).
31. All five major US investment banks were in trouble. Ultimately two were rescued (Morgan Stanley and Goldman Sachs) and three went under (Merrill Lynch, Bear Stearns, Lehman Brothers). The credit rating agencies Fannie May and Freddie Mac were nationalised in September 2008. On Lehman Brothers, see Larnaudie's chapter on Richard Fuld (identifiable by his nickname 'the Gorilla' in the text) – Larnaudie, *Les Effondrés*, pp. 47–55.
32. Ibid. p. 37.
33. This nickname was coined by the journalist Bob Woodward in *Maestro: Greenspan's Fed and the American Boom* (New York: Simon & Schuster, 2000).
34. Larnaudie, *Les Effondrés*, pp. 39–40.
35. Ibid. p. 40.
36. Ibid. p. 34, p. 47.
37. Ibid. pp. 40–1.
38. Mathieu Larnaudie, *Notre désir est sans remède* (Arles: Actes Sud, 2015).
39. Interview with the author.
40. On the relation between traditions of ekphrasis and description in film analysis, see Jessie Martin, *Décrire le film de cinéma: Au départ de l'analyse* (Paris: Presses Sorbonne Nouvelle, 2012).

41. Dork Zabunyan, 'Du défilement à la fragmentation: La description en devenir', in Diane Arnaud and Dork Zabunyan (eds), *Les Images et les mots: Décrire le cinéma* (Villeneuve-d'Ascq: Presses Universitaires du Septentrion, 2014), pp. 181–9.
42. Jérôme Goude, 'Pandémie spéculative', *Le Matricule des anges*, 114 (June 2010), pp. 34–5.
43. This term designates the way that spectators attribute fictive properties to the images themselves that make up a film. This is often at the invitation of the film, but it is also constructed by the spectator in a process that is as much perceptual as associative and intellectual. Emmanuel Siety, *Fictions d'images: Essai sur l'attribution de propriétés fictives aux images de films* (Rennes: Presses Universitaires de Rennes, 2009).
44. Larnaudie, *Les Effondrés*, pp. 41–2.
45. Ibid. p. 42; Committee on Oversight, 'The Financial Crisis', p. 45.
46. Committee on Oversight, 'The Financial Crisis', p. 46.
47. Larnaudie, *Les Effondrés*, p. 42.
48. Ibid. p. 43.
49. Sebastian Mallaby, *The Man Who Knew: The Life & Times of Alan Greenspan* (London: Penguin, 2016), pp. 667–8. For a sympathetic account of Greenspan's response to the crisis generally, see pp. 648–71.
50. Ibid. p. 665.
51. Interview with the author.
52. Larnaudie, *Les Effondrés*, pp. 43–4.
53. Ibid. p. 44. Lordon refers to Minc as 'l'idiot canonique du néolibéralisme' ('the canonical idiot of neoliberalism'). Lordon, *Figures du communisme*, p. 134. See also Lordon's discussion of Minc's failure to foresee the crisis in *Les Nouveaux Chiens de garde*.
54. Larnaudie, *Les Effondrés*, pp. 44–5.
55. 'Il est remarquable que les smartphones [. . .] et les réseaux anti-sociaux se soient développés en pleine crise financière' ('It is remarkable that smartphones and anti-social networks developed during a full-blown financial crisis'). Bernard Stiegler, *Dans la disruption: Comment ne pas devenir fou?* (Paris: Les Liens qui libèrent, 2016), p. 173. It was in the year 2007 that the iPhone was invented and that Facebook and Twitter took off.
56. Interview with the author, Institut de recherche et d'innovation, Paris 75004, 17 October 2017.
57. Besides major texts discussed in this chapter, for other references to Greenspan see also Bernard Stiegler, 'Critique de la raison impure: Entretien avec Bernard Stiegler', *Esprit* (March–April 2017), 118–29; 'Entretien avec Bernard Stiegler', *Rue Descartes*, 91 (2017), 119–40; 'Il faut réinventer le travail', *Politis*, special issue 66 (2017), 4–6.
58. Bernard Stiegler, *L'Emploi est mort, vive le travail!* (Paris: Mille et une nuits, 2015), p. 33.
59. Ibid. p. 33.

60. Ars Industrialis, 'Vocabulaire' (2010), arsindustrialis.org/vocabulaire (last accessed 16 August 2021). For a discussion of the political stakes of *prolétarisation*, see Martin Crowley, '#Automaticpolitics', *Diacritics*, 47: 1 (2019), 136–52.
61. Stiegler, *L'Emploi est mort, vive le travail!*, p. 33.
62. Interview with the author.
63. Bernard Stiegler, *La Société automatique 1. L'Avenir du travail* (Paris: Fayard, 2015), pp. 362–3.
64. Bernard Stiegler, *Automatic Society, Volume 1: The Future of Work*, trans. Daniel Ross (Cambridge: Polity, 2016), pp. 204–5.
65. Interview with the author.
66. Stiegler, *Dans la disruption*, p. 256.
67. Stiegler, *La Société automatique*, p. 15.
68. Ibid. p. 25.
69. This idea is re-articulated as the need for 'pænser', forging together *penser* with the Old French word *panser*, meaning to bandage, to tend (a wound) or more generally to care for, thus suggesting 'to think care-fully' or 'to think and care'. Bernard Stiegler, *Qu'appelle-t-on panser?: L'Immense Régression* (Paris: Les Liens qui libèrent, 2018).
70. Ibid. pp. 172–3.
71. Ibid. p. 91.
72. Stiegler, *Dans la disruption*, p. 28, p. 108, p. 254.
73. Interview with the author. Stiegler is thinking here of Marx and Engels's *The German Ideology* (1846).
74. Interview with the author.
75. Interview with the author. For a discussion of sources, autobiographical elements and major readings of the tale, see Rosa Maria Palermo di Stefano, 'Julien', in Éric Le Calvez (ed.), *Dictionnaire Gustave Flaubert* (Paris: Éditions Garnier, 2017), pp. 628–9. A reference to Flaubert's text can be found in a footnote in Stiegler, *Dans la disruption*, p. 55.
76. Both Flaubert's *Julien* and 'Les Reniements du Maestro' contain ironic hagiographical elements. On the tension between hagiography and Flaubert's modernist sensibility, see Claire Chi-ah Lyu, 'Flaubert's Proposition', *French Forum*, 36: 2–3 (2011), 41–60.
77. Interview with the author.
78. Bernard Stiegler, 'Démesure, promesses, compromis, 1: Crédit et certitude', *Médiapart*, 5 September 2020, blogs.mediapart.fr/edition/les-invites-de-mediapart/article/050920/demesure-promesses-compromis-13-par-bernard-stiegler (last accessed 16 August 2021).
79. Bernard Stiegler, 'Démesure, promesses, compromis, 3: Risque, ouverture et compromis', *Médiapart*, 9 September 2020, blogs.mediapart.fr/edition/les-invites-de-mediapart/article/090920/demesure-promesses-compromis-33-par-bernard-stiegler (last accessed 16 August 2021).

CHAPTER THREE

The Derivative in Film and Literary Theory

DERIVATIVES AND NONKNOWLEDGE

In a textbook for financial professionals, the derivative is defined as 'a financial instrument whose value depends on (or derives from) the values of other, more basic, underlying variables'.[1] In the realm of finance, derivatives are usually defined as legal contracts used to exchange something ('the underlying') at a fixed future date at a fixed price. Through such contracts, the risk of the changing value of the underlying is priced, exchanged as an investment vehicle, and thus theoretically managed and shared. Such instruments appeared in the 1970s and exploded in number in the 1990s before becoming notorious for their role in the genesis of the 2008 global financial crisis. In one of the most important books on derivatives, the anthropologist Randy Martin writes that 'derivatives are a transmission of some value from a source to something else, an attribute of that original expression that can be combined with like characteristics, a variable factor that can move in harmony or dissonance with others'.[2] Etymologically, the word comes from the Latin *derivare*, meaning to redirect a stream of water (*de rivus*). In his gloss on the word's etymology, Martin offers the image of water in a stream exceeding its embankments, allowing us to hear in *de-rive* not just redirection but also overflow.[3] Within the semantic range of derivative, we might think of the term in mathematical calculus, or the French *le dérivatif* as diversion, distraction, outlet. Beyond the brief history sketched above, derivatives have been around for thousands of years in agriculture and other fields (grammar, music, medicine, and so on). It is thus that the literary theorist Peter Szendy – whose work is discussed below – writes somewhat enigmatically that the history of derivatives 'began a long time ago; and it is yet to come'.[4] Nonetheless, even if from a deconstructive point of view derivative logics long predate the actual advent of what we commonly understand by financial derivatives today, as we shall see a social or aesthetic logic associated with them appears contemporary with their expansion on financial markets; for Martin, the derivative is today 'the current edge of capital and the contemporary transformation of the commodity relation'.[5]

In the wake of the financial crisis, derivatives became a matter of European public concern. In October 2008 – the same month as Greenspan's humbling described in the previous chapter – the European Union set up a committee, chaired by the former governor of the Banque de France, Jacques de Larosière, to report on European financial regulation. Recommending Europe-wide macro-prudential supervision of financial institutions, this report led to the creation of agencies such as the European Banking Authority and the European Securities and Markets Authority in 2011.[6] The committee found that there had been a generalised underestimation of risk in an over-leveraged system partly owing to the 'extreme complexity of structured financial products':

> financial institutions converted their loans into mortgage or asset backed securities (ABS), subsequently turned into collateralised debt obligations (CDOs) often via off-balance special purpose vehicles (SPVs) and structured investment vehicles (SIVs), generating a dramatic expansion of leverage within the financial system as a whole. [. . .] *Although securitisation is in principle a desirable economic model, it was accompanied by opacity* which camouflaged the poor quality of the underlying assets.[7]

Leaving aside the desirability or otherwise of securitisation, the ambiguity of this latter sentence in an official report should be underlined: for many commentators, the generation of opacity, and hence of unknowns, is not a side effect but part of the essential labour of derivatives, for it is from volatility and nonknowledge that they profit.[8]

There are many different species of financial derivatives and, as the Larosière report suggests, they have a tendency to proliferate in relation to one another. However, when derivatives are discussed in the humanities and social sciences, a few key protocols are usually being referred to. Going beyond the textbook definition given above – which they would criticise as limited in seeing derivatives as merely secondary to the underlying assets – Dick Bryan and Michael Rafferty identify 'binding' and 'blending' processes as two of these key protocols.[9] Binding refers to the operations which bind the future to the present and give rise to futures and options, while blending allows for radically disparate phenomena to become commensurate and thus facilitates the creation of swaps and securitised or structured products. Blending makes it possible to isolate attributes of an object and trade these independently of the underlying object. As we saw in Chapter 1, this process was core to the constitution of the subprime derivatives implicated in the 2008 crisis, in which investment vehicles (notably in the form of CDOs) were made by cutting up 'tranches' or slices of existing loans and ABS to create a species of 'financial *mille-feuille*'.[10]

While acknowledging that derivative principles have the long history mentioned above, Martin argues that the derivative financial operations that appeared in the latter decades of the twentieth century – notably securitisation and risk management – should be seen more specifically in relation to the history of global struggles of colonisation and decolonisation, which in turn should be understood as historical processes of, on the one hand, binding, possession and property and, on the other, of the unleashing, disassembly and reassembly of diverse hitherto enclosed attributes and the reconfiguration of their boundaries.[11] In this account, the flourishing of finance after the end of the Gold Standard in 1971, the end of Bretton Woods and the appearance of the Black-Scholes-Merton formula for pricing risk in 1973 should be seen in relation to the various critical and cultural movements of the 1960s: both consist in a logic of unbounding, dispersion and recombination.[12] He will thus consider phenomena such as hip-hop, musical sampling, postmodern dance styles, graffiti and skateboarding alongside hedge fund management, start-ups and financial trading as privileged examples of a 'social logic of the derivative' characterised by the bundling of dispersed elements, decentralised lateral movement, the attachment of the future to the present within a context of risk or volatility and the release of 'nonknowledge'. It is thus that 'finance may turn out to be less the originator of this social logic than a particularly prominent expression of derivative principles at work'.[13] In this chapter I trace how derivatives and this broader logic have been thought by theorists in relation to images.

With this reference to nonknowledge, Martin offers a fresh deployment, through derivatives, of Georges Bataille's concept of *le non-savoir*. As the title of Martin's book indicates, derivatives are instruments regulating the frontier between knowledge and nonknowledge (understood, firstly, in the financial sense as uncertainty, volatility and risk). Nonknowledge generates derivative logics and renders uncertainty itself productive for those who can issue derivatives. (In that sense, Martin suggests that the derivative is nonknowledge itself, commodified.[14]) As was suggested in Chapter 2 in relation to Greenspan, 2008 was among other things a crisis of knowledge, in that the models and derivatives designed to hedge or 'manage' risk and to put a price on uncertainty failed. However, Martin restores the Bataillean edge:

> When nonknowledge as the open fields of unabsorbed surplus presses back on bodies in a circuit of joy or laughter, as Bataille describes, it suddenly becomes apparent that the closed circuit of capital is sliced through by another, one that is its socializing predicate and residue.[15]

Martin is here referring to Bataille's text 'Non-savoir, rire et larmes' (1953).[16] For Bataille, the laughable is that which, suddenly, removes us from a world in which things are stable, known and foreseeable to one in which we are overtaken by the unknowable, and this experience is joyful. Martin does not quite put it like this, but we can imagine the common or comparable highs of joy that comes from moments of risk-taking in the different practices or forms of derivative life he mentions above (such as skateboarding and financial engineering). It is in these glimpses of social intercommensurability and mutuality that we can understand Martin's disarming remark apropos of the crisis: 'we might just be able to locate some joy if we know how to look'.[17] For Martin, the implication of this is that a politics specific to this era, rather than nostalgic for another, should apply itself to 'socialising' this surplus of nonknowledge, and this means putting derivatives to positive social use.[18] I will explore what this might mean via discussions of texts and films in Chapters 5 and 6.

Martin notes that poststructuralism in general and deconstruction in particular were about contesting what is between binaries and at the limits of knowledge, and as critiques of representation they emerged in alignment with decolonisation movements.[19] Significantly for scholars in the humanities – interested in representation in all senses of the word – Martin offers a lens for reframing these intellectual currents as symptomatic of a wider derivative logic.[20] How does the logic of derivatives relate to other notions in (deconstructive) criticism and critical theory which, like derivatives, deal with or manage ambiguity, uncertainty and the 'radical indecision' of the text?[21] This tension is brought out in certain formulations proposed by thinkers of derivatives; for example, 'a derivative logos that is remaking the world [. . .] as temporary assemblages of deconstructed parts', which suggests Deleuze's notion of *agencement* (assemblage).[22] The notion of disassembling has a certain resonance with concepts associated with poststructuralism, such as *bricolage*.[23] Does the social logic of the derivative simply refashion such critical topoi with financial accents? As Martin puts it, the work of the derivative is analogous to the work of criticism: it is about looking for 'discrepancies from expectation to discover value and place what was held in reserve into circulation to create liquidity'.[24] Criticism, in this view, is always a negotiation around aesthetic and other forms of value. Discussing the etymological meaning of finance (from the French for end, *fin*), Martin observes:

> 'after' is another name for the derivative as such, that which comes from something else, takes after it, adopts aspects of it, pursues it, and does not replace what was with what is newly original but carries forward the elements of what has been in a different arrangement.[25]

In this case, derivation would also imply a relation with critical concepts such as influence, adaptation and interpretation. While the notion of derivatives is thus potentially extremely expansive – to the point of risking losing all specificity – we will retrain it back on its financial dimension, without losing sight of its inherent mutability, fundamental ambivalence and potential for metaphorical redeployment.

In a text hypothesising 'an analogy, an equivalence' between financial derivatives and rhetorical figures such as metaphor and synecdoche, Peter Szendy echoes Martin's association of derivatives with a particular current of poststructuralist theory:

> Inasmuch as they disassemble or deconstruct the unity, that is to say the individual and undividable form of a commodity or an asset, derivative contracts fully belong to the historical configuration – if there is simply one configuration – described by Deleuze as 'control societies'. Or better: derivatives and derivative logic are the very structure, or texture, of these societies – ours – that 'are taking over from [the] disciplinary societies' described by Foucault.[26]

Martin will also refer to the classic text by Deleuze on control societies, and cite in particular the line on how surfing typifies contemporary dispersed, undulatory societies.[27] It is also from this text that Szendy and the anthropologist Arjun Appadurai make use of Deleuze's concept of the 'dividual' – that is, a kind of 'material substrate' from which the individual emerges – which they both theorise as simultaneously brought about and operated upon by derivative finance with ever more granular precision.[28] The literary theorist Yves Citton – who has translated excerpts of Martin's book – also engages with this text by Deleuze when he puts derivation at the centre of his discussion of what he posits as a new form of governmentality based around *recherche-création* ('research-creation', 'creative research' or 'practice-based research').[29] In this regime, value is increasingly found in potentialities rather than in objects: for example, in financial speculation on start-ups – as he notes, much in vogue in France in the contemporary period – but also in the artistic fixation on the 'underground'. In this context, everyone is increasingly required to be both a researcher and an artist, to improvise and to create derivatives.[30] Citton gives the state of the art of *recherche-création* in France and offers a rationale for the state-funded laboratory and graduate school of which he is the director, ArTeC, based at the Parisian universities of Nanterre and Saint-Denis, where projects are developed in which research intersects with practice in the arts, digital technologies and other forms of human mediation.[31] A good example of an ArTeC project (and to which I will return in Chapter 6) is 'Évaluation générale: L'Agence de Notation comme dispositif artistique' ('General Evaluation: Rating Agencies as Artistic Techniques'), which is currently experimenting with new forms of evaluation, inspired among other things by the faulty credit rating agencies implicated in the 2008 financial crisis.³²

Citton writes that while the previous regimes were oriented around self-enclosed objects, societies of *recherche-création* are concerned with *dérivations*.³³ Providing an image suggestive of differential calculus, he writes: 'Ce n'est pas le mouvement lui-même qui compte (la courbe), mais ce qu'il indique de la pré-accélération potentielle qui l'habite en tel ou tel point (la dérivée)' ('It is not the movement itself that counts [the curve] but what it indicates of the potential pre-acceleration which inhabits it at a given point [the derivative]').³⁴ In a differential equation in mathematics, the derivative refers to the rate of change in a function (which can be mapped on a graph as a curve) at a given point. In other words, what is of interest is the potential or tangent found at any particular point on the curve.³⁵ The explosion of derivatives is a symptom, he suggests, of this underlying change in social logic from objectivation to derivation. Citton's essay effectively conjugates Martin with Deleuze in thinking a shift from the commodity to the derivative. So, when Citton writes that ArTeC is based on the intuition that artistic practices help us to understand 'les potentiels et les ambivalences du numérique ubiquitaire qui est en train de reconditionner nos socialités' ('the potentials and ambivalences of ubiquitous digitality currently reconditioning our socialities') we should hear an echo of Martin's 'sociality' in his 'social logic of financial derivatives'.³⁶ In this way, Martin and Citton give us a clue to how we can break down the various protocols that make up derivative finance in order to connect them to a wider social and by extension aesthetic logic. Echoing Lordon's call for a 'dé-division' of intellectual labour, what Citton seeks to develop in institutional practice is 'une *dé-formation* par et pour la recherche et la création d'inattendus' ('un-learning through and in the service of research and the creation of the unexpected').³⁷ The extent to which these aspirations have been achieved is debatable, but what interests us here is that the aim – of dissolving the boundaries between hitherto discrete categories – fits squarely within Martin's derivative social logic. Part of the reason that derivation fascinates is that it can be thought in terms of research and creation – and vice versa. In this, what is most striking in Citton's account is that he hints at a complicity between financial traders and artists and researchers, describing traders and securitisation – always seeking pre-accelerations for profit – as 'une forme particulière, et particulièrement prégnante, de recherche-création' ('a particular, and particularly significant, form of research-creation').³⁸ Those laboratories which remain within an institutional logic of control will have to produce 'deliverables' or 'results' or 'produced objects', but what is yielded by laboratories like ArTeC (that is, their 'derivative products') is – in theory at least – a matter more of unexpected and unpredictable transformational processes, detours and changes in thought and practice: that is, the release of nonknowledge.³⁹

In terms of tracing the intellectual currents and lineages of these ideas, Citton introduces to a French audience recent American thinking on derivatives in a dossier in *Multitudes*, 'Dériver la finance' ('Deriving/Diverting Finance') – but the thinkers he draws on are themselves at least in part inspired by and develop insights from French thought (notably Deleuze's text on control societies mentioned above, but also Mauss, Durkheim and others).⁴⁰ It is through this dossier that we can see that Citton and *Multitudes* form the nodal point in the constellation connecting Beller, Martin, Massumi and, elsewhere, Feher, Hanna, Lordon and Szendy. Citton broadly follows Martin in seeing derivative finance as, firstly, a manifestation of a much more profound social logic, one 'qui fait de la spéculation un opérateur de réassemblage (pour le moment calamiteux) de nos relations entre humains, ainsi qu'avec les non-humains' ('which makes speculation into a vector for re-assemblages [albeit for now a calamitous one] of our relations with other humans and non-humans').⁴¹ Secondly, it relates to a mode of financial power in which we are all today implicated. Finally, it offers new possibilities of *agencement* in relation to new platforms and technologies such as blockchain. If derivatives reach down to potentially make all aspects of our lives exploitable and monetisable, this reveals an overflowing (literally de-rivative) superabundance of wealth or social value. This source could be channelled, says Citton, if one knew how to divert or *détourner* the current systems which exploit it.⁴² This kind of proposition is not untypical of the branch of left-wing thought associated with *Multitudes*. It also echoes the recent proposition of the Belgian philosopher Michel Feher (who has himself participated in the ArTeC 'Évaluation générale' project), who writes that today we are no longer *patron* and *salarié* ('boss' and 'wage-earner') but *investisseur* and *investi* ('investor' and 'investee'):

> il appartient aux militants d'aujourd'hui d'habiter leur condition d'investis de manière à rivaliser d'adresse avec leurs adversaires dans l'art de la spéculation. Autrement dit, l'objet d'un militantisme d'investis doit être la modification des conditions d'accréditation: il s'agit de favoriser l'appréciation de projets alternatifs, à la fois en promouvant d'autres critères de valorisation et en œuvrant au discrédit des initiatives prisées par les marchés financiers.⁴³

> [it is incumbent on today's activists to inhabit their condition of investee in order to compete with their adversaries in the art of speculation. In other words, the aim of an investee movement must be to change the conditions of the allocation of credit – it is a case of increasing the estimation of alternative projects, both by promoting other criteria of value and by working to discredit initiatives prized by the financial markets.]

It is thus a question of 'contre-spéculer' ('counter-speculating') or appropriating financial concepts and tools in order to extend (financial or other kinds of) credit to alternative causes.[44] Citton reframes this analytic in relation to his work on media and *médiarchies*, opening the question: how could we rethink finance and derivative logics from our individual positions, each in front of our own 'communicational post' or computer, from which our attention is valorised to become financial value?[45] A central, practical project generated by the reappropriation of derivative finance thus lies in developing hypothetical alternative currencies and media platforms (for example cryptocurrencies based on blockchain, which emerged soon after the 2008 financial crisis), which, as Citton puts it, could be put in the service of a contestation or re-evaluation of value; that is, trying to conceive of a qualitative rather than quantitative notion of value, and in particular a qualitative notion of the value of creative or expressive human labour.[46] This question is the ultimate stake and horizon of the engagement of these theorists with derivatives: could there be an alternative way of valorising human creativity? In a series of blog essays written in 2020 on the subject of a post-capitalist society, Lordon suggests that there is nothing inevitable about finance's current form: at the conceptual level, finance refers to institutions and practices which allow economic agents to spend money which they do not have.[47] He suggests, following the sociologist Bernard Friot's proposal for an unconditional income for citizens, a system based not around *financement* (interest-bearing loans) but *subventionnement* (grants).[48] In this way, Lordon hints at how the problem would be to try and think a means by which 'social validation' of one's work and creativity could occur other than via money as we currently understand it. In other words: could there be a non-financial derivative? In the American film and media theorist Jonathan Beller's most recent iteration of this idea:

> we may be entering an era in which *the economic logic of extraction underpinning the financialisation of expression can be reversed* and in which a *détournement* of all that has been subsumed by financialisation is becoming possible. A reformatting of monetary protocols allowing for a horizontalisation of issuance would create opportunities for an inversion of agency, allowing peoples' expression to finance post-capitalist futures.[49]

While this statement raises all kinds of technical and political questions of feasibility (concentrated in the conditionals 'may' and 'would'), let us for the moment hold onto this word 'reformatting', which points to how any new valorisation or financialisation of creativity will entail an intermedial passage.

While Beller's text (to which we will return) looks forward to a possible reformatting of monetary protocols that may lie just over the horizon, Szendy opens the catalogue for his 2020 exhibition *Le Supermarché des images* (*The Supermarket of Images*) with a meditation on the history of reformatting. (The projected four-month run of the exhibition, held at Jeu de Paume in Paris, was sadly cut short to one month by the Covid-19 outbreak.)[50] Szendy writes that what lies beneath the surface of contemporary digital images are the hidden economies of code, formatting and compression. He turns to a myth of the origins of painting according to Pliny the Elder, in which the birth of painting coincides with the tracing of outlines of human shadows, which in turn allowed for the making of reliefs in clay: that is, painting has its origin in an intermedial passage, 'from an exchange, from a substitution of media – or formats'.[51] This also entails, Szendy underlines, a speed differential. Szendy thinks about the materiality of digital images – the vast majority of images today are digital – as transported across internet cables on the ocean floor as flux of data temporarily taking the form of images, as *arrêts sur l'image* or as freeze-frames.[52] All images, he suggests, can be seen as temporarily immobilised speed differentials, and this language of calculus gives another sense in which images can be seen as derivatives.[53] One example of how images around us always have material labour concentrated in them is given in the French artist Martin Le Chevallier's short film *Clickworkers* (2017), which features in Szendy's exhibition.[54] The exhibition is split into five rooms or sections which correspond to themes which also organise the catalogue; *Clickworkers* appears in the room named 'travail' or 'work'.[55] The film features short monologues, spoken over images of bare rooms and windows, by the eponymous workers across the world who watch, label, click and 'like' videos on an industrial scale for a few cents per video (they are often required to watch grisly or explicit material). Unlike the shadows cast in the birth of painting mentioned above, the digital images that surround us today do not seem to 'cast shadows'; they are, however, made of an economy of clicking hands and this is 'our contemporary skiagraphy' or 'shadow writing'.[56] Both Beller and Szendy see, and *Clickworkers* shows, the visible as constructed, as relying on a global material infrastructure, as representing congealed but apparently invisible (or 'shadowless') labour. What I want to stress here and develop below is, firstly, that these accounts think contemporary images as inherently *intermedial*, that is, as *derived* from other media and the exchange between them. Secondly, there is and has always been an economy within the image, but this fact has arguably become ever more visible with the advent of the internet and digital images. Finally, it is significant that in the work of all of these writers there is an overlap between an interest in the contemporary condition of images and in derivatives and, by extension, the 2008 financial crisis. This is also the case for Le Chevallier, whose film on the hidden economy of the image today follows an earlier short film directly dealing with the financial crisis, *L'An 2008* (2010).[57]

DERIVATIVE IMAGES

Szendy's exhibition was, he writes, 'derived' from his book *Le Supermarché du visible* (*The Supermarket of the Visible*),[58] a deconstructive reading of cinema and its relation to money, opening onto a broader reflection on the circulation of images in the world today, which he refers to as *iconomy*: that is, images *as* economy, the economy of images (*eikôn* is one of the Greek names for image and *oikonomia* refers to the management of exchanges).[59] A key part of Szendy's text consists in a meditation on the following formulation from the second of Gilles Deleuze's *Cinéma* volumes: 'L'argent est l'envers de toutes les images que le cinéma montre et monte à l'endroit, si bien que les films sur l'argent sont déjà, quoique implicitement, des films dans le film ou sur le film' ('Money is the reverse of all the images that cinema shows and edits on the obverse, so that films about money are already, if implicitly, films within the film or about the film').[60] For Szendy, it is all images, not just the cinema, which have become 'le recto d'un verso monétaire qu'elles portent structurellement inscrit dans leur dos' ('the recto of a monetary verso that they carry structurally inscribed on their back').[61] Writing in the early 1980s, Deleuze thus offers an account of film in which there are so to speak film images on one side of the celluloid and money on the other. One implication of this is that films about money as it were fold the back of the image (the money side) onto the front (the film image). Szendy glosses the Deleuze quotation thus: 'money, imprinted or inscribed on the reverse of each filmic frame, is *folded back* on the obverse when it appears thematically on the screen'.[62] Money should be understood as pure exchange value: 'ce que l'on trouverait au verso de chaque image, ce n'est sans doute rien d'autre que le principe de son interchangeabilité, c'est-à-dire son potentiel de circulation et sa vocation à la transaction, bref, sa pure valeur d'échange' ('what we would find on the verso of each image is no doubt nothing other than the principle of its interchangeability, that is, its potential to circulate, destined as it is to enter into transactions: In short, its pure exchange value').[63] We might say that exchange value is a vector for the cinematographic potential of images: always already nested in the very 'texture' of images, it is what constitutes them in their 'filmicity'.[64] The fascination of images, in this account, would stem from their interchangeability, which is to say the way in which they resemble money. The connection between images and money of course has a long history going back at least to the Byzantine era.[65] In drawing the connection between cinema and money *qua* exchange, Szendy is therefore not thinking about the financing of films, production costs or box office sales, but rather this connection between filmicity and exchange built into every image.

Szendy does not discuss financial derivatives as such in this text, but in one of the 'supplements' to the book he does consider 'merchandise', which in the French ('produits dérivés') is very closely related: literally, derivative products. The brief section of four pages focuses on *Godzilla* (Roland Emmerich, 1998) – as a remake, clearly itself a 'derivative film' – and the way that 'tout blockbuster qui se respecte doit également se miniaturiser en se déclinant sur d'innombrables supports et produits dérivés' ('every self-respecting blockbuster also has to miniaturize itself by offering a range of tie-in products derived from the film on countless media').[66] *Godzilla* is a paradigmatic example of a commercial film, and Szendy shows how it allegorises the way the blockbuster film 'paraît se morceler et se monnayer, se diviser à l'infini pour se reproduire' ('seems to break into pieces and become monetized, to divide itself infinitely in order to reproduce itself').[67] *Se monnayer* has an alchemical association, suggesting base metal transformed into coins. While the reference here is to blockbusters and physical merchandise (we might think of baseball caps and lunchboxes with Godzilla printed on them), the description of the film yielding innumerable intermedial derivatives, valorising itself by reproducing itself in miniature form, is also highly suggestive of the contemporary economy of digital images, especially social media, in which copies of images of a film can be infinitely reproduced in variety of forms on ever smaller screens. The image is a derivative not just because it is always drawn from an underlying source, but also because it is minted for exchange.

This sense of derivative images also helps us understand Szendy's more recent line: 'C'est de l'entr'images, pourrait-on dire, que chaque image ou fragment d'image tire sa valeur et sa consistance' ('One might say that each image or fragment of an image derives its value and its substance from the inter-iconic zone [*l'entr'images*]').[68] With this reference to Raymond Bellour's notion of *l'entre-images* ('between-the-images'), Szendy here as elsewhere inscribes iconomy within a longer tradition of French film theory and intermedial thought while also updating these to conceptualise the value of images: here, as derived from the space and exchanges between images.[69] Like the supermarket of the visible, *l'entre-images* names both specific instances where we find the interpenetration of images across media and within works as well as a more abstract 'space' in which images move. Bellour thus names an experience, with the arrival of video, of 'a new time of the image' in which there is constant exchange between images (in photography, cinema, video, and so on).[70] While in 1990 Bellour says *l'entre-images* names an experience, twenty-five years later, Bellour remarks that '*l'entre-images* is not a concept, but a place that is both real and mental [. . .] "Between-images," I repeat, is a place of exchanges and passages, not a unifying concept. On the subject, there is no clarity.'[71] The variety of senses of this 'betweenness' extends from the micro level 'between two frames' on a strip of celluloid to the stops and starts between still and moving images to the passages of a spectator at a gallery installation between exhibits. To give a full history, Bellour suggests, one would have to go back to prior moments of the blending of images and words in the Middle Ages and the Renaissance. Bellour's notion of course relates to older French conceptions of intermediality and intersections between the arts – he is implicitly thinking, for example, of Maurice Blanchot's 'literary space' and Stéphane Mallarmé's 'Book' (concepts returned to below).

At the same time as money resides in the very folds of cinema images, Szendy argues that in the course of the twentieth century cinema increasingly 'grafted' itself into our very sight, training our vision like a tracking shot.[72] This process of the 'cinematization of the visible' and therefore the 'monetization and commodification of seeing' stays with us when we finish shopping, thus making our world a 'supermarket of the visible'.[73] As a concept or notion, the supermarket of the visible and its implicit more general hypothesis of 'une archi-économie des images' ('archi-economy of images') allowing us, crucially, to think images on a single plane has been formulated by other French thinkers of cinema, and Szendy summarises various iterations of the idea that the world and our experience of it has a filmic structure.[74] Such metaphysical formulations allow Szendy to conceive of images as today the very matter of the world, rather than seeing images as secondary representations of the world. More concretely, such propositions appear to be borne out in the contemporary digital era in the way our lives in large measure take place across all manner of screens, with a superabundance of things attracting our attention, forming an attention economy where looking – as *la plus-vue* ('surplus-view')[75] – has become a form of capital that can be sold as well as a paradigm for the generation of financial value.[76] At the limit point of his argument, Szendy turns it on its head and hesitates as to whether seeing has become more cinematic or whether it has merely been revealed as having always already been cinematic.[77] The corollary is given in a parenthesis which is easy to overlook at the beginning of the book when he wonders whether there is a 'marché des échanges toujours déjà logé au cœur du sensible' ('exchange market that is always already there within the sensible').[78] This is a constructive tension – and provocative political possibility – that Szendy leaves unresolved, and to which I will return below.

As hinted above, Szendy's text can be usefully read in conjunction with the recent work of Jonathan Beller, who in a different register also articulates a financial conception of the film image.[79] For Beller, contemporary film and digital images can 'increasingly be understood as derivatives': that is, they are acts of composition in which we bundle together semiotic elements derived from life or pre-existing images to 'securitize' them as a wager or hedge against the volatility of the social world.[80] 'Expression has become a hedge,' says Beller, 'a wager, a playing of the spread opened by the volatility of the social, in order to access the upside; it has become a derivative.'[81] Beller's conceptual move here is to literalise the metaphor of the derivative, to see films and digital images *as* derivatives.[82] The use of 'volatility' in these formulations suggests how a logic of risk management has permeated all domains of life.[83] The formulation of composing or bundling elements frames images in terms of the 'blending' of Bryan and Rafferty, while, as bets, digital images here are also 'binding'. We see here how Beller's thinking of the derivative ties in with media theory, with Marxian thinking and with social science studies of financialisation. For Beller, then, it is through the hedges of our comments, expressions, artworks and practices that we seek to stay afloat and avoid 'imminent foreclosure' (here alluding to the mortgage foreclosures in the USA during the 2008 crisis).[84] By 'expression', Beller seems to refer to potentially all human means of expression, but especially those taking place across digital platforms, social media and audiovisual technologies, such as memes and gifs:

> with the digitization of nearly all semiotic activity by computational racial capital, any particular communique, from advertising to a call to arms, can be understood as an edited composition that functions as a kind of protocolized wager to strategically manage the volatility of living imposed by the transnational, transsubjective economy in order to get a return.[85]

Even 'radical' cinema would not as a rule escape this logic, although Beller suggests that certain films can subvert the derivative condition to offer alternative visions of the future.[86] He thus sees the camera as a 'derivative machine': a machine which cuts together in bundles signifying elements before spitting them out – like notes from a cash machine – as derivative images.[87] At its most abyssal, we could read this as suggesting that all images begin by being cut and enframed, bundled.[88] These propositions come from a film theoretical framework, but evidently they have political, technological, economic and existential ramifications. The originality of such affirmations lies in the desire to conceptualise the current situation of film and media in a fully financialised world. In these recent interventions Beller is developing ideas that he has previously advanced under the signs of the 'economy of attention' and 'computational capital' while regrouping and modifying them under the paradigm of financial derivatives.[89] What is new since the earlier work is, firstly, the appearance and massive expansion of social and other media platforms, and, secondly, the 'convergence' of these and all other media with financial processes and 'monetary media'.[90] Beller hints at how social media platforms (such as, for example, TikTok and Twitter) derived from older media forms, in which the image is smashed into innumerable fragments, offer perhaps the paradigmatic manifestations of derivative images.[91] All of this is concentrated in his extensive use of the word 'derivative', which underlines how contemporary digital images are indissociable from financial processes.[92] Beller indicates that financialisation is contemporaneous with the digitalisation and the informationalisation of recent decades, but that these are the fruits of capitalist processes going back centuries. Like Beller, Szendy sees ours as a new age of the image which is a function of the digital, writing: 'Nous habitons un monde de plus en plus saturé d'images. Leur nombre connaît une croissance tellement exponentielle – aujourd'hui plus de trois milliards d'images partagées chaque jour sur les réseaux sociaux – que l'espace de la visibilité semble être littéralement submerge' ('We live in a world that is increasingly saturated with images. Their number is growing so exponentially – each day more than three billion images are shared on social networks – that the space of visibility seems to be literally inundated').[93] Szendy's remark suggests that the sheer quantity of screens and of images generated daily has become its own kind of quality, requiring us to think again about the value of images today, starting from a consideration of the material economy sustaining them. What both Beller and Szendy propose is that the contemporary digital iconomy generalises what were already latent logics, with the derivative always implicit in the commodity form from which price is derived.[94] Beller's is a more pessimistic diagnosis than Szendy's, seeing the totalising financial-media system as founded on capitalist expropriation, racial violence and mass alienation. In this context, we are forced to hedge our bets in order to survive: this is what he calls our 'derivative condition'.[95] The existential condition of traders is thus in some sense generalised for all. Beller's is a severe and militant critique, seeing all human communication and even our dreams as conscripted to a computational capitalist logic. His polemic thus forces his readers to consider their implication within a totalising financial logic. Szendy differentiates his position from Beller's earlier work in a footnote, disagreeing that there might have been in some distant past a hypothetical pre-market gaze or natural state of creative energy that was colonised by capital.[96] In Szendy's account there was no pre-derivative condition, and so all images would in some sense be derivative images.

If for Beller we are nodes within a financialised media field, whose infrastructure is itself fixed capital, then audiovisual media are an extension of the financial system and digital images are necessarily financial derivatives.[97] The resulting political question for Beller is whether it is possible to create a more democratic or even a 'communist derivative'.[98] To this end, he suggests we examine alternative financial technologies like blockchain in the hope that they might lead to a democratisation of financial tools and a 'decolonization' of finance, thus creating the conditions for an expression that would not be based on value extraction and accumulation.[99] This has been the aim of his collaboration with the Economic Space Agency (ECSA), a think tank exploring post-capitalist economic media and cryptocurrencies.[100] Most recently, Beller has stated that we should think of 'economic media' in two categories: all forms of money and 'all other media', including cinema, literature, and so on.[101] These two forms are now 'converging', he argues. The angle of attack here is similar to Szendy's, albeit in a rather different register and to different ends: that is, he collapses all images onto a single (economic) plane. It is this move which consists in seeing the cultural forms that surround us as always in an intermedial relationship with money — that is, iconomic thinking — that leads Beller to propose that we remake our economic media in such a way that they are non-exploitative.[102] (This would be one way of understanding Martin's notion of 'socialising the surplus' of nonknowledge.) Not only might we finance our expressive activities, but finance could itself become an expressive medium.[103] If this was possible, it would allow activists to, in Feher's terms, 'counter-speculate' against the existing economic system, or, as Beller puts it, to 'short' capitalism.[104] In other words, programmable cryptocurrencies and inventing new forms of money might allow collectives to issue credit, futures and options to finance and thus valorise their creative activities, for example through peer-to-peer networks rather than traditional interest structures:

> Such expressive wagers on one another, currently vested in poems, posted on social media, or held as political positions, are already, that is, in actuality, social derivatives on generalised volatility — strategies of survival in a precarious world. These social derivatives may one day provide not just meaningful social returns but meaningful economic returns to anyone and everyone.[105]

Giving another sense to derivative images, these lines hint at how the artistic or expressive phenomena around us not only are socio-economic survival strategies, but may prefigure potential new economic relations. What is also noteworthy in this formulation is that it moves past deploring the exploitation of the qualitative by the quantitative and points to the need to create new quantitative structures that adequately valorise the qualitative. In other words, if the things that give value to our lives — such as, in Beller's examples, poems, political commitments and social media posts — only valorise capital for platforms, then the point would be to reform these monetary media forms such that they generate income based on social value (which, as he states, is the basis of all value).[106] Such a statement is speculative and it remains to be seen if ECSA can realise its promise for post-capitalist economic media. Looking back to Deleuze's point about money being the other side of images, we could however say that we may glimpse on the verso of derivative images a potential alternative cooperative economy in which risk is managed by issuing derivatives based on underlying social or creative value.

Tokenisation based on blockchain technology is a cutting-edge area of practical financing in the audiovisual industry. A pioneer in this field is Patrice Poujol, a French film finance consultant and academic based in Hong Kong who wrote the first PhD on the use of blockchain in creative media.[107] Poujol runs a company, Lumière, which uses blockchain to help independent filmmakers finance their films, and was involved in producing, it is claimed, the first tokenised and securitised film, *Papicha* (Mounia Meddour, 2019), a coproduction between France, Algeria and Belgium, and which was Algeria's entry to the Oscars in 2020.[108] Tokenisation in this context refers to the issuance of digital tokens corresponding to an underlying asset, allowing investors to trade their fractional ownership of a film as a derivative. The advantage of blockchain as a model for the digital securitisation of the asset is that it allows for individuals' rights over the asset to be codified in a transparent, secure and disintermediated way. Using a smart contract, revenue can be collected and then paid out automatically, inexpensively and in real time.[109] The decentralised nature of this technology may allow filmmakers to step outside of the limitations of traditional funding structures, including crowdfunding models.[110] In theory this should also make it easier for retail investors to participate in film financing, who may then act as 'brand ambassadors' for the film.

While Poujol's example shows how tokenisation offers possibilities for the funding of independent films, the major French bank BNP Paribas – which identifies itself as 'Europe's leading bank for the film sector' and which participates, directly or indirectly, in the financing of one out of every two films produced each year in France[111] – is currently partnering with a film production company, Logical Pictures, on a new tokenised film investment vehicle, 21 Content Ventures, which is the first example of its kind in Europe.[112] In the notes for investors, the fund proposes 'audiovisual content' as a strong underlying asset whose 'acyclical profile demonstrates [. . .] resilience in times of crisis' and which is part of a market currently enjoying strong growth (especially given the development of streaming services).[113] Unlike in Poujol's account, where the advantage of blockchain lies in increasing the agency of the filmmaker, for this fund the advantage over traditional shares is that blockchain 'brings liquidity to a usually illiquid investment'.[114] In other words, films are complex assets which are traditionally difficult to quickly resell. Nonetheless, they generate an income stream that can be exploited long after their first box office sales (television rebroadcasts, streaming sales, DVDs, merchandising, and so on). In addition, according to 21 Content Ventures, part of what makes their investment proposition attractive to larger investors is that the films form a diverse portfolio including films with 'social impact themes (environment, civil rights, etc.)'.[115] Clearly, then, while Beller sees in blockchain and cryptocurrencies the potential for a 'decolonisation of finance', the same technology also presents new frontiers for investment and profit for traditional capitalist actors such as banks. Beller, Poujol and 21 Content Ventures offer differing visions of derivative images, in which films are income streams infinitely divisible into parts.

While for Beller the 'derivative condition' is primarily one of alienation, he nevertheless sees, like Citton and Martin, how it at least potentially augurs possibilities for new modes of sociality. For both Beller and Citton, something of this situation was presciently described by the philosopher Vilém Flusser in his 1983 analysis of the handheld camera as a computer which automates or programs thought and social behaviour.[116] While for them Flusser's description of the functionary of apparatuses playing with symbols and executing a programme is prophetic of the contemporary condition of 'post-historical' humankind, it is highly significant for our purposes that it is more specifically the photographer – someone who takes pictures, who could be anyone, and who (as we shall see in Chapter 5), in today's world of ubiquitous smartphone ownership, *is* everyone – can be seen as a prototype of the derivatives trader.[117] Each of us is tied to a machine which yields innumerable derivative images: Beller writes that '[p]hotography is a derivative whose underlier is "reality" – a volatile "reality" that is the basis for contingent claims.'[118] Elsewhere, Beller will suggest that films can be seen as programmes, that is, platforms which instrumentalise information and affects according to economic imperatives, such that filmmakers and critics are now either functionaries, fulfilling the programme, or programmers, who have the potential to create spaces for agency.[119] The importance of Flusser for these writers appears to lie in thinking possibilities for outrunning programmes *qua* that which, like market algorithms, seems always to be ahead of us. The horizon of Flusser's reflections on the camera is the possibility of carving a space for agency or human freedom: 'Freedom is the strategy of making chance and necessity subordinate to human intention. Freedom is playing against the camera.'[120] As these ideas will recur in the coming chapters, it is worth underscoring here the notion of *strategy* as a means of playing against one's position as a functionary, of taking a strategic position in relation to images with the ultimate objective of obtaining some kind of freedom. Clearly something similar is at stake in Beller and Citton's thinking of the relation between derivatives and media, and this explains their investment in Flusserian themes and engagement with potential post-capitalist monetary forms.

What much of the foregoing suggests is that we see the image as in the position of a derivative, and vice versa. Here we are in the logic of the *calque* (tracing). The poet and theorist Christophe Hanna – to whose work I will return in Chapter 6 – offers the concept of the *calque* as akin to filters in Photoshop, which allow one to bring out different perceptual aspects of images, for example by changing images to black-and-white or sepia, or by inserting some extra feature (like a hairstyle).[121] He uses this notion as a way of understanding the functional, relational and structural properties of given poetic works, looking at them as a *dispositif* or as an 'instrument'.[122] While the notion of the literary text as an 'instrument' is one that goes back to aesthetic modernity, the analysis offered by the theorists in this chapter gives us an example of how this can be rethought in our era of derivative financial instruments: they conceive of the literary or filmic work *as* a derivative (Hanna would say '*en* derivative'); that is, they imagine the financial derivative as, so to speak, superimposed over the image or work of art like a *calque*.[123] The point is not exactly to prove that images *are* derivatives, but rather to see how thinking of images as derivatives changes our way of looking at images, thus potentially leading us to change the (monetary) media housing them. This intermedial mode of seeing one thing in terms of another entails exchanging the plane of representation for the higher plane of 'fiction' and is at work in all economic conceptions of the image.[124] 'Fiction', in Hanna's terms:

> désigne finalement toutes les formes d'activité qui ouvrent à des possibilités nouvelles, qui nous mettent en disposition de pouvoir effectuer une *mise à distance de la réalité*, qui nous permettent localement de *dé-réaliser* pour *re-réaliser*, de modifier l'agencement du réel par les infléchissements, les perturbations, les collusions interinstitutionnelles inattendues que les pratiques de fictionnalisation réclament.[125]

> [designates in the end all forms of activity which open onto new possibilities, which allow us to hold reality at a distance, which allow us locally to de-realise in order to re-realise and modify the assemblage of the real by the shifts, disruptions and unexpected inter-institutional collusions required by practices of fictionalisation.]

What Hanna calls 'fiction' we could call speculation or, following Feher, 'counter-speculation'; that is, to engage strategically and imaginatively, through art, with finance in order to remake it.[126] I will show in Chapter 6 how one of Hanna's literary works does this, along with others.

Is the Psyche a Market?

Beller's perspective appears unthinkable outwith the context of the 2008 financial crisis and the putting into question of derivatives which resulted from it. Szendy's case is different. Notwithstanding the 'produits dérivés' discussed in relation to *Godzilla*, *Le Supermarché du visible* makes no direct reference to derivatives or 2008.[127] One would not necessarily expect such a reference in a work of film theory, but this absence is arguably noteworthy in a work about images and money written in the prolonged period of economic difficulty in the wake of the 2008 global financial crisis, which was notable precisely for shaking faith in market ideology among economic elites (the book is based on lectures given in 2014), because this context has potential to influence the interpretation of certain key statements. One might think of a passage at the beginning of the text in which Szendy offers a hesitation within a parenthesis:

> Parler d'un supermarché esthétique, c'était plutôt, d'une part, une manière d'indiquer que l'*aisthêsis*, que la sensation ou la perception sensible sont bel et bien un marché où se produisent des échanges: des images ou des sons y circulent, ainsi que des écoutes, des regards ou des points de vue. (Peut-être est-ce d'ailleurs le caractère intrinsèquement échangiste de la sensibilité ou de la sensationnalité, peut-être est-ce ce marché des échanges toujours déjà logé au cœur du sensible qui rend possible ce qu'il nous faudra bien décrire comme sa marchandisation sans précédent à l'époque du capitalisme globalisé.)[128]

> [Rather, to speak of an aesthetic supermarket was, on the one hand, a way of indicating that *aisthēsis*, sensation or sense perception, is indeed a market in which exchange takes place: Images and sounds circulate there, as do listening, gazes, and points of view. (Moreover, perhaps it is the intrinsically exchangist quality of sensibility or sensationality, perhaps it is this exchange market that is always already there within the sensible that makes possible what we will have to describe as its unprecedented commodification in the era of globalized capitalism.)][129]

Szendy completes this brief two-page section saying this idea of a supermarket was also a way of rethinking Marx's idea of base and superstructure as a (super-)market of sensation on top of the economic market. Our sense perceptions are constructed, Szendy goes on, glossing Marx, they are the result of underlying social and economic relations from below, but they are also constructed by aesthetic productions from above. He then leaves this much larger reflection to one side and goes on to discuss cinema images and money in a similarly theoretical manner. What is striking in this account of the construction of the visible, then, is the idea that our sensibility has been commodified in the contemporary era *because* our senses are in some way already structured like a market.

Such remarks may be read in a radically different way depending on whether they had been written after the crash or, say, in the 1990s, during the height of the fever of the putative 'end of history' associated with the ineluctable triumph of the market and the ascent of global capitalism that is alluded to in the closing words of the quotation. There is thus at first glance something untimely about Szendy's position, which he hedges with the repeated conditional adverb 'peut-être'. How then can we read this parenthesis? What kind of market is this market at the heart of the sensible? What exactly is Szendy claiming about this market structure? More precisely, is he saying there is something ineluctable about markets? We should note that he writes that the market is *always* already there: it is '*toujours déjà logé au cœur du sensible*'. The image would suggest that our ideas, sensations and perceptions could in some sense be seen as goods circulating in a market. We might think of street markets where traders shout and hustle at stalls trying to attract the attention of the buyers who flow past between them. We might imagine the glimmering, or not so glimmering, aisles of a supermarket. Equally it might suggest a financial market, which is one of the themes of several of the artworks in Szendy's exhibition. The postulation of a market within the psyche is a prime example of the recursive relationship between the economic and the existential identified by Emily Apter and Martin Crowley in what they call 'economies of existence'.[130] The contested place of the market in human life and in the calculating human psyche of course has a long history, and may remind us for example of Nietzsche's remark: 'Fixing prices, setting values, working out equivalents, exchanging – this preoccupied man's first thoughts to such a degree that in a certain sense it *constitutes* thought.'[131] Seeing 'the' market as somehow natural, of course, has strong ideological connotations and is a familiar target in French anti-capitalist polemics.[132] Szendy will also cite the Marxian idea that our sensory organs are the historical product of underlying economic and social relations.[133] In a radio programme on the launch of his exhibition, Szendy reiterates that, in this sense, his is a Marxist vision: visibility and images are always produced, they are products and the result of work.[134] But Szendy's supermarket might also remind us of a liberal tradition, such as Adam Smith's view that exchange is the basis for all social relations and the market is 'both the means and the end of organized social relations'.[135] For influential intellectual figures associated with twentieth-century free market reforms such as Friedrich Hayek, the market is a site of knowledge (through price) and freedom (from economic planning and state control).[136] However, the 'neoliberal' market is by no means the only possible kind of market, as Frédéric Lordon writes. The market is, like finance, a very abstract and conceptual term, he says, which can take on a wide variety of specific historical forms.[137] As a concept, he sees it as an extension of the division of labour, a space where private propositions can be offered for social validation, and not necessarily by way of money (Lordon gives the example of those who offer witty propositions on social media in search of the currency of likes).[138] Read this way, almost any social situation where one person's offer is chosen over another's could be seen as a market. Under capitalism, what we call 'the market' is a particular form of social validation conditioning our material survival as individuals. However, in the communist system Lordon advocates for, there would still be, he says with a degree of irony, 'private initiatives', but they would be voluntary, rather than something we are all subject to.[139] What he contests, then, are not markets *per se*, but their dominance over other spheres of life and the way they are experienced as coercive. For him there would potentially at least still be markets even in a hypothetical post-capitalist society.

Szendy has previously postulated a psychic market in *Tubes: La Philosophie dans le juke-box* (*Hits: Philosophy in the Jukebox*, 2008), where he refers recurrently to 'une certaine homologie entre le marché et la psyché' ('a certain homology between the market and the psyche') which helps produce hit pop songs that get stuck in our head and which, inversely, the songs produce (in this passage he again deploys a double 'peut-être').[140] What haunts or persists in pop songs is 'l'hymne intime qu'ils entonnent, au plus profond de nous, à la gloire de l'échange. Comme s'ils suscitaient ou édifiaient en nous, de façon chaque fois singulière, l'inthymnité de l'équivalence générale et du capital' ('the intimate anthem that they belt out in the depths of our self about the glory of exchange. As if they incited or edified within us, each time in a singular way, the inthymnity of capital and of general equivalence').[141] The private anthem named by the portmanteau coinage *inthymne* (combining 'hymn' and 'intimacy'), our secret song we play to ourselves, is a form of access to the psychic economy. The germ for his notion of a psychic economy in which mass-produced articles circulate comes from a text by Walter Benjamin discussing neurosis, but he traces this back to Freud's economic vocabulary discussing jokes and, further, to Kant's understanding of music as being ultimately based on the pure pleasure of exchange. In the final account, jokes and songs 'n'auraient au bout du compte rien à dire d'autre que l'exposition nue de cette structure d'interchangeabilité, d'équivalence générale, de circulation. Ils ne feraient, au fond, que *se prêter à. Se prêter au change*' ('have nothing to say beyond the naked exposition of this structure of interchangeability, general equivalence, and circulation. In the end, they would do nothing more than *lend themselves to*. Lend themselves to *exchange*').[142]

In the closing three pages of *Tubes*, Szendy offers a section that we could compare with the parenthesis near the beginning of *Le Supermarché du visible*. Whereas in that quotation he wrote that it was perhaps the market structure of the psyche that made possible its commodification in the era of globalisation, here he writes – thinking of the 1997 Daft Punk hit 'Around the World' – that hit songs: 'font désormais le tour du monde, ils accompagnent le mouvement même de la mondialisation, de l'expansion du marché. A l'extérieur – vers de nouveaux marchés à conquérir – comme à l'intérieur – dans la marchandisation de la psyché' ('now go all around the world. They accompany the very movement of globalization and the expansion of the market. From the outside – toward new markets to be conquered – and from the inside – in the commodification of the psyche').[143] What makes the song this vector between the psyche and the market is that it is the meeting point where general interchangeability switches places ceaselessly with absolute singularity.[144] That is, the hit tends to be a cliché: it talks of nothing and nobody in particular and it is utterly interchangeable with any number of other songs. It plays and sells in innumerable copies just as it multiplies itself and replays on loop inside our head.[145] And yet the paradox is that it touches us in our singularity: it seems to be our own personal anthem, it speaks to us, it takes us back to a moment or era of our personal history and gives access to our most singular and hidden self.[146] The melancholy of *tubes* is that they commemorate a moment in a life charged with affect, a singular *there was*, repeating it infinitely in our psyche.[147] He is here describing what it is like to be inside this psychic market, to be in the market all the way down. The song reveals 'la réserve d'un excès, en moi mais qui ne m'appartient pas' ('the reserve of an excess is held, in me but without belonging to me'); it is as if the song knew us 'au plus intime de nous-mêmes, mais comme si nous n'étions pas là' ('in our most intimate details, but also as if we were not there').[148] Szendy's account here of our psyche is an abyssal one: it is as if, in our deepest interiority, we are not the individual idly browsing market stalls but rather the market square itself over which sensations and buyers and sellers flow.

This idea of a possible underlying structure of the psyche as a market might seem close to the capitalist subsumption deplored by Beller, but without the pejorative connotation.[149] For both Beller and Szendy, 'il n'y a pas ou plus de vue *hors marché* (à supposer qu'il y en ait jamais eu)' ('there is no – or no longer any – view *outside the market* [if there ever was one]').[150] There is a risk here of ascribing politics to Szendy's aesthetic philosophical reflections, but we could argue that the point is precisely that the reconfiguration and refashioning of the concepts of market and economy take place in a space like aesthetic theory which is seemingly insulated from more frontal political discussions and which has a priori nothing directly to do with the financial crash. We should not interpret Szendy's reading of the psyche as symptomatic (of the way one passively interiorises market norms under conditions of financialisation); rather, Szendy hints at how a derivative logic had always ('peut-être') already been there, at the heart of the sensible. Traversed by these fragments of music and film, it is a market of what we could call derivative aesthetic products. At these limit points of the argument where Szendy has to manage uncertainty, he does not take an agnostic position: he takes a hedge position. In financial terms: at the heart of his argument, he writes an option. This approach to the imponderability of whether the psyche was always configured as a market, or not, could itself be seen to bespeak a market disposition. Even if he does not refer to the financial crisis directly, then, Szendy responds implicitly by offering an at least potentially positive vision of derivative subjectivity (while also, arguably, offering a guarded allusion to the limitations of our capacity for change), by showing how we will never be finished with markets – *peut-être*.

DERIVATIVE CREATIVITY

If in most cases in this book I am interested in writers, artists and theorists who make use of ideas about financial derivatives to conceptualise aesthetic experience and creative practice, with Elie Ayache, one of the most original commentators on derivatives, we have a case of the reverse: a trader who makes use of literary theory to conceptualise his experience of the market. Ayache started his work as a market maker on the French stock exchange on Black Monday, the stock market crash of 19 October 1987, a key moment in the growth of derivatives.[151] Ayache was born in Lebanon but is based in Paris, where he runs a financial software business. Ayache's central philosophical claim – which converges with the 'speculative materialism' associated with Quentin Meillassoux – in the long and complex work *The Blank Swan* (2010) is that we should think of the real in terms of contingency, not probability or possibility, and that the market of financial derivatives is the 'medium of contingency'; that is, it cannot be reduced to a set of possibilities and is that which better than anything else puts one in direct relation to contingency.[152] He insists on the radical novelty of events – here drawing on philosophies of the event, such as in the work of Alain Badiou – of which something will always escape the representational logic of the categories of possibility and probability.[153] '[I]t is as if I were saying,' he writes, 'that the market is a communication channel inextricably coinciding with the unrepresentability of events.'[154] It is thus that Ayache is critical of probabilistic models of derivatives, of which the Black-Scholes-Merton formula is the paradigm example. This is not to say the formula is useless – the paradox is that such models (often using stochastic processes) are needed to make the market, but these models do not and cannot represent contingency in some transcendental sense.[155] The model requires ideal conditions, whereas in real life no calculus of probability works. If, as we saw in the previous chapter, for Greenspan the failure of models could be taken as a plaintive conclusion of the crisis, for Ayache the inadequacy of models only testifies to the contingency of the market as always in excess of models; for him, this is a positive state of affairs.[156] Contingency deals with events, and this is why he calls derivatives 'contingent claims'.[157] Derivatives are quantitative, but the market is a medium of contingency, which cannot ultimately be quantified; using a cinematic metaphor, he avers that the market is 'a kind of numerically constituted soundtrack of the far richer movie of history'.[158] Trading, then, like writing, starts where probability ends.

It is beyond the scope of the present discussion to interrogate Ayache's broader argument; rather, the thread that I want to take up is this analogy between derivative trading and literary creation – Ayache's suggestive claim that 'the trader's work is poetic' – which is the subject of part III of his book.[159] Around midway through the book, Ayache offers a complex metaphorical argument about the origins of creative activity.[160] Later, Ayache will conceptualise creativity by drawing on Deleuze's philosophy of creation,[161] but in this section halfway through the book he describes, via the film *Barton Fink* (Joel Coen, 1991), a highly abstract movement whereby 'thought' overcomes a state of passivity to meet with its 'outside' by making a 'mark' or 'cut' (*entaille*)[162] on the 'surface', which is the market.[163] If I understand Ayache correctly – for some passages are rather enigmatic – he is suggesting that the process of financial derivative trading is a model for literary writing but also creative thinking in general, whereby 'thought' is confronted with a blank page and must overcome its passivity through inspiration in order to make a mark or 'cut' on the blank page: hence, the *blank* swan. Ayache's blank page, like the blank page or blank screen Evelyne Grossman describes, can be read as a synecdoche for the 'crisis' of inspiration, motivation and creation known by everyone involved in creative activity.[164] Describing the issuing of derivatives as a kind of creative cutting,[165] he writes: 'thought issues derivatives payoffs that are destined to trade on the surface of the market (the surface of the mark), the surface of writing'.[166] Ayache's idiosyncratic use of 'cutting' is distinct from the cutting of tranches in the makeup of derivatives mentioned above and in Chapter 1. Here Deleuze is the most proximate reference, whose use of this term is complex and polysemic, with mathematical, cinematic and other resonances; however, numerous acephalic images will also suggest Bataille and the cut that engenders (de-)structural play in French poststructuralism.[167]

What interests us here is how Ayache thinks the activity of the derivatives trader in terms of the work of the literary writer, an account which betrays a deep engagement with the writer Maurice Blanchot and the symbolist poet Stéphane Mallarmé. Blanchot thinks of inspiration and the process of the creation of literary or artistic works as occurring in a 'literary space' of profound solitude.[168] Mallarmé's *Un coup de dès jamais n'abolira le hasard* (1897) is, famously, a poem which makes radical use of the space of the page on which the poem is laid out to reflect on the nature of chance.[169] What is original about Ayache's move is to think analogically literary creation and financial market-making in fundamentally spatial – not temporal – terms. The market is on the side of space, not time, and this is counter-intuitive because derivatives are often thought in terms of time, for example as futures. On the one hand, there is nothing transcendent about the market – it is a contingent, material product, essentially a kind of palimpsest, a space or surface on which the event of pricing as writing takes place; at the same time, it is clear Ayache understands the space of creation and trading in a metaphysical sense, reimagining Blanchot's literary space as a (trading) 'room' and sees 'the market' as having the nature of 'the Book' (*Le Livre*: that is, an ideal totality).[170] Just as Blanchot offers an account of the psychology of the literary writer, Ayache provides an account of the psychology of the trader as he or she creates derivatives. In both sides of this equation, it is a moral or existential ordeal which resembles the trials of Barton Fink. The analogy between writing and trading is centred on their common irreducibility to, and overturning of, probability. Ayache describes how writing involves not possibility and probability but contingency, because it consists in immersion in the text and a forgetting of self and all of the received knowledge about the task at hand.[171] We could say, following Martin, that it is a negotiation with nonknowledge. The moment of the trade or of writing – in Ayache's terms, the moment when one makes a cut on the surface of the market – opens the gap between intuition and planning and execution in the creative process, in which an 'event' takes place in which something new comes into being. The whole creative 'work' exists in this margin or interval when we reach the limit of models and of concepts and engage directly with risk. What Ayache tells us is what is more elegantly put by the philosopher and psychoanalyst Anne Dufourmantelle, that risk is passion and thus the source of our creative endeavours.[172] For Ayache, like for Beller (and indeed Kerviel, as we shall see in Chapter 4, and some of Hanna's artists in Chapter 6), the derivative condition is a matter not of profits but of survival as a market-maker, of trading to survive.[173] 'The medium is of the nature of writing,' Ayache writes, 'and the trader of contingent claims is a writer and a creator.'[174] The trader does not try to predict market events; rather, '[t]he market is his *work*, as when we say that the book is the work of the writer or the poem is the work of the poet.'[175] If I have suggested that we place the derivative as a *calque* over the image, then all of Ayache's effort in this section of *The Blank Swan* is to place the trader over the writer, to see the market as 'a trading/writing capacity'.[176]

Conclusion

The positions of Beller, Citton, Martin and Szendy should be understood together (even if they have important differences) in order to grasp a contemporary financial aesthetic of the image conditioned by the 2008 financial crisis. All in some sense posit contemporary spectators as '*très haut débiteurs d'images*' ('*high-speed debtors-downloaders*').[177] This phrase is at once evocative of cinephilia, widespread addiction to digital images and our implication in a world in which our relation to images is fully financialised. Conjugating the positions of these theorists would be to conceive all images within a single iconomy, but one where fragments of images are constantly in the process of disassembling and reassembling themselves in innumerable derivative products, down to the 'market' of our psyches. It is in taking these positions together that one can put to work the fundamental ambivalence of derivation which, of course, has a violent and hypertrophic logic which engenders precarity and transforms social values into securities. But as Martin shows, the 'omnipresent' logic of the derivatives manifests its own social logic which tends to open new, potentially socially productive forms of association between groups and individuals. The importance of the financial crisis for the theoretical writing discussed in this chapter is thus found in the way the crisis reconfigures a nexus of older questions around images and mediality, but under the sign of financial derivatives and the digital audiovisual image. Derivatives are placed over the contemporary digital image like a *calque* or metaphor, allowing us to see the images around us as derivative images. This thinking of images in economic or financial terms catalyses real projects and works: for Ayache, it allows him to rethink his activity as a trader and financial software developer; for Beller, it is the occasion to directly get involved in changing the conditions of monetary media formats (with ECSA); for Citton, it allows him to conceptualise his laboratory and institutional framework around the derivations of *recherche-création*; for Szendy, it leads him to curate a major exhibition on the economy of images. The creativity of the financial crisis (to adapt the title of Evelyne Grossman's book *La Créativité de la crise*), then, is shown in these derivations it inspires.

Notes

1. Hull, *Options, Futures, and Other Derivatives*, p. 1.
2. Martin, *Knowledge LTD*, p. 51.

3. Ibid. p. 6.
4. Peter Szendy, 'Derivative Shakespeare: *The Merchant of Venice* and Dividual Capitalism', *Diacritics*, 47: 1 (2019), 62–79 (p. 73).
5. Martin, *Knowledge LTD*, p. 4.
6. Jacques de Larosière et al., *The High-Level Group on Financial Supervision in the EU*, Brussels (2009), ec.europa.eu/economy_finance/publications/pages/publication14527_en.pdf (last accessed 16 August 2021).
7. Ibid. p. 8, pp. 6–7. My emphasis.
8. Martin, *Knowledge LTD*, p. 62; Edward LiPuma, *The Social Life of Financial Derivatives: Markets, Risk, and Time* (Durham, NC; London: Duke University Press, 2017), pp. 31–3, pp. 50–1.
9. Dick Bryan and Michael Rafferty, *Capitalism with Derivatives: A Political Economy of Financial Derivatives, Capital and Class* (Basingstoke: Palgrave Macmillan, 2006), p. 12.
10. Cédric Durand, *Le Capital fictif: Comment la finance s'approprie de notre avenir* (Paris: Les Prairies ordinaires, 2014), p. 83.
11. Martin, *Knowledge LTD*, pp. 76–7. The historical decolonising movement releases hitherto silenced voices and generates a surplus of multiplex forms of knowledge and nonknowledge which Martin names an 'excess criticality'. That is, he writes, there is an overflow of the political that today creates a derivative condition of volatility of public opinion and political risk that is sometimes called 'identity politics', in which a person's attribute (such as one's race or gender or nationality) is taken as an organising principle and substituted for the whole person. Ibid. p. 10, p. 123.
12. On Black-Scholes-Merton, see Donald MacKenzie, *An Engine, Not A Camera: How Financial Models Shape Markets* (Cambridge, MA: MIT Press, 2006), esp. pp. 136–42. Ayache points out that Black-Scholes is prefigured in the work of the French mathematician Louis Bachelier, whose *Théorie de la spéculation* was written in 1900 – Elie Ayache, *The Blank Swan: The End of Probability* (Chichester: Wiley, 2010), p. 67.
13. Martin, *Knowledge LTD*, p. 7.
14. Ibid. p. 5.
15. Ibid. p. 75.
16. Georges Bataille, *Œuvres complètes: Tome 8* (Paris: Gallimard, 1976), pp. 214–33. For an English translation, see Georges Bataille, 'Nonknowledge, Laughter, and Tears', in *The Unfinished System of Nonknowledge*, trans. Michelle Kendall and Stuart Kendall (Minneapolis: University of Minnesota Press, 2001), pp. 133–50.
17. Martin, *Knowledge LTD*, p. 50.
18. On the political ambivalences of Bataille's notion of excess, see Eugene Brennan, 'The Politics of Excess and Restraint: Reading Bataille alongside and against Accelerationism', in Will Stronge (ed.), *Georges Bataille and Contemporary Thought* (London: Bloomsbury, 2017), pp. 217–38.
19. Martin, *Knowledge LTD*, p. 224.
20. For an example of something like the reverse, see Suhail Malik, 'The Ontology of Finance: Price, Power and the Arkhéderivative', in Robin Mackay (ed.), *Collapse*

8: *Casino Real* (Falmouth: Urbanomic, 2014), pp. 629–811. Malik connects contemporary theories of finance to core ideas of French poststructuralist thought – specifically, he claims that we can see 'the schematic logic of derivative pricing as a variant of Jacques Derrida's quasiconcept of *différance*' (p. 638). As per the notion of *différance*, derivatives defer exchange and thus create a price differential. Unlike in the case of, say, a spin of a roulette wheel, the derivative price will be influenced by the bets (p. 673). This is what he means when he writes that derivatives 'systemically operationalise an unprecedented modality of the wager that is intrinsic to the standard notion of betting but is theoretically and practically unavailable upon the basis of that standard notion' (p. 638). The derivative contract is founded on an interval of Derridean 'spacing' or, in this case, 'pricing' (pp. 688–91). The theoretical consequence of this would be that the derivative is not 'derivative' of, or secondary to, a price in the 'real economy', but actually sets price differences. Most interesting in Malik's argument is how, while Derrida will follow Levinas to see *différance* as based on an infinitely anterior past, the same does not hold for derivatives, which are constituted by statute (pp. 692–3). As Ray Brassier underlines, what is crucial in this departure from Derrida is that we are no longer dealing with an undeterminable past entailing an ethical relation, but rather a political relation arising from the inscription of the indeterminacy of the future in the derivative contract. Ray Brassier, 'Pricing Time: Remarks on Malik's "Ontology of Finance"' (2017), https://www.youtube.com/watch?v=VPyRdsHoCQk (last accessed 18 September 2021).

21. Leslie Hill, *Radical Indecision: Barthes, Blanchot, Derrida, and the Future of Criticism* (Notre Dame, IN: University of Notre Dame Press, 2010). On deconstruction and financialisation, see also Beller, *The World Computer*, pp. 50–1.
22. LiPuma, *The Social Life of Financial Derivatives*, p. 11. Martin's insistence on the notion of lateral movement may also recall the Deleuzean rhizome.
23. On how derivatives disassemble capital, see Martin, *Knowledge LTD*, p. 61. On bricolage, see Claude Lévi-Strauss, *La Pensée sauvage* (Paris: Plon, 1962). Described in this way, derivative logics would recall collage, a mode of artistic visual production associated with various early twentieth-century European art movements which also bears, according to some of its theorists, the potential for the regeneration of social relations and the urban environment. For recent perspectives, see Kathryn Brown, 'Collage as Form and Idea in the Art Criticism of Tristan Tzara', *French Studies*, 73: 4 (October 2019), 544–60 and Frédéric Martin-Achard and Aude Laferrière, 'La Mouche et le bichon: Style et autorité au risque du collage dans *La Carte et le territoire* de Michel Houellebecq', *French Studies*, 74: 2 (April 2020), 259–74.
24. Martin, *Knowledge LTD*, p. 78.
25. Ibid. p. 214. On the etymology of finance, see Peter Szendy, 'Infinance, or Narration and Solvency', *differences: A Journal of Feminist Cultural Studies*, 31: 3 (2020), 1–11.
26. Szendy, 'Derivative Shakespeare', p. 64. Thinking the derivative in relation to language, rhetoric and textuality, of course, opens a whole line of argument distinct from images.

27. Martin, *Knowledge LTD*, p. 205. Gilles Deleuze, 'Post-scriptum sur les sociétés de contrôle', in *Pourparlers, 1972–1990* (Paris: Les Éditions de Minuit, [1990] 2003), pp. 240–7. For a discussion of this text in relation to changing work conditions in France, see Jeremy Lane, 'From "moule" to "modulation": Logics of Deleuzean "Control" in Recent Reforms to French Labour Law', *Modern & Contemporary France*, 26: 3 (2018), 245–59. For other recent perspectives on the text, see Florian Cord and Simon Schleusener (eds), *Coils of the Serpent*, 5 (2020).
28. Arjun Appadurai, *Banking on Words: The Failure of Language in the Age of Derivative Finance* (Chicago: University of Chicago Press, 2015), pp. 101–24.
29. Yves Citton, 'Post-scriptum sur les sociétés de recherche-création', in Erin Manning and Brian Massumi, *Pensée en acte: Vingt propositions sur la recherche-création* (Dijon: Presses du réel, 2018), pp. 97–124; Randy Martin, 'La logique sociale de la dérivation financière', trad. Yves Citton, *Multitudes*, 71 (2018), 59–68. The allusion here is of course to the three regimes of governmentality previously hypothesised by Foucault and Deleuze.
30. Citton's text is a postface to a translation of a text by the Canadian philosophers Erin Manning and Brian Massumi about the principles guiding their laboratory SenseLab in Montreal, which explores the intersection between artistic practice and philosophy. Manning and Massumi trace the origins of *recherche-création* in Canadian research funding policy and its focus on interdisciplinary research. The main part of the text is a discussion of the specific collective experiments they ran bringing together art and philosophy as well as a reflection on the nature of creativity as such. In their account, *recherche-création*, if it is to avoid the trap of falling into a merely superficial interdisciplinarity, must be based around a process and events rather than deliverable results. Success in this context means such events later giving way, for example, to unforeseen collaborations. For the original, see Erin Manning and Brian Massumi, *Thought in the Act: Passages in the Ecology of Experience* (Minneapolis: University of Minnesota Press, 2014), pp. 83–133.
31. See eur-artec.fr (last accessed 16 August 2021).
32. See evalge.hypotheses.org (last accessed 16 August 2021).
33. Citton, 'Post-scriptum', p. 111.
34. Ibid. p. 111.
35. While it is Citton who introduces and develops the notion of derivatives in relation to *recherche-création*, 'pre-acceleration' is here a reference to Erin Manning, *Relationscapes: Movement, Art, Philosophy* (Cambridge, MA: MIT Press, 2009).
36. Citton, 'Post-scriptum', p. 100.
37. Ibid. p. 115.
38. Ibid. p. 111.
39. Ibid. p. 112.
40. The dossier is in *Multitudes*, 71 (2018).
41. Yves Citton, 'Vers un horizon post-capitaliste des dérives financières?', *Multitudes*, 71 (2018), 33–44 (p. 36).
42. Ibid. p. 44.

43. Feher, *Le Temps des investis*, p. 43.
44. Ibid. p. 44. On 'speculative activism' in relation to the GameStop affair, see Michel Feher, 'Another Speculation is Possible: The Political Lesson of R/WallStreetBets', Progress in Political Economy (PPE) blog, 5 February 2021, ppesydney.net/another-speculation-is-possible-the-political-lesson-of-r-wallstreetbets/ (last accessed 16 August 2021).
45. Citton, 'Vers un horizon', p. 44.
46. Ibid. p. 42. On the re-evaluation of value, see Brian Massumi, *99 Theses on the Revaluation of Value: A Postcapitalist Manifesto* (Minneapolis: University of Minnesota Press, 2018). On blockchain, see Finn Brunton, *Digital Cash: The Unknown History of the Anarchists, Utopians, and Technologists Who Built Cryptocurrency* (Princeton: Princeton University Press, 2019), pp. 153–70 and Guillaume Helleu and Anthony Masure, 'Total Record: Les protocoles blockchain face au post-capitalisme', *Multitudes*, 71 (2018), 70–9. On derivatives and technological innovation, see Donald MacKenzie, *Material Markets: How Economic Agents Are Constructed* (Oxford: Oxford University Press, 2009), pp. 63–73.
47. Lordon, *Figures du communisme*, p. 137.
48. Ibid. p. 140.
49. Jonathan Beller, 'Economic Media: Crypto and the Myth of Total Liquidity', *Australian Humanities Review*, 66 (May 2020), 215–25 (p. 221).
50. At the time of writing, however, the exhibition is enjoying a longer run in Beijing as part of the Sino-French Cultural Spring festival.
51. Peter Szendy, 'Voiries du visible, iconomies de l'ombre', in Peter Szendy, Emmanuel Alloa and Marta Ponsa (eds), *Le Supermarché des images* (Paris: Gallimard/Jeu de Paume, 2020), pp. 17–40 (p. 33)/Peter Szendy, 'Shadow Iconomics and Road Networks of the Visible', trans. Jeremy Harrison, in Peter Szendy, Emmanuel Alloa and Marta Ponsa (eds), *The Supermarket of Images* (Paris: Gallimard/Jeu de Paume, 2020), pp. 17–40 (p. 33).
52. Szendy et al., eds., *Le Supermarché du visible/The Supermarket of Images*, p. 15. Szendy is here implicitly referring to Serge Daney's use of the term, which is a little more idiosyncratic than 'freeze-frame' – see Serge Daney, *La Maison cinéma et le monde: Les Années Libé 1986–1991* (Paris: P.O.L., 2012), pp. 307–13.
53. Szendy, 'Voiries du visible', p. 30/'Shadow Iconomics', p. 30. As Elena Esposito writes, derivatives do not refer to assets directly, but to changes in their value: 'One could say that derivatives are tools located at the second order of observation: they vary on the basis of variations, not in reference to the world [. . .] All the features of derivatives can be traced back to this distance from the world, to which they refer through reference to something else.' Elena Esposito, *The Future of Futures: The Time of Money in Financing and Society* (Cheltenham: Edward Elgar, [2009] 2011), p. 108.
54. On the film, see Szendy et al. (eds), *The Supermarket of Images*, pp. 164–5.
55. The exhibition can be visited virtually, and the exhibition map and guide downloaded, at https://jeudepaume.org/evenement/le-supermarche-des-images-2/ (last accessed 16 August 2021).

56. Szendy, 'Voiries du visible', p. 40/'Shadow Iconomics', p. 40.
57. Le Chevallier's short film *L'An 2008* ('The Year 2008', 2010) is a fable about globalisation and the problem of where to lay blame within a complex interconnected system. In the film, a young Breton man is wandering in a forest clearing when he almost falls into a hole because a manhole cover has been stolen. A series of encounters then take place as the young man interrogates a chain of stereotypical figures who explain their situation in a deadpan style: first the man who steals the manhole cover, who explains that the textile factory where he worked has been moved to Rabat and he thus has no other choice; then he speaks to the Moroccan 'social dumper'; then a Chinese seamstress who says she wants to live like an American. This young man, wearing a simple red t-shirt and jeans, is identified by an intertitle as 'the French consumer' and says he needs cheap t-shirts given his limited purchasing power. Next, we see the 'overindebted American', living in a caravan in his dressing gown, whom the young man berates as his life on credit supposedly caused the subprime crisis. The American then suggests that it was the fault of a trader, noting that he lost his home in the process. Later, the young man will encounter the trader in a clearing in the forest, who arrives on a bicycle and speaks with an English accent. Before riding off, the trader blithely replies that while he is sorry, he has to speculate on something to provide profits to pension funds. The young man will then proceed to interrogate those who rely on pension funds, and so on. On *L'An 2008*, see Frédéric Nau, 'Candide au pays des subprimes', *Images de la culture*, 26 (December 2011), 48–51. For a contrasting example in which the trader is a malevolent figure, see the short film *Confessions financières* (Lionel Bernardin, 2015).
58. Szendy et al. (eds), *The Supermarket of Images*, p. 15.
59. Peter Szendy, *Le Supermarché du visible: Essai d'iconomie* (Paris: Les Éditions de Minuit, 2017), p. 14/*The Supermarket of the Visible: Toward a General Economy of Images*, trans. Jan Plug (New York: Fordham University Press, 2019), p. 4.
60. Gilles Deleuze, *Cinéma 2: L'Image-temps* (Paris: Les Éditions de Minuit, 1985), p. 104. This line comes in Deleuze's discussion of 'crystals of time', where he argues that money is bound up in cinema's relation with conspiracy and with the time-image. Translation from Peter Szendy, 'The Reverse of Images (By Way of an Introduction)', *The Yearbook of Comparative Literature*, 60 (2014), 1–5 (p. 3).
61. Szendy, *Le Supermarché du visible*, p. 19/*The Supermarket of the Visible*, p. 8.
62. Szendy, 'The Reverse of Images', p. 3.
63. Szendy, *Le Supermarché du visible*, p. 35/*The Supermarket of the Visible*, p. 19.
64. Ibid. p. 27, p. 36/p. 13, p. 20.
65. Szendy directs us to the classic study Mondzain, *Image, icône, économie*.
66. Szendy, *Le Supermarché du visible*, p. 125/*The Supermarket of the Visible*, p. 80.
67. Ibid. p. 127/p. 81.
68. Szendy, 'Voiries du visible', p. 28/'Shadow Iconomics', p. 28.
69. Raymond Bellour, *L'Entre-images: Photo, cinéma, vidéo* (Sesto San Giovanni: Éditions Mimésis, [1990] 2020)/Raymond Bellour, *Between-the-Images*, ed. Lionel Bovier, trans. Allyn Hardyck (Zurich: JRP/Ringier, 2012), p. 17. Situating Bellour in relation to other notions of intermediality, see Ágnes Pethő, 'Approaches to

Studying Intermediality in Contemporary Cinema', *Acta Universitatis Sapientiae, Film and Media Studies*, 15 (2018), 165–87.
70. Bellour, *Between-the-Images*, p. 18.
71. Hilary Radner and Alistair Fox, *Raymond Bellour: Cinema and the Moving Image* (Edinburgh: Edinburgh University Press, 2018), pp. 126–7.
72. Szendy, *Le Supermarché du visible*, p. 92/ *The Supermarket of the Visible*, p. 56.
73. Ibid. p. 99, p. 154/p. 61, p. 106.
74. Ibid. p. 20/p. 9.
75. Ibid. p. 121/p. 75. Szendy is here playing on the French for 'surplus value' (*la plus-value*).
76. See Jonathan Beller, *The Cinematic Mode of Production: Attention Economy and the Society of the Spectacle* (Lebanon, NH: University Press of New England, 2006) and Yves Citton, *Pour une écologie de l'attention* (Paris: Seuil, 2014), pp. 15–46, pp. 73–98.
77. Szendy, *Le Supermarché du visible*, p. 72/ *The Supermarket of the Visible*, p. 44.
78. Ibid. p. 14/p. 4.
79. I am of course not the first person to put these thinkers in dialogue; compare for example Mathias Kusnierz, 'L'usure iconique: Circulation et valeur des images dans le cinéma américain contemporain', *Transatlantica*, 2 (2016), doi.org/10.4000/transatlantica.8330 (last accessed 16 August 2021).
80. Beller, *The World Computer*, p. 222.
81. Ibid. p. 228.
82. Ibid. p. 222.
83. Ibid. p. 241.
84. Ibid. p. 230.
85. Ibid. p. 223; cf. pp. 184–90.
86. Ibid. pp. 197–205. He gives as examples *Squatterpunk* (Khavn de la Cruz, 2007) and *Three Times* (Hou Hsiao-Hsien, 2005).
87. Jonathan Beller, 'The Derivative Condition' (2018), youtube.com/watch?v=D29DjMvMAq0 (last accessed 16 August 2021). The screen-capture function on a smartphone might be the most familiar example of such a cut: by clicking two buttons, on the shoulder and base of the device, a shutter sound is made and a copy of the image on the screen is framed and cut, shrinking into a smaller image which shuttles to the corner of the screen to be stored. On this subject, see Laurence Allard, 'Des mobiles, des apps et autant de nuances d'images', in Laurence Allard, Laurent Creton and Roger Odin (eds), 'Mobiles: Enjeux artistiques et esthétiques', *Théorème*, 29 (2018), 165–88.
88. This is what Emmanuel Alloa means when he writes that 'all imagery is abstract'. Emmanuel Alloa, 'Abstracting', in Peter Szendy, Emmanuel Alloa and Marta Ponsa (eds), *The Supermarket of Images* (Paris: Gallimard/Jeu de Paume, 2020), pp. 73–94 (p. 78). On the use of 'abstract' and its cognates to describe finance in the humanities, see La Berge, 'The Rules of Abstraction'.
89. Beller, *The Cinematic Mode of Production*; Jonathan Beller, *The Message is Murder: Substrates of Computational Capital* (London: Pluto Press, 2018).

90. Beller, *The World Computer*, p. 102.
91. Beller, 'Economic Media', p. 216: 'While able to broadcast "personal" thoughts and "values", users, who occupy positions in networked computing analogous to those of workers on the assembly lines of yesteryear, cannot adjust the economic protocols of the distributed machine for which they are in large part functionaries. Consequently, most of the value created by users who are, in effect, working in deterritorialised attention factories composed by a computer-network of screens – is split from its qualitative "content", and subsequently transmitted to platform owners who collect it. The values we project and create in media factories are abstracted by means of new sets of metrics (of which "like" is only the most primitive), and, in the processes of monetisation are converted and collapsed into the value-form priced by the code of money. They are, in short, liquidated and placed on the market. After being sold to attention brokers, this value, realised as money, flows upwards to platform owners. Thus, values are encrypted and stripped of their content as all signals, no matter their content, are reduced to number and then to price.'
92. Fredric Jameson famously discussed fragmentation in relation to the cultural logic of finance: 'What happens here is that each former fragment of a narrative, that was once incomprehensible without the narrative context as a whole, has now become capable of emitting a complete narrative message in its own right. [. . .] Whence the vanishing away of affect in the postmodern: the situation of contingency or meaninglessness, of alienation, has been superseded by this cultural renarrativization of the broken pieces of the image world.' Fredric Jameson, 'Culture and Finance Capital', in *The Cultural Turn: Selected Writings on the Postmodern 1983–1998* (London: Verso, 1998), pp. 136–61 (p. 160).
93. Szendy et al. (eds), *Le Supermarché des images*, p. 14.
94. Beller, *The World Computer*, p. 114. The political theorist William Davies similarly sees the derivative as forming a natural pair alongside digital platforms: together they have been the most disruptive inventions for liberal democracies in recent decades and share a calculating logic which takes a relation or institution based on trust (such as lending or friendship) and exploits it for profit – William Davies, *This Is Not Normal: The Collapse of Liberal Britain* (London: Verso, 2020).
95. Beller, *The World Computer*, p. 20. One might compare Beller's 'derivative condition' with the 'symbolic misery' which in Stiegler's account results from the colonisation of aesthetic experience by the market and especially marketing – Bernard Stiegler, *De la misère symbolique 1: L'Époque hyperindustrielle* (Paris: Galilée, 2004). The 'derivative condition' is also a key term in the work of the writer and artist Gerald Nestler, naming the way that financial derivatives have come to condition sociality beyond the market – see Gerald Nestler, Christian Kloeckner and Stefanie Mueller, 'The Derivative Condition, an Aesthetics of Resolution, and the Figure of the Renegade: A Conversation', *Finance and Society*, 4: 1 (2018), 126–43.
96. Szendy, *Le Supermarché du visible*, pp. 119–20, n. 62/*The Supermarket of the Visible*, p. 147, n. 65.

97. Beller, *The World Computer*, p. 223.
98. Ibid. p. 193.
99. Ibid. pp. 244–54. On blockchain and iconomy, see Catherine Malabou, 'Intericonomics: A Currency Within Sight', in Peter Szendy, Emmanuel Alloa and Marta Ponsa (eds), *The Supermarket of Images* (Paris: Gallimard/Jeu de Paume, 2020), pp. 255–61.
100. On the Economic Space Agency, see economicspace.agency/vision/ (last accessed 16 August 2021).
101. Beller, 'Economic Media'.
102. Beller, *The World Computer*, p. 246.
103. Ibid. p. 180.
104. Jonathan Beller, 'How We Short Capitalism – And Finance the Revolution', September 2020, coindesk.com/post-capitalist-revolution-tokenized (last accessed 16 August 2021).
105. Beller, 'Economic Media', p. 221.
106. Ibid. p. 222.
107. Patrice Poujol, *Online Film Production in China Using Blockchain and Smart Contracts: The Development of Collaborative Platforms for Emerging Creative Talents* (Cham: Springer, 2019).
108. Lumiereproject.io (last accessed 16 August 2021).
109. Poujol, *Online Film Production in China Using Blockchain and Smart Contracts*, pp. 161–9.
110. Ibid. p. 164.
111. '#Blockchain: BNP Paribas is Supporting the Future of the Audiovisual Industry', BNP Paribas press release, 11 December 2020, https://group.bnpparibas/en/news/blockchain-bnp-paribas-supporting-future-audiovisual-industry; 'BNP Paribas et le cinéma', https://welovecinema.bnpparibas/bnp-paribas-et-le-cinema; Cédric Ardouin, 'Tokens and the Audio-visual Industry', 8 December 2020, https://www.linkedin.com/pulse/tokens-audio-visual-industry-c%25C3%25A9dric-ardouin/?trackingId=R13nOA/ZSQS9W%2Biw9vG6Cg%3D%3D (all last accessed 16 August 2021).
112. 21 Content Ventures press release, http://www.21contentventures.com/wp-content/uploads/2020/12/21CV-PRESS-RELEASE-ENGLISH.pdf (last accessed 16 August 2021).
113. Ibid.
114. Ibid.
115. http://www.21contentventures.com (last accessed 16 August 2021).
116. Vilém Flusser, *Towards a Philosophy of Photography*, trans. Anthony Mathews (London: Reaktion Books, 2000). See Beller, *The Message is Murder*, pp. 148–9 and Yves Citton, 'Postface à *Post-histoire*', in Vilém Flusser, *Post-histoire* (Paris: T&P Work UNit, 2019), pp. 183–200.
117. Flusser, *Towards a Philosophy of Photography*, p. 28. As is clear from Flusser, writing, criticism and academic work do not escape this logic – this book, then, would be but one more twist in the attempt to derive, say, the permutations of the 'film studies' programme.

118. Beller, *The World Computer*, p. 153.
119. Jonathan Beller, 'The Cinematic Program', *La Furia Umana*, 23 (2016), lafuriaumana.it/index.php/56-archive/lfu-23/350-jonathan-beller-the-cinematic-program (last accessed 16 August 2021). Compare Flusser, *Post-histoire*, p. 97.
120. Flusser, *Towards a Philosophy of Photography*, p. 80.
121. Christophe Hanna, 'Poétique des concepts-calques (un projet)', *Questions Théoriques*, 1, 'Frontières de la littérature' (2011), questionstheoriqueslarevue.com/blank-5 (last accessed 16 August 2021).
122. See Christophe Hanna, *Nos dispositifs poétiques* (Paris: Questions Théoriques, 2010).
123. Nikolaj Lübecker, 'Mallarmé's Instruments: The Production of the *individu-livre*', *French Studies*, 73: 3 (2019), 367–83.
124. Christophe Hanna, 'La Fiction comme institutionnalisation', preface to Dominiq Jenvrey, *Le Cas Betty Hill: Une introduction à la psychologie prédictive* (Paris: Questions Théoriques, 2015), pp. i–x (pp. iv–v). Clearly, as indicated above, this logic has been around for a long time – Mondzain will write of how 'l'image est dans la même situation que la monnaie elle-même' ('the image is in the same situation as currency itself'). Mondzain, *Image, icône, économie*, p. 197. Szendy glosses: 'ce qu'on pourrait appeler la double équivalence iconomique: non seulement la monnaie est à l'image de l'image, mais l'image, à son tour, est à l'image de la monnaie' ('what we might call the double iconomic equivalence: not only is currency made in the image of the image, but the image, in turn, is made in the image of money'). Szendy, *Le Supermarché du visible*, p. 18/ *The Supermarket of the Visible*, p. 7.
125. Hanna, 'La Fiction comme institutionnalisation', p. x.
126. Feher, *Le Temps des investis*.
127. However, as mentioned above, see Szendy's 'Derivative Shakespeare', which thematises derivatives in relation to language and is thus distinct from the focus on visual images in *Le Supermarché du visible*.
128. Szendy, *Le Supermarché du visible*, p. 14.
129. Szendy, *The Supermarket of the Visible*, p. 4.
130. Emily Apter and Martin Crowley, 'Economies of Existence', *Diacritics*, 47: 1 (2019), 3–15 (p. 6).
131. Friedrich Nietzsche, *On the Genealogy of Morality*, ed. Keith Ansell-Pearson, trans. Carol Diethe (Cambridge: Cambridge University Press, [1887] 2007), p. 45.
132. For example Dany-Robert Dufour, *Le Divin Marché: La Révolution culturelle libérale* (Paris: Gallimard, 2012).
133. Szendy, *Le Supermarché du visible*, p. 15/ *The Supermarket of the Visible*, p. 5.
134. 'La Grande Table', France Culture, 17 February 2020, franceculture.fr/emissions/la-grande-table-culture/peter-szendy-analyse-liconomie (last accessed 16 August 2021).
135. Vogl, *The Specter of Capital*, p. 30, p. 32.
136. F. A. Hayek, *The Road to Serfdom* (Abingdon: Routledge, [1944] 2001).
137. Lordon, *Figures du communisme*, p. 125.

138. Ibid. p. 125.
139. Ibid. p. 128.
140. Peter Szendy, *Tubes: La Philosophie dans le juke-box* (Paris: Les Éditions de Minuit, 2008), p. 77/Peter Szendy, *Hits: Philosophy in the Jukebox*, trans. Will Bishop (New York: Fordham University Press, 2012), p. 65. The idea of *tubes* as a kind of psychic commodity fetishism comes as much by way of analyses of films as songs and tunes (notably Fritz Lang's *M* [1931] and certain films of Hitchcock). The perhaps debatable commensurability of songs and film images seems to come from their being seen not as objects but as *séquençages* ('sequencings'). For more on this, see Peter Szendy and Dork Zabunyan, 'Entretien: Ausculter les images', *Meeting Point*, 2 (2018), lemagazine.jeudepaume.org/2018/02/meeting-point-zabunyan-peter-szendy-fr/ (last accessed 16 August 2021).
141. Szendy, *Tubes*, pp. 77–8/*Hits*, p. 65.
142. Ibid. p. 58, p. 78, p. 80/p. 47, p. 66, p. 69.
143. Ibid. p. 91/p. 79.
144. Ibid. p. 91/p. 79.
145. Ibid. 91/p. 79.
146. Ibid. p. 92/p. 80.
147. Ibid. p. 93/p. 82.
148. Ibid. pp. 93–4/p. 82.
149. Beller, *The World Computer*, p. 69: 'The unconscious of market discipline goes to the core of the subject form and has its basis in the computation of exchange-value.'
150. Szendy, *Le Supermarché du visible*, p. 117/*The Supermarket of the Visible*, p. 73.
151. On the 1987 crash, see MacKenzie, *An Engine, Not A Camera*, pp. 179–210.
152. Ayache, *The Blank Swan*, p. 16; Elie Ayache, 'On Black-Scholes', in Benjamin Lee and Randy Martin (eds), *Derivatives and the Wealth of Societies* (Chicago: University of Chicago Press, 2016), pp. 240–51 (p. 249). For discussions of *The Blank Swan*, see Appadurai, *Banking on Words*, pp. 83–100 and Elie Ayache, 'The Writing of the Market: Interview with Elie Ayache', in Robin Mackay (ed.), *Collapse 8: Casino Real* (Falmouth: Urbanomic, 2014), pp. 517–602.
153. Ayache, 'On Black-Scholes', p. 242.
154. Ibid. p. 245.
155. Ibid. p. 247.
156. Ibid. p. 245.
157. It should be noted that the kind of derivatives that Ayache is most concerned with are options, which best express contingency (using the formula 'if . . ., then . . .'). Ayache, *The Blank Swan*, p. xix. As Jon Roffe points out, Ayache is critical of products such as CDOs involved in 2008 and which do not depend on Black-Scholes for their functioning. Jon Roffe, 'From a Restricted to a General Theory of the Pricing Surface', in Robin Mackay (ed.), *Collapse 8: Casino Real* (Falmouth: Urbanomic, 2014), pp. 603–28.
158. Ayache, 'On Black-Scholes', p. 251.
159. Ayache, *The Blank Swan*, p. 10.

160. Ibid. pp. 217–36.
161. Ibid. pp. 393–403.
162. Ibid. p. 217. Ayache's book is written in English but here as elsewhere he offers French in parenthesis.
163. Ibid. p. 218.
164. Grossman, *La Créativité de la crise*, pp. 9–12.
165. Ayache, *The Blank Swan*, p. 221.
166. Ibid. p. 220.
167. Gilles Deleuze, *Difference and Repetition*, trans. Paul Patton (New York: Columbia University Press, 1994), p. 172; Anne Sauvagnargues, *Artmachines: Deleuze, Guattari, Simondon*, trans. Suzanne Verderber with Eugene W. Holland (Edinburgh: Edinburgh University Press, 2016), pp. 110–22; Patrick ffrench, *The Cut: Reading Bataille's* Histoire de l'œil (Oxford: Oxford University Press, 1999). For the acephalic formulations, see for example Ayache, *The Blank Swan*, p. 225, p. 233. Compare Ayache's account of writing earlier on pp. 100–8.
168. Maurice Blanchot, *L'Espace littéraire* (Paris: Gallimard, 1955). Ayache had previously engaged with Blanchot in Elie Ayache, *L'Écriture postérieure* (Paris: Éditions Complicités, 2006).
169. Blanchot and Meillassoux are, of course, famous readers of Mallarmé. Ayache draws on Blanchot's discussion of Mallarmé in *Le Livre à venir* (Paris: Gallimard, 1959).
170. Ayache, *The Blank Swan*, p. 4.
171. Ibid. p. 104.
172. Anne Dufourmantelle, *Éloge du risque* (Paris: Éditions Payot & Rivages, [2011] 2014). See also Vinzenz Hediger, 'Risk as Aesthetic Virtue', in Bishnupriya Ghosh and Bhaskar Sarkar (eds), *The Routledge Companion to Media and Risk* (New York: Routledge, 2020), pp. 453–67.
173. Ayache, 'On Black-Scholes', p. 245.
174. Ayache, *The Blank Swan*, p. xv.
175. Ibid. p. xv.
176. Ibid. p. 19.
177. Szendy, *Le Supermarché du visible*, p. 73/ *The Supermarket of the Visible*, p. 44. The French *haut débit* carries the sense of high-speed broadband.

CHAPTER FOUR

Trading in Images: The Case of Kerviel

SCREENS WITHIN SCREENS

Much of what goes on in *L'Outsider* (2016, directed by Christophe Barratier and produced by Jacques Perrin) concerns what is happening on the screens of financial trading terminals used by traders at the French bank Société Générale.[1] We are at several moments in the film given screens-within-a-screen (Figure 4.1). In one variation of this, the shot of the trading screen is followed by a reverse shot, from the point of view of the screen, showing the characters looking at it, and therefore almost as if also looking at the audience (Figure 4.2). However, the characters' eyes are not looking directly at the camera lens, but just above it. Another variation of this is when we see the screen with a reflection, in focus, of characters looking at it, thus merging both the data on the screen and those scrutinising it.

Some 40 minutes into the film, the main character has just made a large profit during a frantic trading session and, in a moment of calm after the storm, looks with his colleagues at the numbers. As we see below, the trading screen consists in prices and commands to buy and sell a product. Reflexive moments such as this not only signal that the 'action' of this story takes place

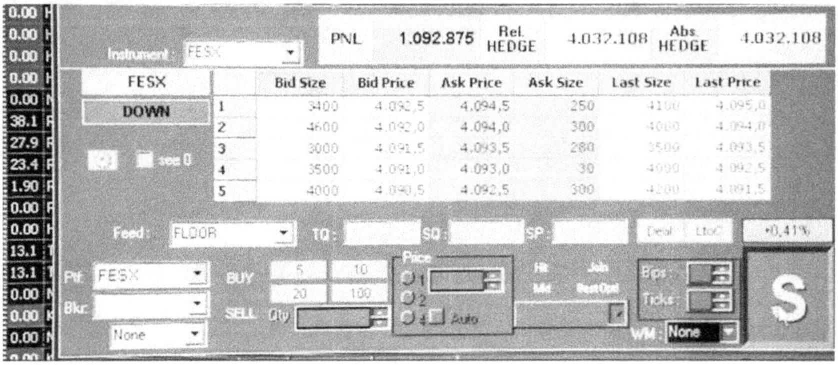

Figure 4.1 *L'Outsider* (Christophe Barratier, 2016) © Le Pacte.

Figure 4.2 *L'Outsider* (Christophe Barratier, 2016) © Le Pacte.

through the data coursing through the trading software and the graphs they translate themselves into, but also that people interacting with screens may itself be suitable material for a film.[2] Like *le boiteux* in Chapter 2, the traders are fascinated by their screen: a form of 'ploutéidoscomanie'.[3] The film's blue palette here creates correspondences between the blue hues of the traders' shirts and those of the screen. That said, *L'Outsider* is a relatively traditional dramatic film, and much of the story takes place outside of the trading hall.

L'Outsider is the film adaptation of the memoir of Jérôme Kerviel, *L'Engrenage: Mémoires d'un trader* (2010). As is well known, Kerviel was a young man who worked as a trader for Société Générale until January 2008 when he became the focus of a major scandal as he was accused by the bank of what was then supposed to be the largest financial fraud in history. The film and the source text can be taken together to form an instructive comparative case study on the complexities of representing derivative finance within a French context. In this chapter I will sketch the history of the affair as recounted by Kerviel and its film adaptation before discussing the image it gives of the nature of the job of the trader. It will be my contention that the film's deployment of the bank's logo and brand identity onscreen responds at the level of the film's visual economy to the derivative trading it depicts.

Kerviel at Société Générale

On 24 January 2008, Société Générale announced that one of its traders had taken unauthorised speculative positions on futures contracts in global markets amounting to €50 billion. The bank had unwound these massive positions, incurring a record loss of €4.9 billion. The announcement came amid a summary inspection of French bank balances demanded by the governor of the Banque de France in the context of brewing anxiety about the extent of the exposure of European banks to the emerging US subprime mortgage crisis. According to Kerviel, the bank was aware of his activities and cynically used his case to deflect attention from its announcement of major losses in subprime derivatives, which were ten times worse than expected.[4] A few days later, on 28 January 2008, Kerviel was charged and placed under court supervision. Eighteen months later, at the end of August 2009, Kerviel was brought to trial before the first-level criminal court (Tribunal Correctionnel) in Paris. In October 2010, Kerviel was found guilty of breach of trust, fraudulent entry of data into an automated processing system, forgery and use of forged documents.[5] He was sentenced to five years in prison, including a two-year suspended sentence, and required to pay €4.9 billion in damages to Société Générale. In October 2012 his appeal was upheld by the Paris Court of Appeal. In 2014 the Court of Cassation upheld the original criminal conviction but overruled the compensation, which was fixed by the Versailles Court of Appeal in 2016 at €1 million. Kerviel has lodged several complaints that are under investigation, and the bank has also filed suits in response. Kerviel was unhappy with the handling of his case, finding that the judge did not understand derivatives; he has demanded a review of his trial.[6]

L'Engrenage was written before the trial, which was a major media event, and clearly the book formed something of Kerviel's defence, but it remains an important primary source on financial culture in France in the run-up to the 2008 financial crisis.[7] In 2016 he published another volume of memoir, returning to issues in the first volume as well as recounting his life since the affair, notably his meeting with Pope Francis.[8] He has continued to be a well-known figure, appearing on multiple French television magazine programmes to discuss his case.[9] The film recounts Kerviel's story but does not deal with incidents after the discovery of his positions by Société Générale, which are covered in the book: his perquisition, his *garde à vue*, transfer to the *pôle financier*, problems with his legal team, *l'instruction*, the seeming impossibility of getting the judge to understand the nature of his job, his stay in La Santé prison, his constantly being pursued by journalists wanting pictures of him, and so on. As he describes it, his struggle against the monolithic institution that is Société Générale is a moral ordeal, sleepless at every turn, in which he feels powerless and alone.[10]

The film was released to mixed reviews in France. Some reviewers were unconvinced by the story of 'le gentil trader', calling it 'une blanchisserie maladroite' ('a clumsy whitewash') and, indeed, effectively part of his legal defence.[11] A reviewer for *Le Monde* claimed, not uniquely, that the film tells us very little about the banking system, noting that it suffered from being released a few months after the American film *The Big Short* (Adam McKay, 2015), which, also dealing with the financial crisis, had more explicatory power, according to the paper.[12] *Libération* argued that what is characteristic of the film is the way it adapts for a French context certain tropes found in American cinema such as the debauchery of bankers.[13]

Describing his trajectory to becoming a trader, Kerviel recounts a relatively modest route of study in Quimper and Nantes which does not include attendance at one of the *grandes écoles* (elite schools), unlike most traders he encounters.[14] It is during a short *stage* (internship) at Société Générale in Nantes that he first comes into contact with derivatives, taking a particular interest in asset-backed securities.[15] After another year of study, this time in Lyon, he takes a *stage* at BNP Arbitrage in Paris, which he enjoys and where he learns about algorithmic trading and securitisation (and where a fund manager intimates to him that this kind of trading is likely one day to cause a major crisis).[16] He is headhunted to join Société Générale in the early 2000s, a period in which it was industrialising its cutting-edge derivatives operation.[17] He is then rapidly promoted from a relatively minor role to become first an assistant trader and then a junior trader in 2005; this was an unusual route to become a trader, he says, and was thanks to the mentoring of one of his superiors.[18] By the mid-2000s, in his guise as a market-maker (someone who gives prices to clients for the buying and selling of products), he sells 'turbo warrants', primarily to clients in the German market but also to Swedes and Finns.[19] These are essentially options, tools for betting on various financial indices:

> Disons, pour faire simple, qu'il s'agit de produits dérivés crées par les banques à destination des particuliers et des professionnels de la finance. Il s'agit d'options d'achat (des '*calls*') ou de vente (des '*puts*') sur les produits les plus divers appelés sous-jacents: actions, indices boursiers, taux de change, matières premières . . . Leur mécanisme est simple et peut s'assimiler à une sorte de pari: je prends une option d'achat sur telle action à un prix que l'on fixe à l'avance et dont je pense que le cours va monter. À l'échéance, je gagne si le cours a monté, et j'empoche la différence entre le cours et le prix fixé au départ, appelé prix d'exercice. Si le cours a baissé, je ne perds que le prix du warrant.[20]

> [To put it simply, these are derivative products created by banks for individuals and finance professionals. They are buying and selling options ('calls' and 'puts') on all kinds of 'underlying' products: stocks, share indices, exchange rates, raw materials . . . Their mechanism is simple and can be seen as a kind of bet: I take a buying option on such-and-such a stock at a price fixed in advance and whose price I think will rise. At expiry, I win if the price has risen and I pocket the difference between the new price of the stock and the price of the contract (the strike price). If the price of the stock has dropped, I only lose the cost of the option.]

Figure 4.3 Screen-capture taken from 'Société générale: produits de bourse' advert (2006): ina.fr/video/PUB3284290102/societe-generale-produits-de-bourse-video.html © Archives Historiques Société Générale.

In the 2000s, these products were being widely advertised and sold. Figure 4.3 shows one example of the TV advertisements used by Société Générale in this period.[21] This example lasts 20 seconds and invites viewers to use the bank for 'investment solutions', in which it claims to be 'the world number one'.[22] A speedy disclaimer running across the bottom of the screen justifies this statement, as the bank had for two years in a row been named the best bank in the world for derivatives; this is followed by a standard warning that investments are inherently risky and their value can be lost. Against a white background, the advert shows innumerable floating tiny square images, each framed by grey corners. The advert stops to frame a selection of these generic images – the Taj Mahal, a group of three smiling figures in suits, an image of cupped hands full of coins from which a plant stem grows – which signify the vast variety of possible underlying products in which one can invest. (Kerviel evokes how he was managing many hundreds of such products.[23]) The camera pulls back from these apparently swirling images to show that they are in fact frozen in space and make up a globe. Fully in the frame, the globe rotates, like a planet, and around this globe move four words: TRACKERS, CERTIFICATS, TURBOS, WARRANTS. The globe speeds up in its rotation and repositions itself in the top left-hand side of the image, while, on the right-hand side are centred the names of these products, this time arranged in the colour and style of the bank's distinctive red and black logo: 'trackers' and 'certificats' in black sitting atop 'turbos' and 'warrants' in red. A voiceover explains over a jaunty commercial tune the range of possible investments and the expertise of the bank. The slogan on which the advert closes is: 'Société Générale: prenez plaisir à réussir en bourse' ('take pleasure in winning at the stock market').[24]

What I want to draw attention to here is how the advert offers an implicit representation of financial derivatives: innumerable generic little *images*, each discretely but unobtrusively framed, swirling in an abstract space. When it comes to derivatives, quantity becomes a kind of quality, their value vastly outstripping global GDP. In this sense, they resemble the vast image space evoked by Szendy in which we are today submerged. In contrast to the cinematic representation in *L'Outsider*, then, where derivatives are represented in the form of the screen of the trader's calculator showing a spreadsheet-like grid of numbers, bars and buttons, here, in an advertisement inciting one to buy derivatives, the images suggest a virtual whole in continual movement: they form an iconomy.

It is at this point — while trading turbo warrants — that Kerviel's life is seemingly completely monopolised by Société Générale: he is now 'chained' to the bank and lives in a perpetual present.[25] Earlier in the book, Kerviel describes his normal routine as a trader: he arrives at the towers of Société Générale at around 7 a.m. to follow the Asian market and to see how particular products have done on the American market the night before. Then he reads the economic press and checks on the internet to see if there is any news that might affect the companies that he follows. Before the European markets open at 9 a.m., he puts some information into the bank's trading software for buying and selling orders (*l'automate*). Throughout the day he gives the price of the products for which he is responsible, following the evolution of the market.[26] Traders take a few breaks during the day to smoke or drink coffee at the base of the tower, and generally for lunch eat a sandwich at their desk.[27] The Parisian market closes at 5:30 p.m., but many of his products follow New York market time, meaning he usually works until around 10 p.m. At the end of the day, he has a drink with colleagues at the base of the tower, where they discuss the market events of the day:

> Étrange moment de décompression, en vérité; nous ne parlions guère d'autre chose que de notre travail, des cours de nos produits, de l'état des marchés, nous échangions des anecdotes sur la tôle de l'un, les gains de l'autre, et

repassions ensemble les événements d'une journée vécue au rythme frénétique des clics de souris et des sommes faramineuses engagées dans nos différentes opérations. Chacun de nous était en quelque sorte devenu une excroissance de la Société Générale. Nous ne vivions que par elle et pour elle, au point d'accepter sans même nous en rendre compte que notre vie privée soit envahie par sa toute-puissance. Même loin de la tour de La Défense, en vacances ou en week-end, c'était comme si un fil invisible continuait de nous attacher à elle; une sorte de cordon ombilical, de lien organique qui à la fois nous maintenait dans son giron, nous nourrissait et nous protégeait.[28]

[A strange moment of letting off steam, in truth: we barely spoke of anything but our work, how our products were doing, the state of the markets, we swapped anecdotes about one person's profits and another's bad luck, and we went over all the events of a day lived at the frenetic rhythm of mouse clicks and huge sums wagered in our different operations. Each of us had in a way become an outgrowth of Société Générale. We only lived through and for the bank, to the point of accepting without realising it that our private life was taken over by its omnipotence. Even far from the tower of La Défense, on holiday or on a weekend getaway, it was as if an invisible thread continued to tie us to the bank: a sort of umbilical cord, an organic link which simultaneously kept us in its bosom, nourished us and protected us.]

He returns home to his flat in Neuilly (a rich western suburb of Paris) around midnight or 1 a.m., exhausted, to sleep for five hours. At 6 a.m., he gets ready for work while reading market news on TV or on his mobile phone.[29] Not only is he tied by an invisible thread to the tower, but he is also glued to a screen: if he is not in the trading hall watching the market on a screen, he has to watch France Info on television; if he is in a car, he must listen to the radio. In Kerviel's account, being a trader means one must continually observe the evolution of the market. Kerviel's case bears out the observation of psychotherapists that, in a condition of derivative images, the screen becomes a vector for exhaustion, to the extent that the screen worker becomes a spectator whose subjecthood has been hollowed out.[30] Kerviel rarely sees his family in Brittany, and no longer eats even breakfast at home.[31] The film adaptation emphasises that he is under considerable stress, showing him smoking increasingly heavily, coughing up blood and becoming aggressive with his love interest. His case thus fits within a wider literature on burnout and stress in contemporary corporate capitalism, in France and across the West.[32] And yet, as this passage makes clear, he is not simply exploited but also 'nourished' and 'protected' by the bank: the invisible thread is also an ambivalent affective bond yoking him to his work. On the temporal horizon, Kerviel remarks that his job is so all-consuming that he is unable to project himself into the future, which is a striking remark given that, as we shall see in Chapter 6, this condition is normally associated not with traders but with the precariat.[33]

Kerviel writes that everyone has in mind an image of trading halls from cinema marked by an intense brouhaha; this image, he says, is only partially accurate. This was what it was like at the beginning of his career, on the sixth floor of the tower:

> Yeux rivés sur leurs écrans et micros au bord des lèvres, les traders passent leurs journées à communiquer avec leurs correspondants tout en envoyant des ordres sur le marché. L'ambiance sonore atteint de tels niveaux et, par moments, l'hystérie est si forte qu'il est quasiment impossible de suivre les conversations des voisins les plus proches.[34]

> [Eyes riveted to screens and microphones at their lips, traders pass their days communicating with their correspondents while also sending orders on the market. The ambient noise reaches such levels and at times the hysteria is so strong that it is almost impossible to follow the conversations of those sitting beside you.]

This is because they are often speaking to several people at once. Each trader has three screens, two keyboards and two phones. A scene evoking this mood in the trading room comes 15 minutes into the film, a scene consisting mainly of shots of tapping keyboards, people holding the phone between their head and their shoulder, being told to hurry up, being passed post-it notes, traders patting or slapping each other, rifling through piles of paper, shouting, shots of screens showing numbers and line graphs, a clock on the wall ticking down to the close of the trading session, when a bell rings, like the bell at the end of a boxing round.[35] Derivatives grew so much that Kerviel was moved to another room higher up the tower, a vast open space full of screens but which was oddly silent and where everyone knew what their neighbour was doing.[36] This, he says, makes it absurd to suggest, as claims Société Générale, that he was acting secretly when he took his large positions. He was part of a group of eight traders, whose screens were about a metre apart from each other, and his line manager was about 2 metres from him.[37]

Kerviel describes his first big operation, which takes place during the London bombing attacks in July 2005.[38] He worked on the German market and followed the insurance company Allianz, whose stock in June 2005 was erratic due to large capital movements. At the same time, the market was falling generally. This reminds him of when he was working in the middle office in 2001, during the 9/11 attack in the USA. During the days before the disaster, derivative products related to American airline companies suffered capital movements. Who knows why, he asks. The graphs giving him a feel for the direction of the market look similar, so he decides to speculate on the fall of the value of stocks in Allianz.[39] One of Kerviel's preferred words is *subodorer* (to scent), which evokes his instinct for the caprice of the market.[40] This is at once a vague intuition but also often based on carefully studying market precedents, as in this case. There is a certain art to this: he looks for resemblances and signs in the data, recognising similarities across disparate fields and temporal gaps. He refers repeatedly to his method as a 'stratégie'.

In trader jargon, the operation he performs here is called a 'spiel' (from the German: 'game'), naming a purely speculative operation.[41] When the attacks take place, the markets in London then Germany start to *gerber* or 'dive'.[42] It is a success: he unwinds his position and wins €500,000. His manager gives him a mixed message, officially saying he will cover up for him, at the same time complimenting him, suggesting he develops his strategy and expanding his limits for speculation in the system. In this way, he says, traders are subject to paradoxical injunctions: they have limits that they should not pass, and yet they are encouraged to do so. They are told not to speculate, but if they do, they are congratulated on their winnings and invited to show their superiors how they did it so the strategy can be modelled.[43] The attitude to dubious practices is one of *pas vu, pas pris* ('you only get punished if you get caught').[44] Nonetheless, traders are under intense pressure to bring in money for the bank; Kerviel's superiors refer to traders as *bonnes gagneuses* ('whores').[45] In 2006, he starts making bigger bets, taking positions on the German Dax index worth several hundred million euros.[46] In 2007, he starts betting on the market falling and on the sale of subprimes, taking colossal positions of €3 billion between March and July.[47] The market does eventually fall when BNP Paribas announces it can no longer calculate its liquidity (as discussed in Chapter 1). He unwinds, earning €500 million. But he thinks the fall in the market is not yet finished, so bets again €30 billion. After a month he unwinds again, earning the unprecedented sum of €1 billion.[48] He is speculating so much that he starts using a broker to expand his operation.[49] Despite the large sums he wins for the bank in 2005–6, he receives relatively modest bonuses.[50]

His problems begin in January 2008. What disturbs the bank is the way he has kept the enormous profit *mis sous le tapis* ('under the carpet'), that is, he kept it aside in case it was needed later.[51] He contends that his operations were legitimate, but that he should not have concealed the risk by putting into the system fictional operations that appeared to cancel out the real positions.[52] His positions were so huge that they destabilised the bank's required capitalisation ratio, which, in theory, guarantees that the bank has enough liquidity in the event that its positions go bad.[53] He had taken positions totalling €50 billion, and if he had to *déboucler* ('unwind') his positions in a hurry, this would entail huge losses.[54]

What is significant about January 2008 is that this is when the subprime crisis was beginning to affect European financial institutions, causing the market to fall and thus negatively impacting on Kerviel's positions.[55] In *L'Outsider*, aerial shots track over the tops of the Société Générale towers over which a radio news programme dramatically announces the arrival of subprime crisis in Europe, communicating something of the shock this caused among banks in Paris, which were expected to announce major losses. On Friday 18 January, Christophe Noyer, the governor of the Banque de France, asks for an inspection of all French bank balance sheets by the following Monday. There is a rumour that Société Générale has lost billions on subprimes.[56] Kerviel is told before he goes for his weekend that things will be resolved, but he is quickly recalled during the weekend and is subject to a long interrogation in the towers.[57] While Kerviel protests that his positions can all be traced on his margin calls, they soon realise that his positions are huge and entail massive losses.[58] Sensing a possible scandal, his superiors move quickly to protect themselves: in order to avoid the suspicion of having covered up his operations, his bosses 'ne pouvaient que me *sacrifier* sur l'autel de la pureté bancaire' ('could do nothing but *sacrifice* me on the altar of banking purity').[59] He is effectively told to go on the run, whereupon the bank performs a clean-up operation.[60] When the markets open on Monday, the CAC 40 – the key French stock market index – loses 6 per cent.

A few days later, on Thursday 24 January, the story breaks of a €4.9 billion 'fraud' at Société Générale. Kerviel recalls his shock at seeing himself on screens being described as the biggest fraudster in history: the front page of *Le Figaro* on 25 January 2008, for example, ran with the headline: 'L'homme qui a fait perdre 5 milliards à la Société générale'.[61] He calculates that his bosses badly unwound the positions, leaving him in the red. At the same time as the fraud, the bank announces €2 billion lost on subprimes (ten times more than they had previously thought).[62] The loss on subprimes is thus deflected by the Kerviel story. Kerviel notes that the bank paints him as an embezzler or even a financial terrorist, and important French financial figures such as Christine Lagarde take the bank's side, describing him in similar terms.[63] He watches France Info and LCI constantly, 'comme un lion en cage' ('like a lion in a cage'), where he has the surreal experience of seeing his professional identity card photo repeatedly projected in the news, as if he were a fugitive.[64]

Kerviel admits that he had 'made mistakes' by going over his limits and concealing his losses and gains – but everyone did the same thing, he claims. He claims his superiors had known since April 2007 that he had fictional operations on his account (he provides documentary evidence in the book's appendix to this effect).[65] Everything he did was made possible 'grâce à une forme de complicité par laisser-faire' ('thanks to a form of complicity through laissez-faire').[66]

Trading as *métier*, the Trader as Functionary

Kerviel writes that he only ever had one passion in life, and that was his *métier*.[67] He repeatedly stresses that he was 'convaincu d'œuvrer dans le seul intérêt de la banque qui m'employait' ('convinced that he was working purely in the interest of the bank that employed him'), with no personal interest.[68] He claims he carried out his work seriously and efficiently, which is why he got quickly promoted.[69] He realises he took excessive risks, that his positions were too big, 'et j'avais d'autant plus succombé à la griserie des chiffres et à la passion de mon métier qu'aucun garde-fou n'était venu me freiner dans mon mouvement' ('and I had all the more succumbed to the intoxication of the numbers and the passion of my *métier* as no barrier came to stop me in my tracks').[70] Kerviel's world outlook is a strangely moral one – throwing himself into his work is a way of doing right by his parents in Brittany. In some ways his fault was to have too diligently made himself an organ of the bank, to have over-identified with it. Kerviel rejects the idea, proposed by some of his colleagues, that trading is a game: it is rather a *métier*.[71] Traditionally, the word *métier* refers to an artisanal, manual work, as distinct from art, industry and unskilled work. It refers to meaningful, skilled work, a profession or vocation that is socially recognised and which involves a specialist training and initiation. As Laurent Creton shows, the word's rich etymology comes from a conflation of the roots of the words 'minister' and 'mystery' (*ministerium* and *mysterium*), thus associating, respectively, the mundane connotations of administration and the sense of ritual and cult knowledge reserved for initiates.[72] In Creton's usage, *métier* takes on a connotation from management strategy: that is, of aiming to ensure, within conditions of uncertainty and volatility, that one has the necessary skills to position oneself competitively within a market, which may imply diversifying or redefining one's *métier*.[73] As Kerviel's discussion of his work as a *métier* suggests, the trader is not exactly an entrepreneur nor a capitalist, but a kind of artisanal worker for banks. His *métier* is a source of deep ambivalence for him. He describes the intense stimulation he gets from using his instinct for the market and his strategies, the pleasure he derives from diligence as such – and yet he is also profoundly alienated.[74] He seems to be the only one at the bank who is not primarily motivated by money. This partly explains why his case is not understood by the bank and the justice system. He claims to have been naive: 'J'étais convaincu qu'il suffisait de faire son métier en allant au bout de soi-même et sans en tirer d'autre profit que la satisfaction de faire au mieux. [. . .] [J]'éprouvais alors un plaisir d'autant plus intense que tout le monde m'encourageait' ('I was convinced that it was enough to do one's job as best as one could and solely for the satisfaction of doing one's best. [. . .] I enjoyed it all the more as everyone was encouraging me').[75] He abandons the sports he previously enjoyed (judo, jogging), smokes more and more, eats poorly, and spends his weekends in recovery from the week.[76]

On 28 January 2008, Kerviel was charged and placed under court supervision. He describes his intense fear of going to prison, which he imagines through film and television images.[77] Seeing things through media is a recurring motif: elsewhere, Kerviel describes his situation in terms of cinema: police film,[78] Luc Besson's *Taxi* series,[79] *Wall Street* (Oliver Stone, 1987).[80] Arrested, he is even keen to stress to the police that, unlike the traders in American films, he is not motivated by money; rather, he is in his situation due to his 'véritable passion pour son métier' ('real passion for his *métier*').[81] And yet, Kerviel does not exactly try and justify trading *as* a *métier*, and he certainly does not attempt any intellectual justification of derivatives or even banking in and of itself. Rather, he offers what are effectively aesthetic reasons explaining the passion. In Lordon's language, we might say he is attracted by the *affects* of finance. Everything he did, he did:

> avec un maximum de plaisir, en y consacrant toute mon énergie et sans compter mon temps. J'aimais le rythme trépidant des journées, le *speed* des opérations, les émotions que j'en retirais, et jusqu'à l'ambiance de la salle dans laquelle je travaillais, ces murs d'écran où s'affichaient des graphiques, des courbes, des colonnes de chiffres. J'aimais, surtout, ce couplage entre une action nécessairement rapide et le temps de la réflexion qui la suivait; pourquoi mon opération a-t-elle marché? Pourquoi me suis-je planté? [. . .] J'aimais avoir l'esprit toujours en éveil, à l'affût des informations, en prise directe avec les vibrations du monde.[82]

> [with a maximum of pleasure, dedicating all my energy to it and without heed to time. I liked the hectic rhythm of the days, the speed of the operations, the emotions that I got from it and even the atmosphere of the hall in which I worked, the screen-walls where charts, line graphs, columns of figures were shown. I liked, above all, the link between a necessarily rapid action and the time for reflection which followed: why had it worked? How did I screw it up? [. . .] I liked having my mind alert, on the lookout for information, directly plugged into the vibrations of the world.]

It becomes clear that his attraction to this world is not economic or venal; rather, it is a function of media images and their association with his childhood. He says that when he was growing up, his father followed current affairs on television, on radio, and in newspapers, discussing them at the dinner table, and it was because of the place of financial markets in these media that Kerviel was attracted to them.[83] Symmetrically, when his world collapses, it is because his image becomes the focus of a media scandal.

Passages such as the above could be read as bearing out Maurizio Lazzarato's remark that the subjectivity of a financial trader is a 'machinic subjectivity'; in other words, the diagrammatic semiotics of line graphs and stock indices, the trading monitors and the wider financial machinery into which he is plugged at least partially condition his subjectivity and, by extension, his 'freedom' (or lack thereof).[84] As a trader he is an individuated subject, and hence he can be identified and blamed by the press as the one at the centre of the scandal; yet at the same time, he is a product of a 'machinic assemblage'. For Martin O'Shaughnessy, drawing on Lazzarato, recent European post-crisis films stage the human as plugged into a 'machinic enslavement', and he gives subprime mortgage derivatives as an example of how machinic assemblages are constructed by processes of subjectivation (the assignation of roles and identities) and machinic enslavement (the tearing of parts of a person's identity into a machinic process).[85] As we have seen, in the case of Kerviel we have someone who powerfully identifies with his job and with the bank's brand; like Larnaudie's *le boiteux* and Greenspan, Kerviel's is a 'monetized subjectivity', meaning his world and psyche are measured financially, commensurable with his performance as a trader.[86] For example, his poor decisions about his choice in friends are described as 'de mauvais arbitrages humains' ('bad human arbitrage').[87] As the title of his memoir suggests, he describes himself as a cog in a machine: 'Engrenage d'un système qui utilise les hommes allant jusqu'à les broyer, engrenage des conduites de ces mêmes hommes qui ne se contrôlent plus, engrenage des mécanismes qui s'affolent, engrenage des intérêts personnels qui bloquent la manifestation de la vérité' ('Cog in a system which crushes people, cog of the behaviour of these same people who no longer control themselves, cog of mechanisms entering crisis, cog of personal interests blocking the manifestation of truth').[88] In another vocabulary, we could say that Kerviel is a perfect functionary, merging with the trading apparatus, like Flusser's photographer mentioned in the previous chapter. Always playing out a logic which exceeds him, this becomes a question of the search for freedom, which is only possible if we understand programmes as an 'absurd game'.[89] Flusser writes that while functionaries function like the 'cogs' (*rouages*) of a black box, for another class of people, the programmers, reality is a game they play with programmes and symbols. Traders, then, are like post-ideological functionaries because they largely do not influence the programme but enact it, unlike figures such as Greenspan (who, as we saw, was supposedly a 'concepteur et décideur'). Kerviel writes that 'comme tous les autres traders, j'étais devenu un être privé d'identité propre, un numéro parmi d'autres au milieu de la foule qui grouillait dans le quartier de La Défense' ('like all the other traders, I have become a being deprived of a personal identity, a number among the others in the crowd which swarmed around La Défense').[90]

The orthodox reading of the Kerviel affair is that he took out positions that were too large and he concealed his trade. He was supposed to be a market-maker and became a speculator. He traded equity indices and was supposed to look for arbitrage opportunities. It is thus that Kerviel has become a case study in a textbook on derivatives for financial professionals:

> Kerviel used his knowledge of the bank's procedures to speculate while giving the appearance of arbitraging. He took big positions in equity indices and created fictitious trades to make it appear that he was hedged. In reality, he had large bets on the direction in which the indices would move. [. . .] The lessons from these losses are that it is important to define unambiguous risk limits for traders and then to monitor what they do very carefully to make sure that the limits are adhered to.[91]

For Lordon, cautioning against focusing critique on individuals rather than structures, the only difference between Kerviel and other traders is that he had 'poussé un peu plus loin les curseurs' ('pushed the cursors a little further than the rest').[92] While this part of his story is not shown in the film, Kerviel's memoir describes deep disillusionment with the world of finance, and he can be seen as one of those myriad actors in the contemporary world Lordon identifies as exhibiting an ethical revulsion with the current state of affairs.[93] On the one hand, Kerviel describes the traders as *engrenages* or gears in a machine; on the other, he describes a system of 'omerta', as if the bank was a kind of mafia.[94] Kerviel does not see himself as a symptom of the 2008 crisis but rather as an isolated case of someone who committed errors.[95] The 2008 crisis was only the trigger for his ordeal, but Kerviel is just as much an *effondré* as the figures in Larnaudie's book, and, in view of his later pilgrimage to visit Pope Francis, perhaps also a 'saint of the crisis'.[96]

Suicide and Société Générale

The first scene of *L'Outsider* is among the most striking in the film. It begins with a sequence showing traders looking around nervously over their screens. We see through the blinds of a private office that a meeting is being held where we surmise a trader is being dismissed by his superiors, who look on sternly. In the main trading hall, the trader, whose face we do not see, switches off his computer monitors and puts some items into two cardboard boxes. With his work bag slung over his shoulder, he is then accompanied out of the building by a security attendant. As the trader exits the building, we have the first shot establishing that we are at the main offices of Société Générale on a damp, grey day (Figure 4.4). This is clear from the conspicuous

Figure 4.4 *L'Outsider* (Christophe Barratier, 2016) © Le Pacte.

presence of the bank's brand logo on the left-hand side of the image. The shot lasts a little longer than those preceding it, at once letting us take in the new surroundings but also suggesting a slower pace of things outside the office. The cold and glassy greyish-blue chromatic landscape here sets the tone for the film as a whole.

The following two, briefer shots show the trader walking with his boxes across the walkways and fortification-like structures, which are typical of the area around the bank's offices in La Défense. The next shot – one of the longest in the film at just under 50 seconds – confirms the location as La Défense. This crane shot begins with an elevated panoramic view of road networks and flyovers looked down on by large office buildings. The camera cranes backwards over a graffiti-covered wall and tracks backwards, close to the ground. The trader enters the shot and the camera follows him as he approaches a large pile of rubbish on this elevated, seemingly abandoned platform – perhaps the top of a disused carpark, now overgrown with weeds. Again, the slower pace of the montage, taking in the real built environment surrounding him, suggests that, dismissed, the character is now more concretely grounded in a sense of place – here, La Défense.[97] He stops before the pile of rubbish and puts down his boxes as the camera reframes him, tracking right and panning left, to show two buildings that can be seen in the distance over the rim of the wall (Figure 4.5). On the right is a shorter, more distant office, clearly identified with the Société Générale logo.

In the centre of the frame, we see the lower-middle section of a very tall skyscraper. The trader begins to climb the mound of garbage and the camera continues to track right and pan left, now also tilting up so that the skyscraper increasingly fills the screen, and the rubbish largely disappears from the bottom of the image. The trader looks up at the building and steps

Figure 4.5 *L'Outsider* (Christophe Barratier, 2016) © Le Pacte.

Figure 4.6 *L'Outsider* (Christophe Barratier, 2016) © Le Pacte.

onto the top of the pile, then stops and straightens up, just a little to the left of the centre of the frame. He now stands still and the camera is also at last still, whereupon the accompanying music reaches its climax. The tower, reflecting the passing clouds against the blue sky, is now clearly identified as one of the Société Générale towers as another logo is visible on the tower at the top of the screen, on the same vertical axis as the trader, who looks up at it (Figure 4.6).[98]

The trader is dwarfed beneath the gleaming towers, among the trash and contrasting with their polished veneer. He then hops over the wall, presumably to his death, and the image fades to black. The films titles begin, explaining that events take place eight years earlier. The next shot shows Kerviel (played by Arthur Dupont) stepping into the frame in close-up and looking up. We see the two towers of the bank from a low angle, followed by a tilt down to show the base of the towers, whence the trader was ejected in the previous sequence, now with people going about their business near the bank's entrance.[99] Kerviel walks straight towards the bank for his first day at work. The film thus invites us to suppose this individual who takes his own life is Kerviel, although this is of course misleading.[100] It is rather the film's way of marking Kerviel's story out from the outset as one of *effondrement* and evoking the existential stakes of derivative trading and the derivative condition.

Among the trash, he is cast off like the useless financial instruments that went bad. If as we saw in Lordon's play the derivatives had turned into *déchets* ('garbage'), we should note this accords with a broader post-crash sentiment in which people also come to be seen as superfluous, as *déchets*.[101] As the trader looks up at the bank's logo on the side of a skyscraper before jumping onto the flyover, the Société Générale tower is here like an obelisk before which the trader sacrifices himself.[102] If we accept Beller's idea that a ramification of the derivative condition is the 'movement of all cultural-semiotic practice toward advertising' – in other words, in that all signs and actions can be seen as positions on underlying social volatility, they increasingly resemble adverts or logos – then the prominent position of the logo can be read as signifying the derivative condition that the trader can no longer bear.[103] Opening the film in this way, associating the Société Générale logo with suicide, suggests dark undertones to the activity of La Défense.[104] To this extent, *L'Outsider* has something in common with the rather different film *Dans ma peau* (Marina de Van, 2002), a film in which a self-destructive sacrificial logic pervades as the underside to the capitalist productivity of the district.[105] The financier who must leave the bank carrying their possessions in brown cardboard boxes was one of the key tropes of the media coverage of the financial crisis, primarily associated with the collapse of American banks such as Lehman Brothers. Suicide is a recurring motif in both Hollywood and French-language films about the crisis, while financial crises generally are strongly resonant with a sacrificial logic.[106] For O'Shaughnessy, recurrent non-proletarian suicides in contemporary European film 'point to a wider crisis of neo-liberal subjectivity as figures (managers, management consultants) whom one might have expected to be heroic, neo-liberal entrepreneurs-of-the-self mutate into characters oppressed by their labour or in search of escape'; many of the films can find no viable exit from the situation and, with a few exceptions, 'highlight the absence of meaningful political alternatives'.[107] As *Les Effondrés* shows, many financiers did indeed take their own lives during the financial crisis. Indeed, during his interrogation, Kerviel's superiors fear that he will take his own life, which had apparently happened previously with another trader at the bank.[108]

Of course, skyscrapers are well-known tropes in the topology of finance. In her study of (primarily Hollywood) representations of the financial crisis,

Miriam Meissner uses the concept of the 'urban imaginary' to explain how narratives of the financial crisis function by metonymy and symbolic correlative; that is, by focusing on financial skylines, indices and, inversely, images of suburban ruin.[109] Meissner argues that the attention to corporate glass façades implies at once 'repellent surface qualities' that stand for the impenetrability of financial institutions for outsiders, and at the same time the 'porous, interactive, electronically connected qualities of an interface'.[110] In general, scholars have shown that, rather than examining the financial flows as such, films on finance often have a tendency to explore the culture and temporal and spatial milieu of finance, and in this respect *L'Outsider* resembles certain well-known Hollywood films on finance.[111] Closer to home, European filmmakers train their cameras on specific financial districts to find 'a material architectural representation for the abstract exchanges of contemporary finance capital'.[112] Jeremy Lane has shown how La Défense has been depicted in certain contemporary French films – notably in *Violence des échanges en milieu tempéré* (Jean-Marc Moutout, 2004) – as 'being *in* France yet not really being *of* France, a non-French space located on the margins of the nation's capital, the locus of global financial forces that threaten to undermine any specifically French polity or society'.[113] In fact, the generic image of skyscrapers is such a cliché that what emerges as significant in this particular sequence is precisely how conspicuous the bank's logo is.[114] In his review of the film for *Libération*, Didier Péron notes that the filmmakers did not have the right to use the Société Générale logo, which we see repeatedly onscreen.[115] Indeed, on the bank's website one can find a statement deploring the 'omnipresent' use of the logo in the film.[116] In an interview, Barratier explains that he did not seek authorisation to use the logo, but he did need to ask permission from the architect in order to film the towers, which he received, and on which the logo is prominently displayed.[117] As I suggest below in conclusion, the Société Générale logo, which we see at three points in the 1-minute sequence discussed above, makes the film, in my view, uncannily resemble an advertisement for the bank.

Société Générale was established in 1864 to support French industry. In 1912, it moved to its historic seat at 29 boulevard Haussmann, opposite the Paris Opéra. Société Générale's highly recognisable red and black square logo came into being in 1986, just before the bank's privatisation in 1987.[118] While Paris has been an international financial centre since the eighteenth century, historically concentrated around the Paris Bourse, in the 1990s Société Générale led the way by moving from boulevard Haussmann to the business district of La Défense, 3 kilometres west of Paris.[119] It is here where the famous towers of Alicante and Chassagne were constructed, each 167 metres tall.[120] A third tower, la tour Granite, was erected in 2008, 180 metres in height, and this is the tower we see in the sequence analysed above.[121] In her useful book on the visual communication strategies of European banks, including a case study of Société Générale, Angela Bargenda describes the fortress-like towers, which we can see when Kerviel looks up at the end of the sequence:

> La symétrie inhérente à ce plan d'ensemble met en place un dispositif spéculaire, où les deux tours isomorphes entretiennent une relation dialogique, suggérant davantage une autoréférentialité hermétiquement fermée qu'une ouverture sur l'environnement urbain. L'inclinaison des toits vers la plate-forme intérieure renforce cette impression visuelle de dialogue intime. La topologie complexe des tours aux reflets multiples, où reluisent tantôt leur propre image réfractaire, tantôt des ombres d'immeubles adjacents, crée un jeu de surfaces éphémères.[122]

> [The symmetry inherent to this overall plan establishes a mirror-like arrangement in which the two isomorphic towers maintain a dialogic relation, suggesting more a hermetically sealed auto-referentiality than an opening onto the urban environment. The inclination of the roofs towards the interior platform reinforces this visual impression of intimate dialogue. The complex topology of the towers with multiple reflections creates a play of ephemeral surfaces where can be seen by turns their own refractory image and the shadows of adjacent buildings.]

Bargenda also notes the strongly postmodern dimension to Société Générale's aesthetic relative to the other banks in her study and in radical contrast to the old bank headquarters, whose façade allegorises the bank's values of social responsibility and service to society.[123] She goes on to say that the 'rhetoric' of the architecture evokes solidity, sovereignty, security, power, protection and defence – and then immediately relativises these notions.[124]

In this way, *L'Outsider* mobilises against the bank its own visual currency – the logo and the trademark iconography of the towers – by incorporating it into the film. The insistent presence of the bank's logo within the diegesis reminds us not only of the non-fictional basis of the story, but, more importantly, of the economic underside of every image. The flat square logo serves as a metonym for the derivatives in the turbo warrant advert discussed above. As with Szendy's discussion of the *Godzilla* remake, what we see here is an example of a more general logic in which images tend to multiply themselves as merchandise or 'produits dérivés'.[125] The logo functions as a trapdoor leaving open the continual possibility of a metaleptic slippage from fiction film to advertisement, thus suggesting a 'fiction of the image' according to which all films would be a species of advertisement or other economic media.[126] Placing the bank's logo over the film image like a *calque*, the fiction of the image proposing itself, then, would be to see *L'Outsider* as not simply a film about derivative products but *itself* a derivative product and by extension ours as a world of derivative images.[127] Kerviel's ordeal is thus a moment when our wider derivative condition comes sharply into focus – a condition whose existential stakes the film underscores.

Notes

1. Perrin is well known for producing politically committed films with Costa-Gavras.
2. *L'Outsider* here is in line with Hollywood representations of the financial crisis, where the market is shown to be not simply reflected by the screens but constituted by it, the way cinema shows the trading screen entering into relation with the way viewers look at the cinema screen. Micky Lee, *Bubbles and Machines: Gender, Information and Financial Crises* (London: University of Westminster Press, 2019), p. 111. However, there is a crucial difference between the trading screen and the cinema: the trading screen is bi-directional – the trader gives it information too. On trading terminals, see also Christopher Wood, Alasdair King, Ruth Catlow and Brett Scott, 'Terminal Value: Building the Alternative Bloomberg', *Finance and Society*, 2: 2 (2016), 138–50. As Meissner writes, finance poses narrative challenges for cinema by its lack of 'eventfulness' – it happens on balance sheets, and in films about the crisis it appears as a 'spectral absence' – Meissner, *Narrating the Global Financial Crisis*, pp. 222–3.
3. Citton, *Médiarchie*, p. 373.
4. Jérôme Kerviel, *L'Engrenage: Mémoires d'un trader* (Paris: Flammarion, 2010), p. 204.
5. See Société Générale's statement on the case, societegenerale.com/en/news/newsroom/kerviel-case (last accessed 16 August 2021).
6. Kerviel, *L'Engrenage*, p. 221, p. 195.
7. The world of financial trading is notoriously hermetic and resistant to sociological study. For an alternative, ethnographic account of life during the same period in a derivatives department in a French bank – which, while pseudonymous, closely resembles Société Générale – see Vincent Antonin Lépinay, *Codes of Finance: Engineering Derivatives in a Global Bank* (Princeton: Princeton University Press, 2011).
8. Jérôme Kerviel with Richard Amalvy, *J'aurais pu passer à côté de ma vie* (Paris: Presses de la Renaissance, 2016).
9. To give but two examples, he has appeared on Laurent Ruquier's *On n'est pas couché* (October 2012) and Jean-Luc Mélenchon's *Pas vu à la télé* (May 2016).
10. Kerviel, *L'Engrenage*, p. 177.
11. Iegor Gran, 'Plus blanc que Kerviel, qu'est-ce que c'est comme couleur?', *Charlie Hebdo*, 22 June 2016. For a more positive review, see Olivier De Bruyn, 'Jérôme Kerviel: Antihéros de cinéma', *Les Echos*, 22 June 2016, p. 12.
12. Thomas Sotinel, 'Un Bas-Breton perdu dans la haute finance', *Le Monde*, 22 June 2016, p. 18.
13. Didier Péron, '"The Outsider", traders en chœur', *Libération*, 22 June 2016, p. 28. This debauchery is largely (with the exception of the corporate weekend

in Deauville) invented for the film adaptation. For example, Kerviel at no point in his memoirs talks of going to lap-dancing bars, yet this is a recurring motif in the film.
14. Kerviel, *L'Engrenage*, p. 76, p. 90.
15. Ibid. pp. 76–7.
16. Ibid. p. 78–81.
17. Ibid. pp. 81–2. On the liberalisation of the French financial sector in the 2000s, see Woll, *The Power of Inaction*, p. 114.
18. Kerviel, *L'Engrenage*, p. 96.
19. Ibid. p. 100.
20. Ibid. p. 91. On options and warrants, see MacKenzie, *An Engine, Not A Camera*, pp. 119–42.
21. On the value of looking at adverts from financial institutions from around the time of the financial crisis, see Christian De Cock, Max Baker and Christina Volkmann, 'Financial Phantasmagoria: Corporate Image-Work in Times of Crisis', *Organization*, 18: 2 (2011), 153–72 and Christian De Cock, James Fitchett and Christina Volkmann, 'Myths of a Near Past: Envisioning Finance Capitalism *anno* 2007', *ephemera: theory & politics in organization*, 9: 1 (2009), 8–25.
22. Kerviel describes how he saw this claim on posters inside the department Dérivés Actions et Indices when he was working there – Kerviel, *L'Engrenage*, p. 82.
23. Ibid. p. 85.
24. The financial crisis marked an abrupt new direction in Société Générale's advertising campaigns. Whereas before the crisis, what was typical of the bank's advertising posters was to use surreal Magrittian and Warholian iconography to position the potential client as a sophisticated, wealthy, risk-prone and somewhat schizoid individual, the post-crisis campaigns use imagery of cross-sections of society to stress the bank's humanistic solidarity and risk-averse sense of social responsibility. In other words, after 2008 the bank moves away from representing anything potentially associated directly with derivatives. Angela Bargenda, 'Sense-Making in Financial Communication: Semiotic Vectors and Iconographic Strategies in Banking Advertising', *Studies in Communication Sciences*, 15 (2015), 93–102. For an official history of the bank's brand identity, see Hubert Bonin, *Banque et identitié commerciale: La Société générale 1864–2014* (Villeneuve-d'Ascq: Presses Universitaires du Septentrion, 2014).
25. Kerviel, *L'Engrenage*, p. 99.
26. Ibid. p. 15.
27. Ibid. p. 20.
28. Ibid. pp. 20–1.
29. Ibid. p. 21.
30. Hélène Romano, 'Écran', in Philippe Zawieja (ed.), *Dictionnaire de la fatigue* (Geneva: Librairie Droz, 2016), pp. 211–16 (p. 214).
31. Kerviel, *L'Engrenage*, p. 99.
32. See Lane and Waters (eds), 'Work in Crisis', *Modern & Contemporary France*, 26: 3 (2018). The post-2008 economic crisis is sometimes associated with a crisis

in masculinity – see Thomas Pillard, 'Crise économique et hommes en crise', in Joël Augros (ed.), 'CinémArgent', special number of *CinémAction*, 171 (2019), 152–8.
33. Kerviel, *L'Engrenage*, p. 99.
34. Ibid. p. 16.
35. One is reminded of Jean-Stéphane Bron's documentary film for Swiss television *Traders* (2009), shot just as Lehman Brothers collapsed, and which covers a Wall Street charity boxing event. The film plays on the metaphor of the trading floor as a boxing ring, where one has to be aggressive to survive, where winners and losers are strictly defined.
36. Kerviel, *L'Engrenage*, p. 17.
37. Ibid. p. 17.
38. Ibid. p. 109
39. Ibid. pp. 109–10. On the various techniques and means of reasoning of traders that inform their trading decisions, see Olivier Godechot, *Les Traders: Essai de sociologie des marchés financiers* (Paris: La Découverte, [2001] 2005), pp. 185–239.
40. Kerviel, *L'Engrenage*, p. 26, p. 40, p. 104.
41. Ibid. p. 18.
42. Other trader argot for the market falling: *dégueuler, caver, partir à la cave, yourzer*. Ibid. p. 55.
43. Ibid. p. 112.
44. Ibid. p. 13.
45. Ibid. pp. 13–14. In the German documentary film *Master of the Universe* (*Der Banker*, 2013) by Marc Bauder, the former investment banker Rainer Voss directly refers to Kerviel while describing his own extensive experience of banking. The banker remarks that people overestimate the role played by individuals such as Kerviel in the banking system. He claims he experienced the same pressure as Kerviel, of having to bring in more and more money for the bank, no matter the method, and being treated like a prostitute. For a discussion of this film, see Alasdair King, 'Documenting Financial Performativity: Film Aesthetics and Financial Crisis', *Journal of Cultural Economy*, 9: 6 (2016), 555–69.
46. Kerviel, *L'Engrenage*, p. 125.
47. Ibid. p. 125.
48. Ibid. p. 126.
49. Ibid. p. 127.
50. Ibid. pp. 117–18.
51. Ibid. p. 27.
52. Ibid. p. 28.
53. Ibid. p. 29. One of the conclusions drawn after the crisis was that the banks were under-capitalised and this led to new macroprudential supervision (notably in the form of the Third Basel Accord) requiring them to have a higher ratio.
54. Ibid. p. 30.
55. Ibid. p. 38.
56. Ibid. p. 39.

57. Ibid. p. 41.
58. Ibid. p. 48.
59. Ibid. p. 49.
60. There is perhaps an echo of Kerviel's case in Enrico Giordano's *Maître du Monde* (2011), a film which shows how, at the moment of the 2008 financial crisis, a forty-year-old broker (Boris Beynet) goes on the run. The film opens with him driving along the motorway, smoking a cigarette and listening to a radio programme where a financier discusses the financial crash. Few words are spoken in this somewhat austere film as we follow the broker wandering in the wilderness, seemingly in search of death, while still holding on to the accoutrements of his profession. As in *L'Outsider*, the trader is shown to be no kind of 'sovereign man' or 'master of the universe' but one who tends to be sacrificed. The crisis is also announced in a similar way by radio in the opening of the documentary *Les Molex, des gens debout* (José Alcala, 2010) – a rather different film – as we hear the film's first words coming over a scratching sound as the frequency is found: 'c'est la crise, la crise'. The film follows the struggle by workers as the American business Molex (a manufacturer of cables and connectors) decides to close its factory in Villemur-sur-Tarn, north of Toulouse. While French films about factory closures, *délocalisation* and deindustrialisation are not unusual, this film shows the direct industrial consequences of a decision taken at the height of the crisis in October 2008.
61. Kerviel, *L'Engrenage*, p. 61. Unlike Bernard Madoff (whose case later in the same year overtook Kerviel's alleged fraud as the biggest in history), Kerviel did not profit from this 'fraud'. The case of Madoff is the subject of Dominique Manotti's short *récit Le Rêve de Madoff* (Paris: Allia, 2013) and is sketched in three chapters of Larnaudie, *Les Effondrés*, pp. 135–54.
62. Kerviel, *L'Engrenage*, p. 63.
63. Ibid. pp. 63–5.
64. Ibid. p. 62, p. 56. See also p. 58. He uses the same expression to describe how he watches news about himself on television while in prison, p. 191.
65. Ibid. p. 19.
66. Ibid. p. 42.
67. Ibid. p. 14. On the notion of trading as a *métier*, see Godechot, *Les Traders*, pp. 253–61.
68. Kerviel, *L'Engrenage*, p. 9, p. 51.
69. Ibid. p. 71.
70. Ibid. p. 54.
71. Ibid. p. 123. Giving a hint of how some traders do see it as a game, he notes how his one-time manager tells him that he misses his work: 'Ma Game Boy me manque.' Ibid. p. 122.
72. Laurent Creton, 'Godard et l'art stratégique de la redéfinition du métier', in Gilles Delavaud, Jean-Pierre Esquenazi and Marie-Françoise Grange (eds), *Godard et le métier d'artiste* (Paris: L'Harmattan, 2001), pp. 315–34 (pp. 326–7).
73. Laurent Creton, *Économie du cinéma: Perspectives stratégiques*, 6th edn (Malakoff: Armand Colin, 2020), pp. 138–43; on strategy, see pp. 109–29.
74. Kerviel, *L'Engrenage*, p. 22.

75. Ibid. p. 19.
76. Ibid. p. 22.
77. Ibid. p. 71.
78. Ibid. p. 43.
79. Ibid. p. 163.
80. Ibid. p. 188.
81. Ibid. p. 151, p. 155.
82. Ibid. p. 155.
83. Ibid. p. 76.
84. Maurizio Lazzarato, *Signs and Machines: Capitalism and the Production of Subjectivity* (Cambridge, MA: MIT Press, 2014), p. 99.
85. Martin O'Shaughnessy, 'Beyond Language and the Subject: Machinic Enslavement in Contemporary European Cinema', *Studies in European Cinema*, 16: 3 (2019), 197–217.
86. LiPuma, *The Social Life of Financial Derivatives*, pp. 267–303, esp. pp. 279–81.
87. Kerviel, *L'Engrenage*, p. 23.
88. Ibid. p. 220.
89. Flusser, *Post-histoire*, p. 54.
90. Kerviel, *L'Engrenage*, p. 23.
91. Hull, *Options, Futures and Other Derivatives*, p. 18.
92. Lordon, *Jusqu'à quand?*, p. 35.
93. Lordon, *Vivre sans?*, pp. 21–3.
94. Kerviel, *L'Engrenage*, p. 220.
95. Ibid. p. 219.
96. Société Générale, close to Goldman Sachs, would end up benefitting from the US bailout deal and managing to survive the crisis. Tooze, *Crashed*, p. 194.
97. No longer plugged into the financial markets, the character leaves the financial chronotope described by Frederik Tygstrup: 'The contemporary debt chronotope teaches us to refrain from conceiving of space – that is, gauging the relation between here and there – in terms of an immediately given territory with tangible gradients of propinquity and distance. Instead, we are situated vis-à-vis a ubiquitously present infrastructural order that relates everything to everything else and constantly readjusts these relations in real-time response to market interventions everywhere on the globe.' Frederik Tygstrup, 'The Debt Chronotope', *differences: A Journal of Feminist Cultural Studies*, 31: 3 (2020), 29–47 (p. 36).
98. In his recent installation *Ici, autrefois* ('Here, in days gone by', 2020), Martin Le Chevallier offers us photographs of closed businesses during the first Covid lockdown in 2020. In each case, the artist affixes a label to the wall or window of the business satirically explaining what function the business hitherto performed in society. His examples are corporations such as McDonald's, Ikea and H&M. One image is of a branch of Société Générale (with logo prominently displayed), to which he adds the label: 'Ici, autrefois, on envoyait l'argent au paradis' ('Here, in days gone by, we sent money to paradise'). In this exhibition as elsewhere, Le Chevallier's work critiques cultures of disposability in the contemporary consumerist economy. Martin Le Chevallier, 'La Stratégie du râteau', Galerie Jousse Entreprise, Paris (2021).

99. Here as elsewhere in the film, the images of workers walking are reminiscent of the artist Vincent Debanne's series of photographs *Les troupes de la Défense* (2004), https://vincentdebanne.fr/les-troupes-de-la-defense/ (last accessed 18 September 2021).
100. This suicide sequence appears to be based on an anecdote given in Kerviel, *L'Engrenage*, p. 221.
101. Anselm Jappe, *Crédit à mort: La Décomposition du capitalisme et ses critiques* (Paris: Éditions Lignes, 2011), p. 17; le Comité invisible, *Maintenant* (Paris: La Fabrique éditions, 2017), p. 93. The image of the garbage here framed at the base of the tower also evokes Nicolas Bourriaud's concept of the 'exformal': that is, that which is normally excluded from representation within a given aesthetic regime. 'The most striking image of refuse and discharge occurs in the economic sphere: *junk bonds* with *toxic assets*; it's as if dangerous materials buried away in the balance sheets of obscure subsidiaries and mutualized portfolios had invaded the financial universe. The matter plainly reveals the *real* of globalism: a world haunted by the spectre of what is unproductive or unprofitable, waging war against all that is not already *at work* or in the process of becoming so. We have witnessed the realm of waste assume vast dimensions. Now it encompasses whatever resists assimilation – the banished, the unusable and the useless.' Nicolas Bourriaud, *The Exform*, trans. Erik Butler (London: Verso, 2016), pp. vii–viii.
102. Advertising is a permanent 'invitation' to suicide, according to Jean-Paul Galibert, *Suicide et sacrifice: Le Mode de destruction hypercapitaliste* (Paris: Éditions Lignes, 2012).
103. Beller, *The World Computer*, p. 184, p. 188.
104. For Dany-Robert Dufour, the details that came to light in the wake of the financial crisis (such as remuneration in the financial sector, corruption and tax avoidance) revealed an obscene underside to the current order characterised by a Sadean liberalism, whose model is Sade's banker Durcet. Dany-Robert Dufour, *La Cité perverse: Libéralisme et pornographie* (Paris: Gallimard, 2012), pp. 18–20, p. 24.
105. Nikolaj Lübecker, *The Feel-Bad Film* (Edinburgh: Edinburgh University Press, 2015), pp. 130–4. Sarah Waters notes how the corporate buildings of La Défense that we see in the documentary series *La Mise à mort du travail* offer 'an image of finance as a purified order that has dissociated itself from a grimy industrial past' – a dissociation belied by the accounts of the real bodily suffering given in the series. Sarah Waters, 'Disappearing Bodies: The Workplace and Documentary Film in an Era of Pure Money', *French Cultural Studies*, 26: 3 (2015), 289–301 (p. 290).
106. Meissner, *Narrating the Global Financial Crisis*, pp. 127–31; Martin O'Shaughnessy, 'Putting the Dead to Work: Making Sense of Worker Suicide in Contemporary French and Francophone Belgian Film', *Studies in French Cinema*, 19: 4 (2019), 314–34; Paul Crosthwaite, 'Blood on the Trading Floor: Waste, Sacrifice and Death in Financial Crises', *Angelaki: Journal of the Theoretical Humanities*, 15: 2 (2010),

3–18. See also Sarah Waters, *Suicide Voices: Labour Trauma in France* (Liverpool: Liverpool University Press, 2020). One might also compare the mischievous entry in the 'Abécédaire de la crise', where the *Multitudes* writers treat us to the synopsis of an imaginary new film by the Dardenne brothers, *Fabulation*, 'un thriller psychologique situé dans le milieu du *trading*' ('a psychological thriller that takes place in the world of trading'), in which two anarchist Belgian IT engineers conspire to bankrupt the French group Suez by putting a bug into the risk assessment algorithms used by their derivatives traders. The financial crisis arrives, bringing this plot to fruition. Their superior, Nicolas, becomes aware of their activities and feels responsible, never having checked the risk assessments himself. As things go to ruin, he murders his wife and children before taking his own life. The film ends with the French and Belgian governments stepping in to save the company, the financial crisis and the complexity of the mathematical models protecting the engineers from discovery. As the writer indicates, the film seeks to combine references to *l'affaire Coupat* and *l'affaire Romand* as well as a family murder by an Electrabel worker in 2001. For the writer, this film is thus a fable about the contemporary 'cognitive' worker's loss of belief in the real world, notably in the case of the traders but also in the utopianism of the saboteurs. The financial crisis thus represents a 'return of the real'. Multitudes, 'Abécédaire de la crise', *Multitudes*, 37–8 (Autumn 2009), 147–9.
107. O'Shaughnessy, 'Putting the Dead to Work'.
108. Kerviel, *L'Engrenage*, p. 45.
109. Meissner, *Narrating the Global Financial Crisis*, p. 2.
110. Ibid. pp. 73–5.
111. Robert Burgoyne, 'Forms of Time and the Chronotope in the Wall Street Film', in Constantin Parvulescu (ed.), *Global Finance on Screen: From Wall Street to Side Street* (London: Routledge, 2017), pp. 42–55 (p. 45).
112. Alasdair King, 'Film and the Financial City', *Studies in European Cinema*, 14: 1 (2017), 7–21 (p. 9).
113. Jeremy F. Lane, *Republican Citizens, Precarious Subjects: Representations of Work in Post-Fordist France* (Liverpool: Liverpool University Press, 2020), p. 182.
114. While we tend to oppose cinema as an art to marketing as commerce, historically this has not been the case – see Chantal Duchet, 'Cinéma et publicité: Le Droit d'asile', in Laurent Creton (ed.), *Le Cinéma et l'argent* (Paris: Nathan, 1999), pp. 88–102. On cinema and advertising, see also Patrick Vonderau, 'Introduction: On Advertising's Relation to Moving Pictures', in Bo Florin, Nico de Klerk and Patrick Vonderau (eds), *Films That Sell: Moving Pictures and Advertising* (London: BFI/Bloomsbury, [2016] 2018), pp. 1–18.
115. Péron, '"The Outsider"'.
116. 'Contrairement à ce que peut laisser penser l'apparition omniprésente de logos Société Générale dans le film, la Banque n'a pas donné son accord pour le tournage de ce film. Sans préjudice d'éventuelles actions judiciaires qui sont actuellement à l'étude, le Groupe déplore l'image caricaturale qui est donnée de ses collaborateurs, qui ont par ailleurs vécu cet épisode comme un traumatisme' ('Contrary to the impression given by the omniprésent appearance of the Société

Générale logo in the film, the bank did not agree to the shooting of the film. Without prejudicing possible legal action currently under consideration, the Group deplores the caricatural image of its employees, for whom this episode was a traumatic experience'). Société Générale, 'Réaction de Société Générale' (2016), societegenerale.com/fr/content/pageqace (last accessed 16 August 2021).

117. Laure Croiset, 'Christophe Barratier: "Dans l'Affaire Kerviel, on a un peu oublié l'humain"', *Challenges* (2016), challenges.fr/cinema/rencontre-avec-christophe-barratier-pour-la-sortie-de-l-outsider_521500 (last accessed 16 August 2021).
118. On the aristocratic associations of this logo, see Angela Bargenda, *La Communication visuelle dans le secteur bancaire européen: L'Esthétique de la finance* (Paris: L'Harmattan, 2014), pp. 160–3.
119. On the historical geography of finance in Paris, see Yamina Tadjeddine, 'Territories of Finance: The Parisian Case', in Isabelle Chambost, Marc Lenglet and Yamina Tadjeddine (eds), *The Making of Finance: Perspectives from the Social Sciences* (Abingdon: Routledge, 2019), pp. 127–34. On the significance of La Défense for the study of increasing inequality in France in recent decades, see Olivier Godechot, 'Pourquoi "occuper la Défense"?', *Savoir/Agir*, 19 (2012), 17–29.
120. Bargenda, *La Communication visuelle dans le secteur bancaire européen*, p. 135.
121. Ibid. p. 141.
122. Ibid. p. 136.
123. Ibid. p. 137, pp. 132–3.
124. Ibid. p. 138.
125. Writing in November 1987 in one of several articles alluding to the financial crisis then under way, Serge Daney wrote that 'la pub fait essentiellement de la pub pour la pub' ('advertising is essentially advertising for the sake of advertising'). He alludes to a recent study which had concluded that very few people absorbed the 'messages' of adverts and reflects: 'Notre époque restera peut-être comme celle qui, faute de se permettre encore le grand gâchis de vies humaines (guerres, etc.) qui fascinait Bataille, se sera rabattue sur un gâchis moins cruel mais tout aussi radical de *signes*. Il y a là un parallèle facile à faire (profitons-en) entre l'inflation des signes et celle des monnaies, avec, dans les deux cas, des risques de krach. Seul le consensus qui exige qu'un produit ne sorte jamais sans son image (son *ombre* en quelque sorte) fait qu'on oublie que le roi est nu' ('Our era will perhaps remain that which, no longer affording itself the great waste of human lives [through wars and so on] which fascinated Bataille, will be pushed back onto a less cruel, but equally radical, expenditure of *signs*. There is an easy parallel to make [so let us do so] between the inflation of signs and that of currencies, with, in both cases, risks of crash. Only the consensus requiring that products never leave home without their image [their *shadow* in some sense] makes us forget that the emperor has no clothes'). Serge Daney, *Le Salaire du zappeur* (Paris: Libération/Éditions Ramsay, 1988), pp. 176–7.
126. Siety, *Fictions d'images*.

127. A recent and comparable example of how a bank's logo can function as a *calque* is given in HSBC's 'Together We Thrive' advertising campaign, launched in 2019 and based around a 'sound identity' or musical logo composed by the French electronic music producer Jean-Michel Jarre. In the adverts, the bank's famous red and white hexagon logo is placed at the centre of seventy-nine different images to frame a visual element or detail brought into relief against the background image. In this way the logo 'becomes a lens through which to look at the world, showing how the influence of the bank can help individuals, businesses and communities to grow and flourish.' HSBC Holdings plc, *Strategic Report 2018*, London: Global Finance, HSBC Holdings plc, inside cover. The campaign, developed by Saatchi and Saatchi, takes the form of both moving and still images; the signature deployment of the still frames is in passenger walkways and jet bridges at a number of major international airports, including Paris Charles de Gaulle. The hexagon is a lens or *calque* for seeing some aspect within a given visual field that could be exploited. A typical motif is to play on connections and echoes between the natural and the technologically modern to stress the continuities of general economy crossing the human and non-human divide. One image shows what looks like a rock pool shot from above, with ripples on the surface of the water. In the centre of the image is a white version of the hexagonal logo, and within the white spaces of the hexagon are glasses of water, shot from above; at some edges the glasses flow over into the surrounding pool image, the curves of the glasses forming a graphic match with the ripples. Taken together with the tagline for this suite – 'Water. The most precious currency of all' – the circles of the glasses are suggestive of silver coins. Seven video edits can be seen online, for example: youtube.com/watch?v=b6PB-XlmS3o and youtube.com/watch?v=IpoNLcMo130; for the airports, see saatchi.co.uk/en-gb/work/hsbc-global-airports/ (all last accessed 16 August 2021).

CHAPTER FIVE

Derivative Films

EFFACING THE VISUAL CURRENCY: *THE FOUNTAINHEAD*

Société Réaliste was a cooperative of two Paris-based artists, the Hungarian artist Ferenc Gróf and the French artist Jean-Baptiste Naudy, founded in 2004 and dissolved a decade later. *Empire, State, Building* was their first major exhibition, held at Jeu de Paume, Paris, in 2011 and then the Ludwig Museum in Budapest, in 2012.[1] The pair's key interest is in the ideological interplay between art and the economy, between the market and institutions. While the pair work in a variety of media, notably installations, their film *The Fountainhead* (2010) is the centrepiece of this body of work. As the art critic Tristan Trémeau notes, Société Réaliste's work was born from an aborted project to put USSR-style Socialist Realism face to face with the 'relational aesthetics' described by Nicolas Bourriaud, which puts into images the network-like relations of human beings today.[2] The work of Société Réaliste thus represents a critical, dissensual art that reflects on the economy and the art world, a work which is often satirical or parodic, for example inventing fictional institutions and agencies.[3]

Société Réaliste's *The Fountainhead* is a reworking of the film of the same name of 1949 by King Vidor, in which all human traces have been digitally removed. This operation was effectuated using postproduction and special effects software at the Academy Jan Van Eyck in Maastricht.[4] Société Réaliste's version is silent; there is no trace of the Max Steiner score from Vidor's film, nor the dialogues. Even the names of the actors are erased during the credits, which instead shows simply the turning pages of an empty book. In divesting the film of its characters, much of the plot is also evacuated. We are left to attend to the formal properties of the image itself. Where in the Vidor original we would have been absorbed in the narrative, in this version we are left to study empty chairs, the corners of walls and other background details that would perhaps otherwise have been overlooked – indeed, in many cases they would have been eclipsed by the characters, and are now revealed by a digital sleight of hand. We are given a much more static film: doors do not open as characters enter rooms, telephones do not magically levitate into the air in Société Réaliste's version when they are picked up in the original film. Seconds are trimmed here and there to accommodate this, so the two films are not in perfect synchrony, but they are quite close. Given to view the uninhabited sets, there is sometimes a sense that we are exploring a doll's house. This operation of erasure was carried out practically frame by frame and took a year to achieve. One of the artists, Ferenc Gróf, suggested to me that ultimately the film is therefore an animation film, or a 'Photoshop in motion'.[5]

The Vidor film of 1949 is an adaptation of the novel of the same name of 1943 by Ayn Rand.[6] Rand was a Russian-born American novelist who developed Objectivism, a philosophy of laissez-faire capitalism and the cult of the individual.[7] The final screenplay was written by Rand, and she exercised considerable influence over the production.[8] While her novel was a bestseller and continues to sell well (particularly among architects), the film was a critical and commercial failure (though now enjoys a cult following).[9] The story follows a struggling architect called Howard Roark (Gary Cooper), loosely based on architects such as Le Corbusier and Frank Lloyd Wright, as he attempts to realise his modernist architectural visions against a backdrop of pervasive establishment corruption. However, Rand's story takes place in an exaggerated world of herd-like conformity in which individualism is a heroic dissident value exemplified by Roark, who refuses to compromise with clients on his architectural design. They want buildings that refer to established historical styles, such as Greek temples and Gothic cathedrals, while he wants to develop his own style of modernist skyscrapers and, as the film dialogue repeatedly states, he 'refuses to give the public what they want'. A typically cynical Randian apophthegm is given when Roark avers: 'A building has integrity, just like a man, and just as seldom.' The ideological struggle is played out between Roark and his nemesis Ellsworth Toohey (Robert Douglas), an architecture critic for the New York *Banner* newspaper who champions mediocre popular taste ('The Newspaper for the People') and who runs a smear campaign against Roark. Toohey states that '[a]rtistic value is achieved collectively by each man subordinating himself to the standards of the majority.' While Rand would later become a fierce anti-communist campaigner, and while her experience was surely influenced by her upbringing in revolutionary Russia, the target of her critique in *The Fountainhead*, a text from the very beginning of the Cold War, was in fact New Deal social democrats.[10]

For Gróf, Rand's novels are wildly overlong and badly written, but as pulsing ideological documents they are fascinating.[11] Rand's most famous text, *Atlas Shrugged* (1957), continues to inspire a cult following particularly among libertarian Republican politicians in the USA.[12] Her most important disciple is Alan Greenspan, where the influence of Rand was arguably significant in the policies of financialisation of the US economy beginning in the 1980s, with which he was closely associated.[13] Like Rand's novel, Vidor's *The Fountainhead* is not a film directly about money and finance, but it is a film that served – among its many other signifying and artistic functions – as kind of myth of the individual justifying what would become a new financial regime. As such, it has a significant relationship with the world of financial flows that we live in today, and whose ideological underpinnings were shaken in 2008 as a crisis in the value of financial derivatives threatened its stability. Société Réaliste 'efface' Vidor's film at the moment of the humbling of the Randians, notably Greenspan, who, as we saw in Chapter 2, in one of the most infamous moments of the crisis conceded to senators on Capitol Hill that there was a 'flaw' in his doctrine of self-interest as unchallengeable motor of free market capitalism. Gróf confirmed to me that it was indeed the connection between Rand and the financial crisis that inspired Société Réaliste to make *The Fountainhead*.[14] The project started from a reflexive joke: what happens, asked the artists, if we 'objectivise' this film (a work of 'Objectivist' philosophy)? What would happen if one were to focus exclusively on the objects within the film, and remove the people? One impulse behind the film was thus a *détournement* of Rand's work. The film was conceived in 2008 during the acute period of the crisis, launched in 2009, finished in 2010, and exhibited in 2011.[15] Despite the fact that it does not apparently represent or directly reference the 2008 crisis, the context and intent of Société Réaliste's film confirms it as a film of the crisis.

Szendy borrows the English expression 'face value' to develop his reading of the Deleuze line discussed in Chapter 3 about money being on the reverse of every image.[16] In our dealings with money, we are interested in the face value because the material or metal value is less. Szendy entertains the metaphor of the film as a series of frames like banknotes, circulating one after the other.[17] While Szendy is often thinking reflexively of examples of film images of faces and money, it seems to me that by virtue of the operation of erasure practised by Société Réaliste, *The Fountainhead* gives us an example where the image-currency of cinema has been devalued, defaced or effaced. By effacing the currency, Société Réaliste erase the narrative of this classical Hollywood film, leaving an underlying stream of images exchanged one after the other. This brings forth the film's underlying currency function, and by extension the imbrication of images within a wider contemporary financial and iconomic logic of incessant circulation and exchange, as theorised in Chapter 3. Société Réaliste's *The Fountainhead* is a useful example to think through these ideas not only because, through its Rand source, it has a talismanic relation to the financial regime, but also because it is literally derived from another film. As a 'Photoshop in motion', we might think of Société Réaliste's film as an 'appropriation film', meaning one which transforms a pre-existing film or video into a new work (famously in Douglas Gordon's *24 Hour Psycho* [1993], but which we also see all over websites like YouTube in amateur montages).[18] However, given its context as a film of the 2008 financial crisis, we should conceptualise *The Fountainhead* in relation to this crisis by seeing the artists' film: firstly, as a filmic derivative; and secondly, as one which through the operation of erasure has lost its 'face value' – like those subprime derivatives triggering the crash.

One scene that this notion of defaced currency may allow us to read, that readings focused on the more overtly architectural parts of the film do not help us with, is that in the quarry.[19] In this sequence in the Vidor film, we see that, as a result of his refusal to compromise on his designs, Roark has failed to find work as an architect and is working instead as a labourer in a quarry. The quarry happens to be owned by the father of Dominique Francon (Patricia Neal), who is a wealthy socialite who also writes for the *Banner* newspaper which is leading the campaign against Roark. In this sequence Francon, who greatly admires Roark's work, happens to pass the quarry and sees him for the first time (though she does not know it is him she sees). Francon will come to love Roark and will urge him to give up architecture as she fears his genius will be crushed in this world of conformism; she will refer back to this moment with the bewitching line: 'stone quarries are all you can expect in the end'. In other words, his plans will never get off the ground. It is for this reason that Francon will marry Gail Wynand, a magnate who owns the *Banner*, before coming back to Roark's side later in the story.

The scene contains twenty-four shots and lasts for 2 minutes and 15 seconds.[20] (In Société Réaliste's version, it lasts for 7 seconds fewer.) The first three shots establish the setting in a quarry where men are at work, and where Francon is walking, in an elevated position, on the lip of the quarry. The fourth and fifth shots show her stopping at a high point and surveying the scene. The sixth shot is a medium shot of Francon as she sees Roark for the first time, drilling a large boulder, and it is here that romantic music begins to play. The subsequent series of shots, until the eighteenth, is a series of shot-reverse shots of Francon looking at Roark, and, when he sees her, him looking back at her too. These become increasingly close, climactic shots of their faces as their eyes meet (Figures 5.1 and 5.3). Two further shots show Francon walking away and exchanging one last look with Roark. Four final shots conclude the scene, in which the music stops as Francon hears the voice of the foreman calling her and accompanying her away. She asks: 'Who is that man?', before thinking better of it: 'Never mind.' In the final shot, we see Francon and the foreman walking away, passing Roark, with a final fleeting exchange of looks. The sequence is one of the most celebrated in the film and, as Luc Moullet notes, it can be paired with the most famous sequence, the close of the film in which Dominique, by this point Roark's wife, ecstatically rides the elevator to the top of Roark's skyscraper, the largest in the world, as if ascending to the empyrean.[21]

In the Vidor version, this is a crucial moment establishing the relation between Francon and Roark. One of the most important shots of the whole film is that in which we see Roark from Francon's point of view, the first time she lays eyes on him. The camera first shows his drill in close-up, then pans left to show his arm, before tilting up to his sweating brow and look of determination. The music here reaches a dramatic climax. The sexual connotations of this image and the importance of Francon's physical position looking down at Roark have been discussed by scholars of the film.[22] Within the Randian universe, this image of a female gaze drawn by the physical attraction of the man at work naturally has ideological connotations, as Merrill Schleier shows:

> The melding of body and machine communicates male power and virility, which are themselves embodied in the phallic skyscraper. Roark's physical mastery of tools is the conceptual and political inverse of what Rand saw as Communism's use of men as tools – extensions of the state. His triumph over raw, inert rock (nature) and his singular command of machinery implies that determined individualism triumphs over fate and robotization.[23]

This shot in which Roark brushes his brow with his forearm is also strengthened by the stoic, stereotypically manly attitude with which Gary Cooper's laconic star persona is associated (Figure 5.1), a conservative actor and a known Republican that Rand was delighted to have play Roark.[24] Roark is a character who lives for work and in a sense incarnates work.[25] Both the sexual politics and the anti-communist symbolism written into this shot are erased by Société Réaliste's operation.

In Société Réaliste's version, the exchange of looks between Francon and Roark is no longer a moment of romantic attraction, but a series of images of rocks where Roark should be (Figure 5.2) and images of a grey sky in place of Francon (Figure 5.4). In the effaced shot of Roark wiping his brow, the workers in the background are gone too; the only movement within the shot is the crane (Figure 5.2). Without their faces, these close-up shots are literally effaced or de-faced. For Szendy, the shot-counter shot dynamic we find in duels onscreen (paradigmatically in westerns) can be read as reflexively illustrative of the very idea of exchange. A similar dynamic is at work in this exchange of the gazes of future lovers. With this sequence in the quarry, then, the simple back and forth of exchange shown in the film image has been voided. The images unfold, but without the diegetic content that logically constructs the exchange or development between shots. What this sequence exemplifies is how, without the exchanges of characters, the narrative flow or circulation has halted, leaving the spectator to labour to establish or reconstruct meaning.²⁶ It becomes unclear where scenes begin and end and we have no sense of relative dramatic climax: we are adrift in a continuous voided present of contemplation.

Figure 5.1 *The Fountainhead* (King Vidor, 1949) © Warner Bros.

Figure 5.2 *The Fountainhead* (Société Réaliste, 2010).

130 *Derivative Images*

Figure 5.3 *The Fountainhead* (King Vidor, 1949) © Warner Bros.

Figure 5.4 *The Fountainhead* (Société Réaliste, 2010).

One could argue speculatively that something like this puzzling voided exchange happened during the acute moment of the financial crisis which inspired the artists' film. In 2008, there was what we might broadly consider a crisis of value as well as a crisis of exchange: a crisis of value, because the toxic assets that triggered the crisis (the subprime mortgages and the derivatives based on them) became worthless; and a crisis of exchange, because this led to a situation in which the banks could no longer trust each other enough to lend to each other. From the banking crisis came a crisis in public finances (deficits, austerity) then a crisis in the 'real' economy (recessions).[27]

Drawing on data from the Bank for International Settlements, Adam Tooze points to international capital flows for a striking image of what happened in the crisis. Before the crash, gross capital flows accounted for almost 33 per cent of world GDP. With the crash, these flows fell by 90 per cent (Figure 5.5).[28] Tooze writes:

> No other aggregate in the global economy was affected on anything like this scale or with this suddenness. It was as though a gigantic stabilizing flywheel suddenly came crashing to a halt, sending a shuddering jolt through the entire financial system.[29]

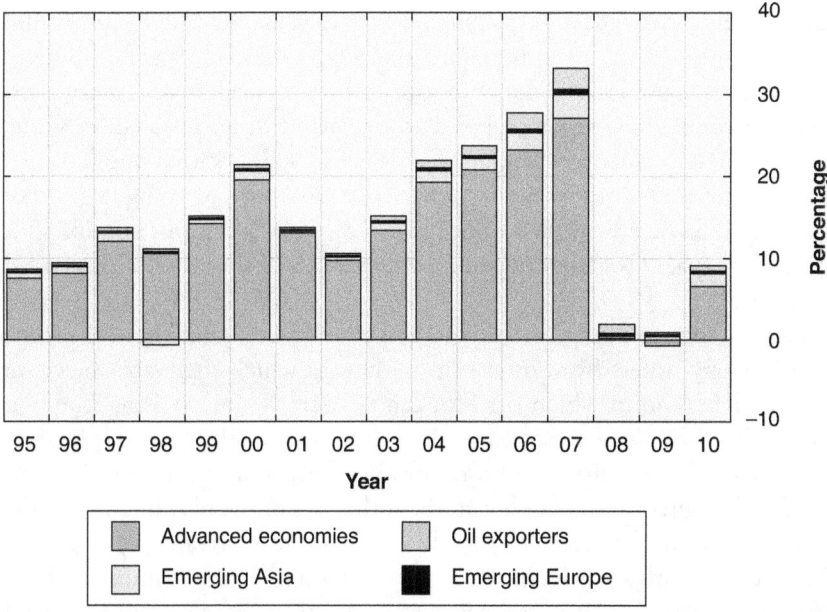

Figure 5.5 Gross capital flows as a percentage of world GDP. Source: This graph, adapted from Tooze, *Crashed*, p. 163, is originally from Claude Borio and Piti Disyatat, 'Global Imbalances and the Financial Crisis: Link or No Link?', BIS Working Paper 346 (2011), graph 5.

Tooze's perspective allows us to conceptualise a key stage of the crisis as a generalised crisis of the circulation of capital and credit. One of the virtues of Tooze's book is to insist on how the crisis that arose from the subprime mortgage bubble and the subsequent eurozone crisis are inseparable. As he suggests, many European politicians were reluctant to acknowledge the degree to which European banks were exposed by the seizure of the interbank dollar lending markets.[30] In other words, one of the things the graph in Figure 5.5 shows is how a huge part of the business of European banks consisted in borrowing in dollars to lend in dollars (hence the importance of gross rather than net flows in the figure). This issue was resolved by the US Federal Reserve becoming the global lender of last resort through the establishment of unlimited currency swap lines between the Fed and the European Central Bank, as well as other central banks around the world, the US dollar thus emerging as the sovereign currency of the crisis.[31]

If the crisis was a moment of seizure in the global circulation of capital, then *The Fountainhead* displaces onto the level of form something of the crisis that inspired it. The halt in capital flows was the consequence of the systemic uncertainty concerning the value of the derivatives – their face (nominal) value had been wiped off. Thinking Société Réaliste's film together with the concepts discussed in the previous chapter, *The Fountainhead* can be seen as constructing a derivative and wiping off its face value. Société Réaliste's film then becomes the site of a suspended exchange or crisis in the economy of images, prolonged for the duration of a feature film. Here one must recall that *The Fountainhead* was designed to be shown in an installation space, where – unlike a cinema screening of Vidor's original – visitors would see the film without necessarily expecting a narrative, coming and going in front of the images. Société Réaliste do not just efface Vidor's film but also install it in a gallery space. Together these operations enhance the sense of suspended exchange.

Because there are no props, skyscrapers or architectural models, the scene in the quarry differs from others in the film in which there are objects to contemplate (and in which the film can be seen as 'objectivising' the film appropriated by Société Réaliste). But when we are left with simple greys and blurs, what the artists' film creates is suspension and uncertainty. As Martine Beugnet remarks in her study of the uses of the blur in cinema, the blur that appears for itself (unrelated to a possible distinct image) confronts the spectator with a particular kind of uncertainty.[32] What is unusual about *The Fountainhead* is that its images started out as clear and distinct and have been subject to a process of erasure that has left blurry remainders. As a derivative, the artists' film is necessarily in a lower resolution than the original and thus arguably constitutes a 'poor image'.[33] Due to the residual imperfections of the process of erasure, furthermore, the image trembles in Société Réaliste's film, enhancing the sense of nervous uncertainty which is both the inspiration for and effect engendered by the film. Seeing the film as a financial derivative may seem an anti-aesthetic approach, but the transformation in derivation and erasure creates a new aesthetic value in this uncertainty. While effacing the face value of Vidor's film may seem to 'impoverish' it on a technical level, the derivative film is a wager on a different plane of value: as a rare and unusual artistic object (only a handful of DVD copies of the film exist), it opens a site not just of attentional capture and aesthetic transformation but also of financial speculation, where value may be added.

As noted in Chapter 3, Szendy does not directly discuss financial crises as such, but in a highly evocative passage he describes the famous scene in the Rome stock exchange in Michelangelo Antonioni's *L'Eclisse* (*The Eclipse*, 1962). In this sequence, all the hitherto frenetic activity of the trading floor stops so a minute of silence can be offered in homage to a trader who died that morning. In this minute of silence:

> tout se passe comme si le film déplaçait l'enjeu de la valeur du temps sur un autre plan: non plus dans la diégèse mais dans l'expérience même du visionnage, dans le vécu des spectateurs que nous sommes. Nous aussi, nous sommes livrés à la fluctuation des valeurs narratives pendant cette minute durant laquelle tout ancrage stable dans un récit est suspendu: nous vivons une pure *spéculation* filmique sur le temps qui passe.[34]

> [it is as though the film were displacing the question of the value of time onto another plane: no longer in the diegesis but in the very experience of screening, in the experience of the spectators we are. We too participate in the fluctuation of narrative values during this minute in which every stable anchoring in a narrative is suspended: We live in a pure filmic *speculation* on the passage of time.[35]]

What Szendy says about this minute of silence could equally apply to *The Fountainhead*. However, in Société Réaliste's film, we are not dealing with a moment of metalepsis within a film, but a speculation on the value of the film as a whole. By suspending narrative and effacing the visual currency, *The Fountainhead* transposes into spectatorial experience something of the historical context out of which it is born. The 2008 crisis saw financial speculation give way to a more radical uncertainty: a speculation on the viability of the world financial system itself. Leaving us to contemplate the circulating image-derivatives, the film thus performs the move prescribed by thinkers in Chapter 3: to grasp the iconomy of derivative images around us and to speculate on how they could be reimagined.

'L'ARGENT EST UN BIEN PUBLIC': *FILM SOCIALISME*

At the Cannes Film Festival in May 2010, where *Film Socialisme* was competing in the *Un certain regard* category, Jean-Luc Godard explained his absence at short notice in a fax, saying that it was owing to 'problems of a Greek style'.[36] This was a reference to the fact that it was only two weeks previously that the International Monetary Fund, the European Central Bank and the eurozone countries had agreed to a Greek bailout loan of €110 billion, conditional on the implementation of austerity measures and the privatisation of government assets. This was a key moment in the mutation of the 2008 financial crisis into a wider European debt crisis. The film was four years in the making and is exactly contemporary with the financial crisis. Godard's boycott of the festival seems to have been intended as a symbolic rejection of the European political-economic order itself in solidarity with the Greeks, and this was part of the reason the film was received with ambivalence. He has in fact subsequently offered a solution – perhaps only partly in jest – to the Greek crisis in the remark that, since the world owes an intellectual debt to the Greeks for inventing philosophy and logic, every time someone uses the word 'therefore' they should have to pay €10 to Greece.[37]

Film Socialisme has a tripartite structure: the first part, 'Des choses comme ça' ('Things like this'), follows a luxury cruise liner as it sails the Mediterranean Sea, stopping off at various places which echo familiar Godardian preoccupations, such as Palestine, Odessa and Greece; the second part, 'Notre Europe' ('Our Europe'), tells the story of a family who run a garage in rural France and are soon to fight a local election; and the third part, 'Nos humanités' ('Our humanities'), returns to the stop-off points of the ship in the first part and gives way to a more abstract montage of the sort seen in Godard's long video-work, *Histoire(s) du cinéma* (1988–98). In this way, the narrative of the cruise liner works to frame the film as a whole and to anchor what is a loose and abstract play of themes. It is 'Des choses comme ça' that I will focus on in this discussion.

In 'Des choses comme ça', there are no fully developed characters, but rather archetypes of sorts – secret agents, young women reading Balzac, Nazi war criminals – all of whom make a number of gnomic utterances which never quite add up to dialogue as such. Part of what makes the film difficult to follow is that there are many voiceovers and it is not very easy to connect them to figures who appear onscreen. Consulting the script, one finds that not all of them even refer to characters who appear onscreen at all, and they frequently speak independently of each other.[38] In addition to these 'characters', there are the actual passengers on the ship. Godard's vision of the ship's tourist passengers *qua* crass consumerism – eating, dancing, gambling – is one of the clearest sentiments expressed in the film. Godard mixes a variety of types of footage together, and the use of low-grade material, apparently taken on a mobile phone, of tourists dancing at the on-board disco, complete with harsh dissonant sound, is one example of how the film renders visible how heavily mediated by images and technology their lives are. (This is Godard's first film shot entirely digitally.) It thus makes sense to read in this an indictment of a rich Western society metaphorically adrift, all at sea, cut off from the rest of the world and sure soon to find itself on the proverbial raft of the Medusa. The irony, of course, is that the ship Godard used for the setting, the *Costa Concordia*, did actually later crash on the Italian coast three years after the shoot.[39]

One figure among the eclectic cast who does stand out and who seems to be the mouthpiece for the film's critique of the contemporary economic situation in the film is Bernard Maris (1946–2015). Before his murder at the offices of the satirical weekly magazine *Charlie Hebdo* on 7 January 2015, Maris was well known in France as a left-wing economist and journalist who made regular media appearances. Maris was known for promoting alternative economic concepts such as basic income and was also highly critical of France's membership of the single currency.[40] As well as sitting on the General Council of the Banque de France, Maris wrote a weekly column on economic issues under the name of Oncle Bernard for *Charlie Hebdo*, where he was also a shareholder. A selection of these columns from 2005–12 was published in 2013, titled *Journal d'un économiste en crise* after the column.[41] In the final edition of the magazine published before the attack, Maris wrote on ecotaxes and ethics, and favourably reviewed the latest novel of his friend Michel Houellebecq.[42] The final book published by Maris in his lifetime was a study of Houellebecq's fiction in relation to economics.[43]

The significance of Maris in *Film Socialisme* is given in the fact that he speaks in voiceover the first line of the film: 'L'argent est un bien public' ('Money is a public good'). To this, a female voice answers 'Comme l'eau alors?' ('Like water?') and he concurs: 'Exactement' ('Exactly'). This exchange is set to an image of a gently shifting dark-blue surface of water. The shouts that can be heard on the soundtrack and the relative calmness of the water both suggest that the image may be of water in a swimming pool. There follows a sequence of images of waves on the open sea and people on the deck of a ship, and in voiceover an exchange between three other characters. At this stage, Maris's line serves in part to open the film and establish some of its themes, namely, money and the contested idea of what constitutes a public good. The montage effects a conceptual connection between money, the 'public good' and water.

Of course, it is through consulting the script that one knows for sure that it is Maris speaking the opening line. The script reveals that the female voice is that of a character named Alissa. Of the viewers watching the film for the first time, only those familiar with Maris's radio and television appearances would be likely to immediately recognise the voice as that of Maris. Maris's death makes this aspect of the film particularly time-bound. Maris does appear onscreen later in the film, where he would be identifiable to many in a French audience as apparently playing himself, and this line is consonant with his real-life persona. In having Maris speak the opening line, Godard is at least in part signalling for this line to be read in the context of Maris's own work. Tyson Stewart writes that in Godard's films 'the public intellectual is already an icon of representation (in the political sense) when he or she enters the terrain of the fictional', thus giving scenes a 'documentary appeal'.[44] Stewart considers examples of Godard's films from the 1960s in which this phenomenon is more explicit, but it is also true of Maris, even if his presence is more withdrawn. So as well as recalling Maris's media appearances, the presence of Maris in *Film Socialisme* may recall his only other film credit, the Québécois documentary *L'Encerclement – la démocratie dans les rets du néolibéralisme* (*Encirclement: Neo-Liberalism Ensnares Democracy*, 2008).[45] In this film – which consists of interviews with left-wing economists and philosophers – Maris argues that economics, conceived as an institution and a discourse, is not, as it purports to be, either 'neutral' or an exact science, but rather a rhetoric. Maris states that the shibboleths of the 'invisible hand of the market' and 'supply and demand' are fictions that do not work in reality. In giving lines of voiceover to Maris, Godard is implicitly giving some suggestion as to the place of 'socialism' in *Film Socialisme*, that is, in a critique of contemporary 'neoliberalism'. However, the specific phrase 'money is a public good' is a direct reference to Maris's columns in *Charlie Hebdo*. Maris uses variants of the phrase in two back-to-back weekly columns from October 2008. This is significant in being the peak moment of the financial crisis: this is when the bailout in the US takes place, after the fall of Lehman Brothers. Maris writes humorously, rhetorically, but also despairingly, during the crisis years of 2008–10. To read his weekly columns consecutively is to read a record of exasperation.

In the article of 8 October 2008, Maris laments that, as the crisis is under way and is crossing the Atlantic, America is acting energetically to contain the fallout while Europe does nothing. Either the bankers will crash the system and bring about a depression or politicians will step in and 'referont de l'argent un bien public et de la banque un service public' ('change money into a public good and the bank into a public service').[46] Maris concludes predicting a repeat of the 1930 depression. The following week, Maris reports that European nations are beginning to act by guaranteeing deposits and nationalising the banks. Maris notes that in the course of the nationalisations almost everything surrounding the banking culture that led to the crisis remains untouched and lessons of the folly of the past remain unlearned. Bretton Woods was supposed to stop speculation on currencies, Maris writes, and until around 1970 French banks did not lend to each other. 'L'argent était un bien public, qui pouvait être créé à l'occasion par le Trésor public' ('Money was a public good, which could be created on occasion by the public treasury').[47] Then, with the deregulation of the banks, which Maris associates with Giscard, speculation was out of control.

These two articles appear to be the source of the phrase in *Film Socialisme*. We might imagine Godard cutting out the line from *Charlie Hebdo* and sticking it into his script, a quotation that Maris is then given to read. I have not found an example of Maris making the connection between money and water from before the time of the film's release, but afterwards, in September 2011, Maris can be found writing apropos of the banks' failure to circulate money: 'L'argent est un bien public, comme l'eau, comme l'air' ('Money is a public good, like water, like air').[48] In an interview in a documentary on the theme of debt, broadcast on Arte within a month of his death, Maris said that money 'is like the air we breathe. It is that which allows us to live. Like water and like air, it should be a public good.'[49] Maris is rethinking the purpose of money: not as that which has to be earned but as that which is required to live and to which we should be entitled. This gives a sense of the meaning of the statement used in *Film Socialisme*: although it might seem at first a cryptic remark, it is in fact a contention. While the exact phrasing of the line in the film is that money 'is' a public good, when we read this against Maris's other iterations of the idea, in which money *was* a public good between the 1940s and the 1970s and should be made so again as a response to the crisis, it becomes clear that the real sense of the line is close to the articulation in the Arte documentary, according to which money *should be* a public good, as we need it to live.[50] The first line of Godard's film thus does not so much reflect on actually existing conditions as posit an ideal state of affairs.

More generally, the idea of money as a 'public good' has a certain resonance with the work of the British economist John Maynard Keynes. This is not surprising as Maris is noted for his advocacy of Keynes, on whom he wrote a book.[51] For Keynes – unlike classical economics – money is not a simple and neutral means of exchange but has properties in and of itself and is therefore indispensable to thinking about how an economic system functions. The idea of money as a public good stands for the proposition that the money supply should be under public control. For Keynes in *The General Theory of Employment, Interest and Money* (1936), money itself 'cannot be readily produced' by labour or private enterprise. It can only be produced by the 'monetary authority', in other words, a publicly owned central bank.[52] As he puts it in a memorable passage:

> Unemployment develops, that is to say, because people want the moon; men cannot be employed when the object of desire (i.e. money) is something which cannot be produced [by labour] and the demand for which cannot be readily choked off. There is no remedy but to persuade the public that green cheese is practically the same thing and to have a green cheese factory (i.e. a central bank) under public control.[53]

Owing to the fact that money's only utility lies in exchange value, it does not matter how much money there is, people still want more. Central banks can however simply print money. Keynes here indicates the need for a central bank, and this is part of the thinking behind Maris's argument for the need to nationalise the banks in the wake of the crisis. Keynes was a long-term interest for Maris, and at the time of the making of *Film Socialisme* he had recently published a book with the economist Gilles Dostaler, *Capitalisme et pulsion de mort* (2009), which relates the Freudian death drive to Keynesian economics.[54] (In *Film Catastrophe*, which I come onto below, this book is at one point shown among a pile of others that Godard arranges on a bed in front of a camera.) Key to the revival of Keynes's work in response to 2008 was the idea that government action in the form of fiscal stimulus is the most effective way to help sustain the economy during a recession.[55] Maris and Dostaler reread Keynes with a strongly Freudian edge, seeing the love of money as a manifestation of the death drive – a danger in a society in which money is not a public good.[56]

There is an inflection of this kind of pessimism in the other lines spoken by Maris in *Film Socialisme*. Following the line about money as a public good, after further establishing shots we hear Maris offer the cryptic comment: 'Ce qui s'ouvre devant nous ressemble à une histoire impossible. Nous voilà en face d'une sorte de zéro . . .' ('What is opening up before us resembles an impossible story. We're facing a sort of zero'). This is heard over a shot on the deck at night, as if that zero point was the dark abyss of the night that the ship sails through. While the line may have its own provenance, in giving it to Maris to speak, its sense is brought into association with the lines from Maris. In other words, among multiple hermeneutic possibilities, the 'zero point' and 'impossible story' can be read as elliptical allusions to the ongoing financial crises Maris details in his writings. In a classic essay discussing the relation between image and text in Godard's films, Raymond Bellour writes that the voices in Godard's works are 'always addressing the spectator, at least somewhat – even when talking to a partner, whether on- or off-screen. Thus, they constantly double the film with a critical layer that isn't commentary, since the voices remain engaged in the fiction.'[57] This phenomenon is raised to a further level in *Film Socialisme* as Maris speaks, but it is unclear as to whom he speaks. The 'we' thus could also be 'we' the viewer. By the same token, the critical layer to 'money is a public good' serves to offer the idea for the viewer's consideration. In having Maris speak, the film is imbued with the economic context that is his preoccupation. However, this is always complicated by the montage: after this line there is a bathetic cut to footage of a woman relaxing in a pool with Madonna's 'Material Girl' playing in the background, as if to suggest that the spectacle of materialism itself constituted the zero point. While money may ideally be, like water, a public good, the luxury swimming pool on board a cruise liner symbolises how such commodities are in fact private. There is another fragmentary dialogue shortly after that discussed above, a dialogue in voiceover between Maris and a student at Stanford who says that she leads seminars on the relation between literary and monetary creation. Maris is here given a pedagogical role, which is both a familiar Godardian trope and a role that typifies Maris's persona as Oncle Bernard, in which he interprets economic events and provides scholia or a 'moralité' at the end of his columns. Yet, bizarrely, this dialogue is heard over a grainy image of an elderly tourist couple eating in the on-board restaurant. While the promiscuous play of references suggests possible meanings, it also keeps the viewer in a state of negative capability as to any final meaning. In both cases, what the montage and Maris's gnomic utterances accomplish is to collapse the economic discussion and context onto an image of ordinary consumerism, yoking those banal images into a general iconomy, comparable to *The Fountainhead*. However, what is different with *Film Socialisme* is the inclusion of rawer, low-grade images from all kinds of sources and quasi-documentary style images of Maris. In other words, the iconomy extends across media, meaning we are less obviously in a fiction. Godard's film here explores the connection between the context of the financial crisis and the contemporary condition of technical images, showing the capacity of the cameras in the tourists' hands to produce innumerable derivative images.[58] It is due to this derivative aesthetic that Guillaume Bourgois notes the convergent ways in which Godard brings new media apparatuses into his film and Szendy's idea that the grafting of cinema into our gaze in the twentieth century also made our gaze an exchange market.[59]

A key sequence for understanding the place of Maris in the film takes place in the ship's casino. Here, Maris can be seen playing at a slot machine and making notes on the results, while a loudspeaker advertises bingo in different languages. Maris is speaking to another of Godard's enigmatic cast, Bob Maloubier (1923–2015), a decorated French secret agent during the Resistance, famous for being recruited as one of Winston Churchill's Special

Operations Executive (SOE) agents behind enemy lines in occupied Europe where he cheated death in many daring missions.[60] Maloubier, like Maris, appears to be playing himself as his role is uncannily similar to his real-life persona, especially with his famously large moustache. 'Normal,' says Maris, 'l'argent a été inventé pour ne pas regarder les Hommes dans les yeux' ('Of course, money was invented so that people wouldn't have to look each other in the eye'). Maris of course does not make eye contact. This is the second occasion in the film in which Maris pronounces on the nature of money. While Maris has generally written about the alienating effects of capitalism, it is notable that this line echoes a line in Maris and Dostaler's text: '[L'argent] joue un rôle dominant dans les sociétés où les rapports de domination sont plus anonymes, il permet de ne plus regarder les hommes dans les yeux, pour paraphraser Georg Simmel' ('[Money] plays a dominant role in societies in which the relations of domination are more anonymous, it allows one to no longer look people in the eye, to paraphrase Georg Simmel').[61] This level of abstract philosophising is again simultaneously undercut and extended in Godard's montage with the subsequent image of a coin pusher machine, on which hundreds of coins and a wad of US dollar notes are sitting statically, the pushers making no impression on the pile (Figure 5.6). The image offers a mute reply to the critique of money and economy articulated by Maris, as if mimicking the indifferent, downturned eyes he describes. That the pusher does not push the coins, however, fixes this as a faltering or stuck iconomy, like the suspended exchange in *The Fountainhead*, rather than one fluidly

Figure 5.6 The coin pusher. *Film Socialisme* (Jean-Luc Godard, 2010) © New Wave Films.

circulating. The next image shows a row of players of slot machines with their backs to the direction the ship is sailing, in shadow and out of focus in the foreground, while a window looking out to the sea can be seen more sharply in the background. The bells and buzzing of the machines can be heard over the sound of the ship's engine. The relatively long duration of the take works to set the gambling in relief against the continual advance of the ship. The ship approaches the zero point, but those on board are blithely or listlessly engaged with their games. Maris sits disinterestedly in front of the paradigmatic form of the *ploutéidoscope*, the slot machine, and thus, as with *le boiteux* and Kerviel before their trading monitors, the film stages the blank dissociation before financial media seen elsewhere during the crash.[62]

Before the cut to the coin pusher, Maloubier replies: 'Alors, on revient à zéro, cher monsieur. Heureusement, les Arabes l'ont inventé. On ne leur paye même pas de droits d'auteur, poor chaps . . .' ('So we come back to zero, mister. Luckily the Arabs invented it. They don't even get *royalties*, poor chaps'). In the use of English 'poor chaps', Godard seems to be gesturing to Maloubier's work for the SOE, a British connection Maloubier himself played up to. As if to hint at this, at another point Maloubier poses on the deck with a copy of *The Observer*. Maris then remarks to Maloubier on the history of negative numbers, how they came from the Indies through the Arab world and how Fibonacci was the first to use them. Turning to Maloubier, Maris then asks, provocatively in light of this British connection, what the British did with the gold of Palestine when they left Israel. (While he lionises Keynes, Maris in his columns for *Charlie Hebdo* is frequently critical of Britain.) Maloubier then leans in to look him in the eye. While this might seem to signal a momentary connection between the two men, the film cuts to the coin pusher. With the point about not looking another in the eye, money is almost posited as responsible for the sense of a breakdown of communication which typifies this polyglot and fragmentary work. With Maris's comment about Palestinian gold, this line on the putative money owed to the Arabs leads associatively to the film's complex subplot about the gold that went missing from Spain during the civil war and that spies on the ship are seeking involving a character named Otto Goldberg. It can be observed from this brief sketch that there is a constellation of ideas around the motif of debt, encompassing ideas of royalties, lost gold, theft. Thus when Maloubier says that '[l]uckily the Arabs invented [zero]', it is as if the hypothetical royalties would be due if, say, it was a product of France or Britain. Zero thus represents: the loss on the slot machine; the 'sort of zero' as the crash that Maris predicted and towards which the gamers are blindly headed; and zero as an abstract numerological concept. Furthermore, in response to the 'sort of zero', Maloubier can be heard saying that he once encountered 'le néant' ('nothingness'). This remark is made twice and in context suggests his many scrapes with death. Within the context of Godard's oeuvre, zero may also bring to mind his films of the 1960s in which political intractability led Godard to call for a 'return to zero'. Douglas Morrey has tracked this motif and points to *Le Gai Savoir* (1968) as representing the return to zero associated with the events of May 1968.[63] In *Le Gai Savoir*, two students 'return to zero' in the sense that they examine the basic protocols of language and the fundamentals of images and sounds. The film was shot in a studio against a black backdrop, suggesting that these elements are being re-evaluated in abstract isolation. In the complex web of senses surrounding the idea of zero, then, it is not only a crass figure on a gambling machine (and synecdoche for the financial system castigated in Maris's writings), but also signifies mathematics, nothingness *qua* death and a point from which to start again. However, if we are facing a 'sort of zero' in *Film Socialisme*, it does not seem to be a return to such a starting point but rather the breaking down of communication and a halting iconomy to the point that it fails to function; again, not unlike *The Fountainhead*.

In Maris and Dostaler's book, they imagine Keynes witnessing today's events and laughing at his prescience in foreseeing the crisis of a system fragile on account of its dependence on credit.[64] The rhetorical question closing their book asks: 'Where today are the Condorcets, Keynes or Freuds who can help us to open our eyes?'.[65] While one might be tempted at first glance to argue that Godard's use of Maris constitutes an endorsement of him, Maris is like Godard a melancholy, disillusioned figure of the left. In fragmenting Maris's words, Godard points to the failure of the communication or dissemination of Maris's ideas. What I have identified as the effect of bathos or undercutting in the montages featuring Maris also contributes to this sense. On this point, the case of Maris fits with the thesis of Stewart: Godard 'has persistently made the partial uselessness of intellectuals explicit [. . .] What is interesting in the later films is how they show that the winds of history have been increasingly blowing against the politicized Western intellectual for many years now.'[66] Stewart concludes that 'Godard's films mourn a certain intellectually communicative, active, and moral temperament [. . .] But his politics of mourning are actually constructive and even hopeful. In the cameos, the performativity of the intellectual is at its most playful and memorable.'[67] The case of Maris is particularly complex when looked at today after Maris's murder, in which it is difficult to find the 'hopeful' aspect.

Nevertheless, that hopeful dimension is found dispersed from the figure of Maris on the plane of the film's form. At the end of the film, a standard-issue FBI copyright warning appears before dissolving to the lines 'quand la loi n'est pas juste la justice passe avant la loi' ('when the law is unfair, justice precedes the law'), followed shortly by a title card reading 'NO COMMENT'. Godard's abuse of copyright, cutting derivatives from many different films and sources, points to a conception of the image as something which should not incur a debt or yield royalties: in other words, like money, images *should* be a 'public good'.[68] More recent debates around the limits of freedom of images have only increased the political stakes of such an affirmation.[69] Maris's formulation thus gives another angle on Godard's claim that the 'socialism' of the film consists in the rejection of the idea of intellectual copyright.[70] The film is, in short, partly a strident deconstruction of the idea of debt and ownership, much as Maris critiqued these ideas in political-economic terms. If to make money a public good is to 'socialise' it, then *Film Socialisme* is a film whose images have been socialised. This is one way of conceiving the film as an '"allegory in form" [. . .] for a future social organization': in other words, Godard's appropriation of images that do not belong to him points to a wider potential reimagining of visual and monetary media.[71] As Laurent Creton shows, throughout his long career Godard has always been concerned with the economic and with money, both as a thematic in his films and as an ineluctable exigency conditioning the practical realisation of his art.[72] His position vis-à-vis this exigency is not that of a Romantic artist's contemptuous disavowal of money, but one of realism in which he strategically appropriates the economic in the service of his art. The notion from management strategy conjugated in Creton's title – 'the strategic art of the redefinition of one's *métier*' – can thus be read together with the idea discussed in relation to Kerviel, Flusser and Citton according to which freedom consists in a strategy of mobilising chance and (economic) conditions to play against one's function and reappropriate expressive media. In this way, Godard too offers a glimpse of a possible productive attitude to take in relation to derivative images.

'THE IMAGES ARE THERE FOR THE TAKING': *FILM CATASTROPHE*

Paul Grivas's *Film Catastrophe* (2018) is at first glance a 53-minute 'making of' *Film Socialisme*, showing Godard and his three assistants at work on board the ship.[73] Grivas is Godard's nephew and worked as his assistant on *Film Socialisme* and previously on *Notre Musique* (2004). The film is made of left-over material from the *Film Socialisme* hard drives, outtakes or bloopers, his filming of the shoot, what looks like promotional material for the cruise ship, and the panic and confusion shot by passengers as the boat was sinking.

In an obvious sense, Grivas's film is derived from Godard's and extends its derivative logics in all directions. A good example of this is found in the sequence beginning around 5 minutes into the film. At this point we are on the ship's deck. The sequence lasts 1 minute and 45 seconds and can be divided into nine shots:

1. Medium close-up of a boy, in profile, looking out to sea. We hear Godard giving instructions to actors, but seemingly from another moment of the shoot. Godard's hands enter the frame to act as a clapperboard.
2. The same moment of shooting, but now the image is in lower resolution and in the 4:3 screen ratio (Figure 5.7). The camera is now handheld and moves behind and above another camera on a tripod, which presumably took the previous shot. The camera moves to the side and refocuses on the boy. Godard claps. There is a lot of background noise.
3. High resolution image of waves and their foam, taken looking down at the water and suggesting the continued advance of the ship.
4. Medium shot of Godard leaning on the rail of the boat and watching a small device in his hands.
5. The same moment, but this time the image is taken from behind and above Godard's shoulder. The device looks like a dictaphone but with a screen on which we see images of the waves being filmed.
6. Blurred image of waves, almost in slow motion – presumably the image filmed with Godard's device.
7. Medium shot of Godard on the deck beside a tripod, still filming the waves like shot 4 (Figure 5.8). He moves towards the railing. An assistant dashes towards the base of the tripod. The camera moves forward and positions itself near the camera on the tripod to see the display, where we again see waves.
8. Image of waves recognisable from *Film Socialisme*, in high resolution and 16:9 screen ratio (Figure 5.9). One supposes that it is the image that was being filmed by the camera on the tripod in the previous shot.
9. Image of a piece of debris floating in the sea, also familiar from *Film Socialisme*. The sea is calmer in this shot, as if the ship was now still, and is a greyer, less lush blue than the previous shot. Maris states in voiceover a line mentioned above, 'Ce qui s'ouvre devant nous ressemble à une histoire impossible', but without the line about the 'sorte de zéro'.

Film Catastrophe documents Godard on the prowl for images, and this sequence illustrates this process. Throughout the film we see him, cigar in mouth, using his hands as a clapperboard to synchronise sound and image. We see images familiar from *Film Socialisme*, but now we can hear Godard's gentle, precise directorial instructions on delivery and intonation to the actors. The clap in the first shot of the sequence marks the creation of an image with

Derivative Films 145

Figure 5.7 *Film Catastrophe* (Paul Grivas, 2018) © Petit à petit production.

Figure 5.8 *Film Catastrophe* (Paul Grivas, 2018) © Petit à petit production.

Figure 5.9 *Film Catastrophe* (Paul Grivas, 2018) © Petit à petit production.

a slicing or tranching gesture, while the repetition of the clap in the second shot thus serves to put all the images onto a single plane (Figure 5.7). Here as elsewhere, Godard and Grivas valorise images of low resolution and give them a structural equivalence with higher resolution images (Figure 5.9).[74] At the same time, the whole sequence plays on the opening of margins or spreads within and between the images (for example the desynchronisation of sound in shot 1) and of between-spaces (the handheld camera's movement in shot 7) in a context of the inexorable onward movement of the ship (shot 3). The ninth shot indicates the value of 'debris' as latent raw material ready for reappropriation. During her discussion with Grivas following the film's screening at the Cinéma du réel festival, Nicole Brenez declared that the film has an 'esthétique du rush, de la prise brute' ('an aesthetic of the rush and of the rough take').[75] She noted that this aesthetic of the rush tended to contaminate all the images of the film and, in turn, the original film. This is what happens in the sequence analysed above: through its style and its relation with the film from which it is derived, *Film Catastrophe* allows us to discern a world made of rushes where all images are in some way always already derivative. It is therefore no surprise to learn that Grivas's project has also yielded a short film, *L'Incomparable du pas comparable* (*The Incomparable of the Non-Comparable*, 2019), about the way Godard adapted the *scénario* and 'pre-production collages' of *Film Socialisme*.[76] The 7-minute short matches twenty-four images from the script with shots in the film to show how they were planned and executed. An example is given in Figures 5.10 and 5.11, showing the script and film versions of a shot of

Figure 5.10 Script for *Film Socialisme* in *L'Incomparable du pas comparable* (Paul Grivas, 2018).

Figure 5.11 Maris and Maloubier in *L'Incomparable du pas comparable* (Paul Grivas, 2018).

Maris and Maloubier on the ship's deck. The script is already constituted in part from extracts of other films, screen-captures, drawings and photocopied quotations furnishing a bundle of elements attached by hand, like a scrapbook.[77] Grivas thus shows how the logic of derivation extends backwards from the finished film to its script and then further back again. Of course, this is not a new theme in the work of Godard, who has previously remarked that films and film scripts can be seen as derivatives of the simpler economy of the accounting statements of the making of a film.[78] In that case, derivation goes both forward, as it were, from the script and backwards from the shoot. By framing the moment of the *Film Socialisme* shoot from multiple perspectives and on multiple devices in the sequence above, Grivas stages shooting as the cutting of derivatives.

Douglas Morrey writes apropos of *Film Socialisme* that 'water can be seen as a cinematic image par excellence' given its capacity for capturing the elements of light and motion, central to cinematic images; yet at the same time, water functions as a symbol for the circulation of money.[79] As we saw, for Maris, money should be a public good, 'like water'. If in Godard's *Le Mépris* (1963) the image of the sea, on which the film famously closes, is 'l'image du vide et de la fin' ('the image of the void and the end'), as Marie-Claire Ropars-Wuilleumier puts it in a classic essay,[80] then in *Film Catastrophe* the rippled surface of the water figures a world in which everything has been liquidated, a world 'littéralement submergé' ('literally inundated') in images, or, we might say, recalling the etymology of *derivative*, a world overflowing with images.[81] Among its multiple signifying functions, the sea offers itself in the sequence analysed above as a figure of the 'social surplus' described by Martin: that is, as a common resource to which we can appeal, albeit in conditions of great volatility. What Grivas shows is that creation in an era of derivation is a matter of releasing a new potentiality from something already existing.

Grivas's film is not a simple 'making of' *Film Socialisme* but a distinctive and experimental composition. Perhaps the most striking sequence is the closing one, which starts with footage taken by the alarmed passengers as the boat begins to sink, before giving way to an extremely complex and sped-up montage lasting some 40 seconds, beginning with Godard using his hands as a clapperboard. It is impossible to count how many images we see in this sequence – it is almost a supercut of the film within the film.[82] We see Godard filming on the deck; tourists at slot machines and taking photos; the scream of the mother in the famous Odessa Steps sequence of *The Battleship Potemkin* (Sergei Eisenstein, 1925); unused footage of Bernard Maris; sights at the cruise ship stops; and many others. The sequence revisits all of the themes of the two films in a hyper-accelerated montage, but emphasising images of the garish games and displays as well as the diegetic on-board casino sounds: roulette wheels, fingers putting coins in slots, croupiers serving blackjack tables, calls of bingo, flippers bashed, coins dropping into winnings trays. The sequence is dizzying, as if to produce the effect of being inside a pinball machine. The film ends shortly after this with what looks like black-and-white drone footage of the crashed cruise ship over which the mournful refrain of the Israeli composer Betty Olivero's *Nehardt Nehardt* (2006–7) plays. The credits begin, overlaid with the casino bells and buzzers.[83] The film ends with an enigmatic dialogue between a male and female speaker playing on the senses of 'fond(s)', meaning both 'depths' or 'bottom' and 'funds'.[84] A deluge of images, then, like the water flooding the ship – but also like the coins spat out by the slot machines. The sequence is a hallucinatory extension of the sequence with Maris and Maloubier discussed earlier. Grivas thus extends the casino motif such that the images take on the iconomic aspect of coins. To these associations must be added the frenetic taking of images by the tourists. The camera as derivative machine is placed over the slot machine to figure the overheating of the contemporary iconomy – and the risk of a crash.

Evoking the freedom of his way of working with images in the edit, Grivas offers a maxim: 'the images are there for the taking, you just got to pick them up'.[85] Here, we could say, as with *Film Socialisme*, images are proposed as a public good. He continues: 'I film a lot of my quotidian life, of my trips, and save it somewhere. Later I watch the images, I edit them, like a game, and often discover things I didn't see when first filming, and I like that.'[86] It was after the release of *Film Socialisme* that he started 'playing' with the images from the shoot. This possibility of deriving art from our daily life is a theme in *Film Catastrophe*, which begins with a voiceover: 'Au XXIème siècle, se filmer ou filmer ses proches est devenu banal' ('In the twenty-first century, filming ourselves or our loved ones has become routine'). This theme of how widespread digital technologies were enabling anyone to film and take pictures – which Godard showed by incorporating YouTube clips and mobile phone footage – was prescient in *Film Socialisme*, and Grivas extends this in *Film Catastrophe*. While 'derivation' or reusing existing material is as old as art itself, the reuse of images has, as Martine Beugnet points out, massively intensified since the arrival of the digital and the internet, leading to an array of new artistic, amateur and commercial forms.[87] As indicated above and as is well known, Godard was a pioneer in reusing film material, while collage more widely has a history going back at least to the 1950s.[88] Without production company or budget, it took Grivas a decade, working on and off, to realise his film, which is freely available online and which he refers to as an 'a-commercial product'.[89] The point of Grivas and Godard's practice here is not to do history, as in *Histoire(s) du cinéma*, nor to contest a system of control, but rather to stage the massive extension of this possibility to create images and to orient the spectator in this condition. If, as Solange Manche suggests, *Film Socialisme* enjoins the viewer to become an amateur and, opposing the 'cognitive mapping' of Toscano and Kinkle (discussed in the Introduction), incites future creation, then *Film Catastrophe* can only redouble this logic.[90] The 'value' of this a-commercial product is thus not so much in the film itself as in the unexpected derivations it inspires. Like *The Fountainhead*, *Film Catastrophe* allows us to grasp the economy of derivative images and, going further, enjoins us to participate in their circulation and remaking. In this way, all three films discussed in this chapter – each illustrative of how many filmmakers address the crisis on the level of form – help us to better make sense of their context and status as cinematic and artistic responses to the 2008 financial crash.

Notes

 1. Société Réaliste, *Empire, State, Building* (Paris: Éditions Amsterdam, 2011).
 2. Tristan Trémeau, *In Art We Trust: L'Art au risque de son économie* (Marseille: Éditions Al Dante, 2011), p. 11; Nicolas Bourriaud, *Relational Aesthetics*, trans. Simon Pleasance and Fronza Woods (Dijon: Les Presses du réel, [1998] 2002).
 3. Trémeau, *In Art We Trust*.
 4. Société Réaliste, *Empire, State, Building*, p. 26.
 5. Interview with the author, Café Gambetta, Paris 75020, 12 December 2017.
 6. Ayn Rand, *The Fountainhead* (London: Penguin, [1943] 2007).
 7. Key Randian positions are given in Ayn Rand, *For the New Intellectual* (New York: New American Library, 1961).
 8. On the adaptation process, see Jeff Britting, 'Adapting *The Fountainhead* to Film', in Robert Mayhew (ed.), *Essays on Ayn Rand's* The Fountainhead (Lanham, MD: Lexington Books, 2007). Rand has been seen as a 'virtual codirector' with Vidor – Merrill Schleier, *Skyscraper Cinema: Architecture and Gender in American Film* (Minneapolis: University of Minnesota Press, 2009), p. 126. On Rand's early love of cinema and her time in Hollywood, see Jennifer Burns, *Goddess of the Market: Ayn Rand and the American Right* (Oxford: Oxford University Press, 2009), pp. 16–17, pp. 20–9.
 9. On the film's reception, see Luc Moullet, Le Rebelle *de King Vidor* (Crisnée: Yellow Now, 2009), pp. 97–103.
10. Schleier, *Skyscraper Cinema*, p. 121.
11. Interview with the author.
12. Burns, *Goddess of the Market*; François Flahault, 'De l'individu créateur à la droite américaine', *Communications*, 78 (2005), 245–68.
13. For Greenspan's relationship with Rand, see Mallaby, *The Man Who Knew*, pp. 64–75.
14. Interview with the author.
15. Ibid.
16. Peter Szendy, 'Face Value (the Prosopa of Money)', *Qui Parle*, 27: 1 (2018), 99–119.
17. Thus the play on 'coupure' as both a banknote and a cut in montage – Szendy, *Le Supermarché du visible*, p. 130/ *The Supermarket of the Visible*, p. 84.
18. Richard Misek, 'Trespassing Hollywood: Property, Space, and the "Appropriation Film"', *October*, 153 (Summer 2015), 132–48. Gróf indicated to me that the more

proximate reference during the making of the film was the Situationist film *Can the Dialectic Break Bricks?* (1973).
19. See for example Giovanna Zapperi, 'Temporal Architecture', in Société Réaliste, *Empire, State, Building*, pp. 119–47.
20. A complete shot breakdown of the film is given in *Avant-Scène Cinéma*, 522 (2003).
21. Moullet, *Le Rebelle de King Vidor*, pp. 90–6.
22. Schleier, *Skyscraper Cinema*, p. 134; Moullet, *Le Rebelle de King Vidor*, pp. 74–8.
23. Schleier, *Skyscraper Cinema*, p. 128.
24. Ibid. p. 126.
25. That said, we never actually see him doing any architectural work, as pointed out in Moullet, *Le Rebelle de King Vidor*, p. 62.
26. All the thinkers discussed in Chapter 3 subscribe to some notion of looking as a form of working; for Beller, notably, 'to look is to labor' – Beller, *The Cinematic Mode of Production*, p. 2.
27. Streeck, *Buying Time*, pp. 6–10.
28. Tooze, *Crashed*, pp. 162–3.
29. Ibid. p. 163.
30. Ibid. p. 13.
31. Ibid. pp. 202–19.
32. Martine Beugnet, *L'Attrait du flou* (Crisnée: Yellow Now, 2017), p. 27.
33. Hito Steyerl, 'In Defense of the Poor Image', *e-flux*, 10 (2009), e-flux.com/journal/10/61362/in-defense-of-the-poor-image/ (last accessed 16 August 2021).
34. Szendy, *Le Supermarché du visible*, pp. 134–5.
35. Szendy, *The Supermarket of the Visible*, p. 89.
36. 'Jean-Luc Godard absent à Cannes', *Le Figaro*, 17 May 2010, www.lefigaro.fr/flash-actu/2010/05/17/97001-20100517FILWWW00436-godard-ne-sera-pas-a-cannes.php (last accessed 18 September 2021).
37. Fiachra Gibbons, 'Jean-Luc Godard: "Film is over. What to do?"', *Guardian*, 12 July 2011, theguardian.com/film/2011/jul/12/jean-luc-godard-film-socialisme (last accessed 16 August 2021).
38. 'Continuitée Dialoguée + Cartons' (2010), newwavefilms.co.uk/assets/465/Film_Socialisme_English__subtitles_plus_dialogue.pdf (last accessed 16 August 2021).
39. Xan Brooks, 'Costa Concordia Provided Setting for a 2010 Jean-Luc Godard Film', *Guardian*, 15 January 2012, theguardian.com/world/2012/jan/15/costa-concordia-jean-luc-godard (last accessed 16 August 2021).
40. Bernard Maris, 'Pourquoi le Revenu minimum d'existence est-il une nécessité de la société post-capitaliste?', *Charlie Hebdo*, 27 December 2013, revenudebase.info/2015/01/09/hommage-bernard-maris-revenu-existence/ (last accessed 16 August 2021).
41. Bernard Maris, *Journal d'un économiste en crise* (Paris: Les Échappés-Charlie Hebdo, 2013).
42. Bernard Maris, 'Domination', 'L'utile et l'inutile' and 'La Conversion de Michel', *Charlie Hebdo* 1177 (7 January 2015), p. 3, p. 6, p. 13.

43. Bernard Maris, *Houellebecq économiste* (Paris: Flammarion, 2014). For an overview of Maris's work, see Gilles Raveaud, *Bernard Maris expliqué à ceux qui ne comprennent rien à l'économie* (Paris: Les Échappés, 2017).
44. Tyson Stewart, 'The Romance of the Intellectual in Godard: A Love–Hate Relationship', in Douglas Morrey, Christina Stojanova and Nicole Côté (eds), *The Legacies of Jean-Luc Godard* (Ontario: Wilfrid Laurier University Press, 2014) pp. 169–82 (p. 169, p. 171).
45. Maris's complete contribution was released as a standalone film after his death: *Oncle Bernard: L'anti-leçon d'économie* (Richard Brouillette, 2015).
46. Maris, *Journal d'un économiste en crise*, p. 93.
47. Ibid. p. 97.
48. Ibid. p. 273.
49. Laure Delesalle, *La Dette, une spirale infernale?* (Arte France: Yuzu Productions, 2015).
50. The point is echoed in Vogl, *The Specter of Capital*, p. 129: 'The finance industry's recent and entirely understandable appeal to be rescued through socialization involuntarily demonstrated that even money, capital, and liquidity are not simply private goods held in private hands for private ends but a public good, one that concerns and affects the entire citizenry.'
51. Bernard Maris, *Keynes, ou, l'économiste citoyen* (Paris: Les Presses de Sciences Po, 1999).
52. John Maynard Keynes, *The Essential Keynes*, ed. Robert Skidelsky (London: Penguin, 2015), p. 231.
53. Ibid. p. 235.
54. Bernard Maris and Gilles Dostaler, *Capitalisme et pulsion de mort* (Paris: Albin Michel, 2009).
55. See for example Robert Skidelsky, *Keynes: The Return of the Master* (London: Penguin, 2009).
56. Maris and Dostaler, *Capitalisme et pulsion de mort*, p. 63. Compare Keynes, *The Essential Keynes*, p. 51 and Maris, *Keynes*, pp. 25–6.
57. Raymond Bellour, '(Not) Just An Other Filmmaker', in Raymond Bellour and Mary Lea Bandy (eds), *Jean-Luc Godard: Son + Image, 1974–1991* (New York: MOMA, 1992), pp. 215–31 (p. 220).
58. On the importance of cameras within the film, see Roland-François Lack, 'A Photograph and a Camera: Two Objects in *Film Socialisme*', *Vertigo*, 30 (2012), closeupfilmcentre.com/vertigo_magazine/issue-30-spring-2012-godard-is/a-photograph-and-a-camera-two-objects-in-film-socialisme/ (last accessed 16 August 2021).
59. Guillaume Bourgois, 'Le Trésor de Godard le Rouge: *Film Socialisme*', *La Furia Umana*, 33, (2018), lafuriaumana.it/index.php/66-archive/lfu-33/749-guillaume-bourgois-le-tresor-de-godard-le-rouge-film-socialisme (last accessed 16 August 2021).
60. Bob Maloubier, *Agent secret de Churchill* (Paris: Tallandier, 2011).
61. Maris and Dostaler, *Capitalisme et pulsion de mort*, p. 63; Georg Simmel, *The Philosophy of Money*, trans. Tom Bottomore and David Frisby (Abingdon:

Routledge, [1900] 2004). In a similar fashion, Maris considers the estranging effect of statistics, in which 'figures' (*chiffres*) allow us not to consider the real people in question: 'Il permet de ne pas voir.' Maris, *Journal d'un économiste en crise*, p. 140.

62. Citton, *Médiarchie*, p. 372.
63. Douglas Morrey, *Jean-Luc Godard* (Manchester: Manchester University Press, 2005), pp. 84–5.
64. Maris and Dostaler, *Capitalisme et pulsion de mort*, p. 122.
65. Ibid. p. 141.
66. Stewart, 'The Romance of the Intellectual in Godard', p. 180.
67. Ibid. p. 180.
68. Godard's practice of reusing copyrighted film extracts has a long history – see Christa Blümlinger, *Cinéma de seconde main: Esthétique du remploi dans l'art du film et des nouveaux médias*, trans. Pierre Rusch and Christophe Jouanlanne (Paris: Klincksieck, 2013).
69. Jean Breschand, 'De la libre circulation des images', *Libération*, 10 December 2020, liberation.fr/debats/2020/12/10/de-la-libre-circulation-des-images_1808269?fbclid=IwAR1Uvak5-Q-TlRgxtiq_nDVwcLHwltiZpz11szu7XlVjXikaTA5FUH90sFM (last accessed 16 August 2021).
70. Jean-Luc Godard, 'The Right of the Author? An Author Has Only Duties', interview with Jean-Marc Lalanne, trans. Diane Gabrysiak, *Les Inrockuptibles*, 18 May 2010, included in *Film Socialisme* Pressbook, newwavefilms.co.uk/assets/465/Final_Film_Socialisme_pressbook_27_may.pdf (last accessed 16 August 2021).
71. Christopher Pavsek, *The Utopia of Film: Cinema and Its Futures in Godard, Kluge, and Tahimik* (New York: Columbia University Press, 2013), p. 70.
72. Creton, 'Godard et l'art stratégique de la redéfinition du métier'.
73. Grivas's film can be seen at filmcatastrophe.com (last accessed 16 August 2021).
74. On the stakes of resolution, see Francesco Casetti and Antonio Somaini, 'Resolution: Digital Materialities, Thresholds of Visibility', *NECSUS: European Journal of Media Studies*, 7: 1 (2018), 87–103.
75. Discussion with Paul Grivas, Cinéma du réel festival, Centre Pompidou, 23 March 2019.
76. See filmcatastrophe.com/lincomparable (last accessed 16 August 2021).
77. While not exactly the same document, see debordements.fr/pdf/Socialime-JLG.pdf (last accessed 16 August 2021).
78. Notably in *Scénario du film Passion* (1982), discussed in Szendy, *Le Supermarché du visible*, pp. 21–3/ *The Supermarket of the Visible*, pp. 10–11. See also Jacques Aumont, *Le Cinéma et la mise en scène*, 2nd edn (Malakoff: Armand Colin, 2015), p. 39.
79. Douglas Morrey, 'The Forest for the Trees: Political Contexts for Godard's Nature Imagery in *Film socialisme* and *Adieu au langage*', *Studies in French Cinema*, 19: 1 (2019), 55–68 (p. 55, p. 58).
80. Marie-Claire Ropars-Wuilleumier, 'Totalité et fragmentaire: La réécriture selon Godard' [1988], in *Le Temps d'une pensée*, ed. Sophie Charlin (Saint-Denis: Presses Universitaires de Vincennes, 2009), pp. 153–66 (p. 162).

81. Szendy et al. (eds), *Le Supermarché des images*, p. 14.
82. On supercuts, see Martine Beugnet, *Le Cinéma et ses doubles: L'Image de film à l'ère du* foundfootage *numérique et des écrans de poche* (Lormont: Le Bord de l'eau, 2021), pp. 37–8.
83. On sound in *Film Socialisme*, see Danae Stefanou, 'Music, Noise and Silence in the Late Cinema of Jean-Luc Godard', in Mervyn Cooke and Fiona Ford (eds), *The Cambridge Companion to Film Music* (Cambridge: Cambridge University Press, 2016), pp. 294–307 and Albertine Fox, *Godard and Sound: Acoustic Innovation in the Late Films of Jean-Luc Godard* (London: I.B. Tauris, 2018), pp. 167–81.
84. 'À fond la caisse. Le fond du problème. À fonds perdus. Retirer des fonds. Les bas-fonds. Au fond de tout. Le fond et la forme. Le fond du problème. À fonds perdus. Retirer des fonds. Les bas-fonds. Le fond et la forme. Au fond de tout.' 'Il n'y pas de raison à s'inquiéter,' says an attendant, 'on a juste touché le fond'.
85. José Sarmiento Hinojosa, 'Paul Grivas: "The images are there for the taking, you just got to pick them up"', *desistfilm* (2019), desistfilm.com/paul-grivas-the-images-are-there-for-the-taking-you-just-got-to-pick-them-up/ (last accessed 16 August 2021).
86. Ibid.
87. Beugnet, *Le Cinéma et ses doubles*, p. 24.
88. See Jacques Aumont, 'Ceci n'est pas un collage: Notes sur certains films de Bruce Conner', *Cahiers du MNAM*, 99 (2007), 13–31 and Daniel Fairfax, 'The Experience of a Gaze Held in Time: Interview with Jacques Aumont', *Senses of Cinema*, 83 (2017), sensesofcinema.com/2017/film-studies/jacques-aumont-interview (last accessed 16 August 2021).
89. Hinojosa, 'Paul Grivas'.
90. Solange Manche, 'Montrer l'invisible: The Politics of the Amateur in Jean-Luc Godard's *Film Socialisme* and the Medvekin Group', paper presented at NECS conference, Gdańsk, 13 June 2019. 'Amateur' here is understood in Stiegler's terms – see Martin Crowley, 'The Artist and the Amateur, from Misery to Invention', in Christina Howells and Gerald Moore (eds), *Stiegler and Technics* (Edinburgh: Edinburgh University Press, 2013), pp. 119–34.

CHAPTER SIX

Dreaming Futures

ARGENT AND VALUE

Argent ('Money', 2018) by the poet Christophe Hanna is a book somewhere between a sociological report and a work of 'poetry'.[1] The book's formal strategy is based on an econometric which divides the French population into 'tranches' of net monthly income (as French income is normally quantified). Each chapter corresponds to one of twenty €200 income brackets. The book recounts Hanna's discussions on the subject of money with one hundred (real) individuals, each individual corresponding to a percentile of income distribution and identified only by their forename followed immediately by the figure corresponding to their net monthly income. Thus, for example, Charlotte433 is an intern or *stagiaire* in a publishing house, Julien1042 is the performance poet Julien Blaine, Nathalie2400 is the writer Nathalie Quintane and Anne-James2500 is the poet Anne-James Chaton. Hanna's process is to ask people he meets – most often writers and poets – about their financial situation, sources of income and their experience of money. This allows him to insist on the real-world conditions of literature: that is, not simply with the cost of material reproduction of poets, but with the economic conditions of the possibility of literary works.[2] The book gives real insight into the economic conditions of the publishers he is involved with (Al Dante, Éditions Amsterdam, P.O.L, Questions Théoriques).[3] Hanna also foregrounds the conditions of the writing of his book, recounting how he obtained the interviews, describing his use of a dictaphone and how he takes the pictures that appear in the margins of his text.[4] Hanna inquires not simply about literary works, but all that escapes a quantitative measure of value: how much, for example, does a love affair cost? 'On ne sait pas vraiment ce qu'on doit comptabiliser' ('We don't really know what to count').[5] Some of those with whom he speaks believe that there is a more or less direct connection between the value of their work and their income, whereas for others the relationship is aleatory or even inverse.[6] Some interviewed feel there is little meaning or dignity to their work. Many of those interviewed by Hanna are those fellow travellers identified by Nathalie Wourm as constituting a loose network of contemporary French writers sometimes inspired by the notions of deconstruction and deterritorialisation.[7] At the same time as offering an image of this community of artists and poets in Paris, Lyon and Marseille, through its organisation Hanna's book practises a derivative operation of disassembling people by attribute and then ordering them into tranches – that is, they are literally priced and profiled according to their income, and hence their risk exposure or creditworthiness. Martin writes: 'derivatives treat people not as whole but in parts, less as subjects who must meet a threshold for participation than as attributes of risk that can be profiled, collected, and ranked'.[8] The book is a literary derivative or a derivative image in the form of a book. This is represented in the bar chart in Figure 6.1 showing the distribution of revenues, repeated at the beginning of each chapter to illustrate each character's place within the spread.[9]

Few of Hanna's securitised interviewees who are writers or artists make a living solely from their literary or artistic work. Many teach, for example, or work for publishers or other cultural institutions. Furthermore, if they do substantially survive from their writing, the key part of their income will be from derivative functions of the writing, such as readings, workshops and selling adaptation rights. Even those in full-time work describe innumerable tactics to make ends meet, including working 'on the black', illegal downloads, shoplifting and stealing at work. Many rely on assistance from their parents.[10] As some of the writers signal, writing a work actually costs money, and like a love affair it is not clear where one should stop in counting the

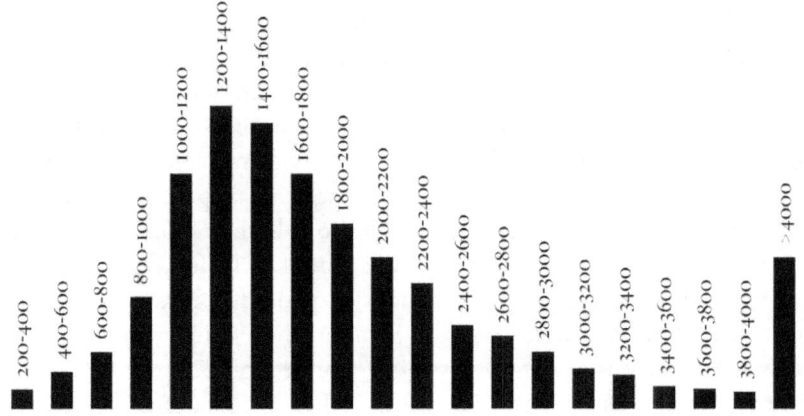

Figure 6.1 French monthly net income distribution (from *Argent*, p. 7) © Christophe Hanna/Éditions Amsterdam.

costs.¹¹ The interviewees sometimes imagine alternative lives in which they had more money, and even those on above-average earnings struggle to 'se projeter dans l'avenir' ('project themselves in the future').¹² Hanna teaches in a lycée in Villeurbanne, near Lyon, and notes that his own academic writings are never paid; at best, he receives a copy of the journal containing his text.¹³ Hanna's own engagement with the legacy of the financial crisis is clear from his participation in the ArTeC project at Université Paris 8, 'Évaluation générale: L'Agence de Notation comme dispositif artistique' ('General Evaluation: Rating Agencies as Artistic Techniques'), run by Nancy Murzilli, which, inspired among other things by the failed credit rating agencies involved in 2008, is currently experimenting with new and poetic forms of evaluation, especially with evaluating that which is not normally evaluated: for example, the condition of the office of the director of an art gallery, or the behaviour of the visitors to a gallery rather than the works of art.¹⁴ What *Argent* documents is at once the precarity afflicting many in post-crash France, but also the experience of a price order seemingly traversing everything in this period. The book does not directly refer to 2008, but one of its themes is the inequality and stagnant standards of living in Western societies which were highlighted and deepened by that event. The book's derivative formal operation clinically exposes the disconnection between remuneration and the unquantifiable care and time that goes into work in the widest sense. *Argent* thus puts into question not just the notions of value, price and money, but also – recalling the discussion of Stiegler in Chapter 1 – the meaning and purpose of work and economy more generally.

The book is made up of blocks of text interspersed with images relating to the financial situation of Hanna's interlocutors. Hanna is extremely interested in the price of things and provides many screen-captures and photographs of documents containing prices: spreadsheets, receipts, bills, online order forms, café menu chalkboards, author copyright clearances, handwritten calculations of expenses and domestic accounts, payslips, telephone screen-captures of account balances on banking applications, gas meters, cheques, honoraria and subscription forms. By my count, there are twenty-five such images in the book. *Argent* thus shows how such quotidian forms of accounting and exchange – which are financial media in their own right, like Maris's slot machine – are imbricated in the iconomy of our daily lives. Hanna will often emend these images to render the proper names in the style of his book. These are found among a total of a little over a hundred images of documents and commodities, including notes, advertisements, websites, artworks, photographs of buildings, homes, bars and shops Hanna visits (without people in view), a screen-capture of GoogleMaps indicating where several of his interlocutors live in the 18th arrondissement of Paris, photographs of products in shops, handwritten essays from his students, online reviews, photographs of clothing, certificates, prizes, tweets, emails, text messages, letters, questionnaires, book covers, shop windows, invitations, CVs, polaroids, floor plans, dedications, professional ID cards, diagrams and police witness statements. Except for three images of a conference where Hanna participates, facial photographs of the personae are almost never shown. (*Argent* seems to confirm Maris's remark that 'l'argent a été inventé pour ne pas regarder les Hommes dans les yeux'). The sense that the faces are as if redacted gives the images the quality of documentary evidence and also foregrounds how the literary text is derived across media. If in *Les Effondrés* Larnaudie crystallises the media image of the acute moment of the 2008 crisis, in *Argent* Hanna assembles derivative images to show how financial flows reach into every corner of the lives of his subjects.

The book begins by describing a reading given by the poet Christophe Tarkos in Marseille twenty years earlier. Tarkos's poetry collection *L'Argent* (1999) is a key intertext for *Argent* and similarly meditates on the phenomenology of money.[15] Tarkos, identified as Christophe254, is the poorest character in the book and the only author in the €200–400 bracket that Hanna could find. Tarkos does not seek any other work, even a part-time job on the side, unlike the other poets in the book. The €254 calculation refers to the monthly value of Tarkos's royalties in 2014 – that is, ten years after his death (Tarkos was born in 1963 and died in 2004, and is thus, unusually but not uniquely, a non-living figure in the book).[16] Pressing open gaps between modes of accounting for literary value, Hanna observes that while Tarkos's work generates limited financial revenue, it is the object of speculation on another plane of value: doctoral theses are now written on his work, and in this way Tarkos is becoming 'monnayable sur le marché du travail universitaire' ('monetisable on the academic labour market').[17] While Tarkos is discussed in terms of a 'crisis of representation' and other critical topoi, Hanna remarks that it would be better ('plus profitable') to describe him as a writer who 'confère un aspect préhensible aux formes des échanges ordinaires auxquelles on s'est accoutumé au point qu'on n'arrive plus bien à les sentir et les observer. Il vaudrait mieux se demander quels moyens, pour parvenir à cela, il a exploités dans l'institution-poésie' ('helps us grasp the ordinary forms of exchange to which we are so accustomed that we no longer even notice them. It would be better to ask how he used the poetry-institution to achieve this').[18]

'Institution' is a key conceptual term for Hanna, and for him poetry is an institution just like, for example, publishing or finance.[19] We get a sense of what this means when Hanna relates a presentation he delivered at the Fondation Pernod Ricard art gallery in Paris, where he says, 'être écrivain, c'est être un homme qui instrumentalise l'institution littéraire pour infiltrer d'autres institutions' ('a writer is someone who uses the literary institution to infiltrate other institutions').[20] We might gloss this by noting that, while many of his interviewees are writers, others are not, and it is as a writer that he persuades, for example, his bank advisor and a lawyer to discuss their financial situation openly with him. In the course of his encounters, Hanna is asked more than once in what sense his work constitutes poetry. Can poetry even be considered a form of work, asks another.[21] *Argent* is not poetry in the conventional sense of a verbal arrangement using such techniques as prosody and lineation. For Hanna, poetry is that which gives consistency to 'notions floues' ('vague notions') used in everyday life.[22] Hanna offers us an extract from his oral presentation for a post at the University of Aix-Provence to explain his research. He is interested in texts arising from 'un travail d'hybridation' ('a work of hybridisation') combining normally discrete institutional logics, such as those by the writers Francis Ponge, Olivier4000 (Olivier Cadiot) or Manuel1300 (Manuel Joseph).[23] He thus develops the concept of 'dispositif d'écriture' ('writing apparatus'): 'tout réagencement d'éléments langagiers dans un contexte donné, visant, par la dynamique même qu'induit la redisposition, à mobiliser dans une synergie nouvelle des compétences cognitives habituellement isolées' ('all reassemblages of linguistic elements in a given context which, by the very dynamic which leads to the rearrangement, aim to mobilise normally discrete cognitive capabilities in a new synergy').[24] Crudely, a *dispositif* is an arrangement of disparate semiotic objects which enter into a new relation with each other and which, combined, potentially produce new effects.[25] Conceiving of writing as a *dispositif* which can potentially disrupt the linguistic system in which it takes off, like a computer virus, Hanna's theory of writing has (neo-)pragmatist and Situationist influences.[26] The *dispositif* of *Argent* can also be understood in derivative terms: that is, as a bundle of heterogenous elements organised by an accounting procedure (selecting and profiling individuals by income) which exploits what Randy Martin calls the 'social surplus' (in the form of the verbal and visual rendering of the lives of individuals) and which is leveraged in a speculative manner with a view to yielding new (literary) value. The hundred or so derivative images in *Argent* document our iconomic condition at the quotidian level of gas meter readings and second-hand purchases, revealing what Feher gestures towards when he states that today we are witnessing not the dominance of the economic over the non-economic, but rather 'the dissolution of the frontier between the economic and the non-economic' – or at least the 'pertinence' of this opposition.[27] *Argent* can equally be seen as testifying to the correlative of this idea, which is the parallel identified by the critic Frederik Tygstrup between increasing speculation in finance over the last forty years and a trend within literature in which '"fictionality", a speculative mode par excellence, has become less well delineated as a feature of literature', this fictionality increasingly insinuating itself in the discursive construction of the real, such that the fiction/non-fiction divide 'is simply becoming increasingly irrelevant'.[28]

In his review saluting *Argent*, Citton explicitly theorises the book in relation to financial derivatives, setting it against a backdrop of financial hypertrophy which he sees as symptomatic of the inability of contemporary societies to appropriately value people's contributions to social life:

> La multiplication de 'produits dérivés' dans le monde de la finance essaie en vain de conjurer l'affolement de nos boussoles en instaurant une sorte de méta-capital financier chargé de 'gouverner' la distribution du capital économique. La finance reste une affaire de prix (quantitatifs), là où nos inter- et intra-actions humaines trament des relations qualitatives. La tyrannie conjointe des évaluations (administratives) et de la financiarisation sont les deux faces réactionnelles d'un même effondrement de toute référence substantielle à la notion de valeur.[29]

> [The proliferation of 'derivatives' in the world of finance tries in vain to steady our spinning compasses by instituting a sort of financial meta-capital which is supposed to 'govern' the distribution of economic capital. Finance remains a question of (quantitative) prices, whereas our human interactions and intra-actions are woven from qualitative relations. The twin tyrannies of administrative evaluations and financialisation are the two reactionary faces of the same collapse of all substantial reference to the notion of value.]

For Citton, *Argent* counters the notion of economic rationality according to which the market establishes the just price for everything, showing not only how work is often insufficiently remunerated but also how price and value are not equivalent. Derivatives are a symptom of an impoverished grasp of qualitative value in the world. He goes on:

> Il y a poésie, d'une part, en ce qu'un dispositif scripturaire de captation produit *un ovni documentaire* qui met en crise les catégorisations à travers lesquelles nos appareils de programmation reconnaissent, classifient et traitent les données qui régissent désormais nos vies. Il y a poésie, d'autre part, en ce qu'un travail de socio-écriture contribue activement à *tramer une certaine forme de commun*, selon une 'poiétique' (une fabrication) opérant par collages, implantations, implémentations à la fois concrètes, inattendues et potentiellement proliférantes.[30]

> [On the one hand, there is poetry in that this literary technique of capture produces a *documentary UFO/unidentified verbal object* which puts into crisis the categories through which our programming apparatuses recognise, classify and process the data which govern our lives. On the other hand, there

is poetry in how a work of sociological writing actively contributes to the *weaving of a certain form of commons*, according to a 'poetics' (a making) operating through collages, creations and implementations at once concrete, unexpected and with the potential to proliferate.]

Citton here extends Hanna's conceptions of poetry and *dispositif*, developing the idea that poetry is the name for writing that reorganises the form of human groups.[31] Certain expressions here ('inattendues et potentiellement proliférantes') show how Citton sees *Argent* as comparable to the kind of work he hopes will emerge from ArTeC, and which, as we saw in Chapter 3, was thought in terms of derivative potentialities. As we saw with Grivas, the futurity of the work lies in its capacity to yield unexpected derivatives. An example of this potentiality is given in how he signs off his review in the style of *Argent* and notes that others have adopted the style too. Citton's reference to Flusser ('appareils de programmation') indicates how Hanna's textual operation might create a space of freedom by short-circuiting our programmed categorisations. The book concretely shows mutual indebtedness and social interdependencies across the tranches of income – how the director in the top tranche depends on the *stagiaire* in the bottom, for example. Again, we should underline the ambivalence of this situation, for Hanna's textual operation of affixing individuals' revenue next to their names equally lays out on the page our tendency to exploit each other as commodities or derivatives. The derivative form thus reveals the social surplus that is harnessed by the economy but which it cannot adequately measure, thus allowing us to glimpse how we might cut derivatives differently.

'FIN DE RÈGNE': *RÊVER SOUS LE CAPITALISME*

In a rather different key, Sophie Bruneau's documentary *Rêver sous le capitalisme* (*Dreaming Under Capitalism*, 2017) also blends poetry with an organising principle that profiles individuals by attribute – in this case, twelve individuals recount a dream to do with their working life.[32] If in *Argent* the people we meet are organised by income to reveal what overflows this, in *Rêver* by contrast we begin from an intimate aspect of the individuals' psychic lives to reveal the oppressiveness of the financial matrix into which they are sorted, the managerial gears in which they are painfully caught. The tenth and eleventh dreams in particular attest to an intrusive regime of quantification and evaluation of productivity which oppresses the central nervous system and causes work to lose all meaning for the employee.[33] The recitations are in most cases given in voiceover over crepuscular, prismatic images of glass windows of offices being cleaned at night, construction sites, and other work locations and transport hubs in Brussels. The dreams are surreal and reflect how the speakers are overburdened with work. The dreamers work in various jobs and professions; as in *Argent*, one of the dreamers works at a supermarket checkout, while others have administrative or industrial roles; one is unemployed. The film is of a beautiful formal economy, lasting 63 minutes and containing just twenty-four shots, all save one of which are static. While in fact just over half of the shots take place in daylight, one of the film's strongest effects is the sense it evokes of the moment just before dawn, as if to suggest the time of having woken too early, of having badly slept, woken by stress, and the dread of knowing one has soon to go to work in a fatigued state. This is the case in the eleventh shot, in which we see a dark room and two windows looking out onto a violet sky. Over some 4½ minutes, perhaps sped up, light enters the room as the sun rises, slowly tracing the outlines of objects, such as a desk and a lamp. In the dream recounted during the shot, a woman is injured and finds herself on a gurney in an infirmary in which her colleagues are wrapped up to their eyes in bandages, like mummies. Starting from a dark room looking out to the morning sky, one might suppose the shot is of a bedroom, suggesting the dream remembered to consciousness in the morning vigil before rising from one's bed. As the light outside becomes the pale blue of day, the outline of a computer in the room is limned to confirm that in fact the shot is of an empty office: the dreamer, even asleep and in bed, is still at work.[34]

The first shot of the film shows a distant half-moon on a night sky amidst passing clouds. With the next shot, the first dream begins to be recounted:

> Je travaillais, c'était une fin d'après-midi, et puis la nuit commençait à tomber, ça devait être en hiver. Je me suis aperçu que quelques collègues s'étaient transformés. Enfin, en tout cas dans mon rêve, ils ressemblaient presque plus à des morts-vivants qu'à des collègues. Ils s'étaient complètement transformés et ils étaient lents, donc ça me laissait quand même une certaine liberté.
>
> À un moment, je me suis dit 'il faut absolument que je fasse quelque chose, que je les dégage de là'. Je suis parti dans le placard à balai, là où les femmes de ménage rangent leurs outils: aspirateurs, balais, machin chose, ramassettes, les petits charriots.
>
> Et puis là, je trouve une pelle. Une pelle en métal avec un beau manche en bois. Je m'en suis emparé. Et puis, dans le bâtiment, il n'y a pas de cave mais je me suis rendu compte que je pouvais ouvrir l'ascenseur et taper les collègues avec la pelle dans l'ascenseur, pour essayer de les coincer là. C'est à ce moment-là où je me suis réveillé . . . je pense que j'ai dû un peu m'agiter en les tapant dans leur dernier retranchement.
>
> Si je devais relier ça à l'ambiance du boulot, effectivement, il y a une espèce de, à la fois de torpeur, parfois il y a des crispations de la direction mais qui sont totalement dénués d'intérêt. Et puis il y a une espèce d'ambiance diffuse, de malaise. C'est quelque chose, une espèce de fin de règne comme ça . . .

Parfois, on rit entre nous, d'ailleurs en se disant 'au revoir', on dit 'peut-être, peut-être à demain', ou le matin on se voit, on se dit 'tiens on est combien aujourd'hui?'. Parce que parfois t'as l'impression, tu rentres dans les bureaux et il y a une ambiance un peu sinistre comme ça, où chacun, évidemment tout le monde est fort occupé à travailler dans son bureau mais du coup, on se croirait un dimanche quoi. Là, où il devrait y avoir une dynamique, de la vie.

Mais il y a aussi, par exemple, c'est assez trivial, mais un verre au départ de quelqu'un, on sent bien, après une heure, il est question d'arrêter parce qu'on ne voit pas bien l'intérêt que les gens se rassemblent parce que quelqu'un a fini sa carrière de 40 ans de service. C'est du temps perdu.[35]

[I was at work, it was late afternoon. Night was falling, it must have been winter. I noticed that a few colleagues had changed. In my dream they looked more likes zombies than colleagues. They had completely changed and they were slow, which left me a certain freedom.

At one point, I said to myself 'I must do something, get rid of them'. I went to the broom cupboard, where the cleaning ladies keep their cleaning tools, hoovers, brooms, dustpans, little carts and stuff. I found a shovel. A metal shovel with a nice wooden handle. I took it. There's no basement in the building, but I realised that I could open the lift and bat the colleagues into it with the shovel and trap them in there. And just at that moment I woke up . . . I must have got a bit excited batting them into a corner.

If I have to link that to the ambience at work, there is a sort of torpor. Sometimes there are tensions from management, which are totally devoid of interest. Then there's a diffuse ambience of unease. A kind of end-of-era feel.

Sometimes we joke amongst ourselves. When saying goodbye we say 'see you tomorrow . . . perhaps'. Or in the morning, we see each other and say: 'How many of us are here today?' Because sometimes you go into the offices and there's a sinister atmosphere. Obviously, everyone's busy working in their office and so it feels like Sunday, whereas things should be dynamic and alive.

Another trivial example is the drink when someone leaves. You sense that after an hour, things wind down because they don't see the point of getting together simply because someone's 40-year career is ending. It's a waste of time.[36]]

As we see here, the dreamers recount but also interpret their dream, relating it to their working lives.[37] Echoes between the testimonies are created in the film by the chance use of similar or even exactly the same phrase, which repeat like a refrain: 'c'est très sinistre' ('it's ominous') and 'à quoi je sers?' ('what use am I?'). In terms of rendering suffering at work, the film fits squarely within a rich body of sociological, psychoanalytic and French studies work on the representation and experience of work in contemporary France.[38] As Jeremy Lane and Sarah Waters write: 'The workplace gives material and localised embodiment to otherwise abstract and distant economic forces grounding these in everyday social realities and identifiable spaces.'[39] Bruneau suggests that the lived experience of work cannot be filmed 'frontalement' or directly and so her film proceeds by testimony.⁴⁰ In perhaps the most startling monologue, a doctor describes a dream to camera in which she witnesses the opening of her cranium and little chairs being set around the opening by minuscule figures who plunge very long fine spoons into her head to feed themselves. As the example quoted above shows, the dreams not only relate individual cases of suffering but also describe a sense of systemic collapse. While there is no direct reference to the 2008 financial crisis in the film, nonetheless it is striking that the theorist Anselm Jappe uses a near-identical phrase to that given in the above quotation – 'fin de règne' ('end of an era') – to evoke the fear brought about by the crisis in October 2008, noting that ordinary citizens were generally only aware of the crisis through the media:

> Pas de licenciements de masse, pas d'interruptions dans la distribution des produits de première nécessité, pas de caisses automatiques qui ne distribuent plus de billets de banque, pas de commerçants qui refusent les cartes de crédit. Pas encore de crise 'visible', donc. Et pourtant, une atmosphère de fin de règne. [. . .] Quand la crise a éclaté, aucun individu contemporain ne semblait, dans son for intérieur, davantage surpris qu'un gros fumeur à qui l'on apprend qu'il a le cancer.⁴¹

> [No mass redundancies, no food shortages, no ATMs refusing to distribute bank notes, no shops refusing credit cards. So no 'visible' crisis. And yet, a mood of the end of an epoch [. . .] When the crisis happened, no one who was there at the time, in their heart of hearts, was any more surprised than a heavy smoker who finds out that he has cancer.]

As we will discuss towards the end of the chapter, the reason why seemingly 'nothing happened' during the financial crisis was because what was happening was happening on the level of the future.⁴²

The monologue quoted above is split over three images. The first shot, which lasts 1 minute and 10 seconds, shows a train passing a deserted station platform during the night, passing relatively slowly at a slight diagonal angle from right to left of the shot. The train looks almost empty, but brightly lit inside. The speaker begins as the train is most of the way out of shot. The darkness suggests it is early in the morning, before the sun is up – so, an early commuter train. The cut comes just after the word 'liberté', after about 20 seconds of an empty frame. The second shot shows two floors of what appears to be an office building, still at night (Figure 6.2). On the top floor a man can be seen driving a floor-scrubbing machine. On the lower floor a number of tables with chairs are arranged; this is perhaps the office canteen. The walls are made of glass, with steel partitions forming a matrix of rectangles. About halfway through the shot a passing train is reflected

Dreaming Futures 165

Figure 6.2 *Rêver sous le capitalisme* (Sophie Bruneau, 2018) © alter ego films.

in the middle of the image, on a darkened strip of the façade. With the word 'malaise', there is a cut to another image, which appears to be a closer shot of the same office building but taken from a different angle. The same yellow walls can be seen on the floor below, unlit and uninhabited, but upstairs another office space can be seen where two people sit at separate ends of the space. The city has not quite awoken, and groggily reflected on the exterior glass walls we see a train as well as the passing lights of a car, a streetlamp and a rotating street advertisement. Similar geometric compositions of the exteriors of office buildings recur later in the film.[43]

These opening shots are typical of how the film works, the shots lingering for around a minute after the end of the monologue, leaving us to contemplate the image in which chance comes into play and apparitions take place; as the director comments, it is 'une sorte de pari sur le hasard dans le mouvement du réel' ('a kind of bet on chance in the movement of the real').[44] The words spoken – often as if under pressure of speech – work over the images as over a canvas, writing meanings into the images of the worksites of contemporary capitalism. The images do not illustrate the dreams, leaving a gap between the verbalised content of the dreams and tableaux in which a free association can take place. This disjunction between sound and image could be seen as a modernist technique and thus reveal an affinity with the work of other contemporary filmmakers who return to modernist techniques to render the experience of the everyday and to critique contemporary liberalism.[45] Like *Argent*, *Rêver* does not simply invite the spectator to reflect on their own imbrication in a larger financial and economic system, but also locates a creative residue that escapes the quantitative matrices and accounting procedures which put pressure on the interviewees. If Bruneau's film uses dreams almost as clinical documents to expose how psychic life is 'travaillé' ('worked') by econometrics, then this would be the negative sense in which we are in the market 'down to the psyche', as suggested in Chapter 3.[46] With the images suggestive of the dawn before the commute and the inertia upon waking, in which one lies in bed while the dream is still lifting, the film proposes this nonknowledge as the source of creative energy which could remake the world of work. In this sense the film shows, as the psychoanalyst Josh Cohen puts it, how '[t]he creative act consists, paradoxically, in sustaining the inactive state'.[47]

'ÇA IMPRIME, ÇA IMPRIME': *L'ÉPOQUE*, *ESCAPARATES*

While *Rêver sous le capitalisme* explores the night and early morning as the time of anxiety for the coming day, Matthieu Bareyre's *L'Époque* (*Young and Alive*, 2018) takes the end of the day and the working week as its starting point: the time in which people leave work and are free to do as they wish.[48] Bareyre remarks that the night is when time slows down and we are no longer plugged into a logic of efficiency and calculation, and in this sense his film is a search for a kind of freedom.[49] The documentary was inspired by the events surrounding the *Charlie Hebdo* shooting in 2015 and covers the period from then until the presidential election of 2017. The film follows a number of young people in Paris during their night life, often in chance encounters in the street or in cafés, sitting by the Canal Saint-Martin, on the Place de la République, in the northern *banlieues* and taking part in protests and street skirmishes with CRS riot police (a familiar image in French cinema of the 2010s).[50] From a variety of different social backgrounds, the young people discuss their career prospects, the notions of freedom and happiness, and the future generally. Several express a sense of feeling lost, of futility; one describes their radicalisation as a black bloc participant.

As in *Rêver sous le capitalisme*, the documentary works by an oneiric logic while also offering a report about people's feelings about the world of work. In a different tone from *Rêver sous le capitalisme*, those interviewed sometimes discuss dreams, and the related formulation of 'faire rêver' recurs across speakers. Some 10 minutes into the film, for example, a young business school student by the canal says that becoming an economist is absolutely not 'ce qui me fait rêver' ('the stuff dreams are made of'); he feels lost doing what is expected of him. Both Bareyre and Bruneau suggest that dreams and the unconscious offer a mode of access for grasping an essential characteristic of our epoch, and that is that today the economic is the existential.[51] The critic Romain Lefebvre evokes the dreamlike logic of *L'Époque*:

> L'une des conséquences du caractère flottant des images et de la libre circulation à travers le montage est en effet de faire basculer l'ensemble vers une dimension inconsciente qui affecte à la fois les éléments qui s'y mélangent et le mode de signification du film. Le retour au fil des séquences de certains noms comme McDonalds [sic], mais aussi Valls et Macron, ne s'accompagne pas d'une analyse mais signe plutôt leur appartenance à une forme d'imaginaire collectif – ce sont des paroles dans l'air du temps, comme un mauvais tube qui, contre notre gré et à force de matraquage, nous est rentré dans la tête au point d'alimenter nos cauchemars.[52]

> [One of the consequences of the floating character of the images and of the free circulation in the montage is to tip the whole thing into an unconscious dimension which affects at once the elements which are found there and the film's mode of signification. The recurrence of certain names like McDonald's, but also Valls and Macron, does not come with an analysis but indicates rather their belonging to a form of collective imaginary – they are words in the spirit of the times, like a bad hit song which, against our will and like being hit over the head, is now stuck in our head to the point of contributing to our nightmares.]

Comme un mauvais tube: while Szendy describes how *tubes* constitute a psychic economy to the glory of exchange, Lefebvre evokes a dark psychic economy in which these brands and names circulate like the derivative products in a polluted ecology of mind. This could be called the 'symbolic misery' resulting from the colonisation of aesthetic experience in what Stiegler calls the 'hyper-industrial epoch'.[53] The recurring attention to media forms and cameras in *L'Époque*, repeatedly focusing on spotlights, camera lenses and screens, as in *Film Socialisme* and *Film Catastrophe*, is one of the means by which the film examines the psychic economy of its subjects.[54]

The theme of 'ce qui fait rêver' is carried forward by Rose, the principal character of *L'Époque* and celebrated by many critics as the real discovery of the film, a young black woman who, like Bareyre, engages in nocturnal wandering during the Nuit debout period (the 2016 social movement based around nightly gatherings at the Place de la République and opposition to labour reforms).[55] At the end of the film, she will vow to leave France because of the racism she has experienced, writing in a Facebook post to the President of France: 'mes icônes font rêver, les vôtres font crever' ('my heroes are the stuff of dreams, yours kill'). Some 27 minutes into the film she offers a monologue at the Place de la République where she speaks movingly about a variety of injustices: apathy towards suffering in foreign countries, the refugee camps in France, police brutality that she has witnessed and experienced.

Her speech starts with the humour that typifies her character, but as it goes on tears rise to her eyes. She says she feels ashamed of her French nationality and feels like giving it up, adding 'liberté pour qui? Égalité pour qui?' ('whose liberty? Whose equality?'), before also asking 'C'est quoi l'argent?' ('What is money?'). She makes a gesture, bringing her right hand down on her left, in a slow, repeated and mechanical rhythm, to signify money being printed: it's a bank, she says, and it is printed and cut: 'ça imprime, ça imprime'. We then all queue up, she says, to collect our banknotes to play Monopoly with them.

At the end of the speech, there is a cut to an image of the monument of the Place de la République reflected upside down in a flat reflecting pool water feature. The monument dates from 1883 and stands, surrounded by a water basin, at the centre of the square. The monument consists of a large stone column, on top of which stands a bronze statue of the Marianne (the personification of the ideals of the French Republic), an olive branch held aloft and carrying a tablet inscribed with 'Droits de l'Homme'. Three stone statues sit around the column, allegorising the terms of the French national motto of liberty, equality and fraternity, while at the base of the monument a bronze lion defends a voting urn, symbolising universal suffrage. Twelve relief sculptures around the base illustrate key scenes from the revolutionary history of the Republic between 1789 and 1880. It was only relatively recently, in 2013, that the Place de la République was redeveloped as the largest pedestrian public square in Paris and the water features added. Since then, features have also been installed specifically for the use of skateboarders. Today the square is regularly used as a meeting point for demonstrations and was notably a gathering spot following the January and November 2015 terrorist attacks in Paris and occupied during the Nuit debout movement: this is the context for the use of the Place in *L'Époque*.[56] Unlike the sheer verticality associated with that contrasting Parisian geography of excess, La Défense, some 10 kilometres to the west (examined in Chapter 4), the Place thus gathers together associations of horizontality, commons, protest, revolution. More specifically, however, skateboarding (which he sees as derived from surfing) is one of Randy Martin's privileged examples of the social logic of the derivative, alongside postmodern dance (derived from the pedestrian) and hip-hop (derived from African American popular culture).[57] Blending images of electronic music culture and rapping as well as Manuel Valls opening a glitzy *soirée* proclaiming France a land of *startuppers*, the film reminds us of Martin's remark that financial engineers can be seen together with extreme sports players, start-ups and 'moshers' as embodying a wider shared derivative logic.[58] For Martin, these are all forms of risk-generating activity based around lateral decentralised movement involving a group taking some kind of ruin and using it as a scene for self-production and self-representation.[59] Such a statement, I would argue, is a good description of what Bareyre does with *L'Époque*. The Place de la République is not a 'ruin' in the sense of an abandoned or dilapidated space, but in Rose's speech the ideals monumentalised there are in a state of disrepair. In the montage, shots of the Marianne are used as counterpoints to those of the goings-on in the square below. The relation between these two sets of images is not straightforward. Nonetheless, we might suggest that they form a configuration in which the Marianne's gesture of holding aloft the republican ideals serves to propose them as an inheritance to be interpreted and used, while the framing of her somewhat inscrutable expression offers the exigency that they be carried forward or derived.[60]

Later in the film, riot police arrive at the Place, where there has been a demonstration. A montage shows the aftermath: taped broken windows, a smashed ATM machine (Figure 6.3), its card reader blinking green, and a broken window of an LCL bank branch on the nearby rue de Turenne. Police sirens can be heard. Rose examines the damage to a McDonald's window, gesturing to the man inside that she is only looking. He offers a gesture of solidarity in return and she laughs. While she will also address issues of identity and equality, Rose's question 'What is money?' is also Hanna's question. While the various interviewees in the film struggling to find meaningful work suggest that it is not just the ideals of the Republic but also the economy that is in 'ruins', the montage here concentrates this sense in the image of a broken, blinking ATM screen. The ATM machine is – like *le boiteux*'s stock tracker, Kerviel's trading terminal and Maris's gambling machine – a monetary audiovisual medium, a *ploutéidoscope*.

Figure 6.3 *L'Époque* (Matthieu Bareyre, 2018) © BAC Films.

We may be reminded of walking through the 'valeurs' ('values') rooms of the *Supermarché des images*, in which ATMs are the subject of two exhibits: firstly, the artist Sophie Calle's installation *Cash Machine* (1991–2003), featuring a wall of black-and-white prints of CCTV footage of users at a cash machine (which Calle obtained from an American bank in the 1990s), and accompanied by a video work, *Unfinished* (1998), in which Calle recounts how she struggled to complete her project; and, secondly, a trailer for Robert Bresson's *L'Argent* (1983), which consists of the door of an ATM machine opening and closing and money being withdrawn.[61] Midway through *Unfinished*, a sequence begins with an image of a 200 French franc banknote, emblazoned with the face of Gustave Eiffel, followed by nineteen images of the faces of the individuals withdrawing money each with different franc denominations over the image to form a parodic graphic match. While Calle's work shows how the cash machine can be the theatre for a range of private dramas between individuals and their account balance while simultaneously a structure of surveillance and control, and while Bresson's film can be seen as allegorising how exchange subtends filmicity in general, *L'Époque* points to the contemporary moment as one in which banks and cash machines are the targets of frustration and violent anger.[62] The shots of the smashed screens and windows each hang for up to 7 seconds in the montage, rhythmically and metonymically figuring halted iconomic circulation, like others in the French cinema of the financial crisis in which, as posited in the previous chapters, 2008 is more often alluded to than directly represented, but which is nonetheless a withdrawn, animating context.[63]

The Paris-based Catalan photographer Anna Malagrida's series of eleven photographs *Escaparates* ('Shop Windows', 2008–9) are images of shop windows in Paris that closed down in the aftermath of the financial crisis.[64] The photographs are close to life-size, taken frontally close to the windows with a heavy camera apparatus, creating for the viewer the sense of looking at a real shop window, but in this case the windows have been whitewashed or painted over to conceal the insides of the shops. Windows form a recurring motif across the whole of Malagrida's photographic work and play on effects on the surface of the glass as well as themes of voyeurism. Many of the images of this series are palimpsestic in that they show: the brushes of white paint (sometimes partially scraped off) on the surface of the glass; the Haussmannian façades and balconies of the street reflected in the window; stickers or advertisements stuck to the glass; and the dejected remainders inside the shop. In *Boulevard Sébastopol* (2008), for example, broad brushes of white paint cover the lower half of the image, while above we can see reflected balconies, trees and windows, another layer coming from the hanging lightbulbs behind the glass.[65] If in Bruneau's film the reflected details appear by chance and drift by on the surface of office building walls, in Malagrida's images they are sedimented. Part of what she is photographing in this example, then, is the readymade painting made by a non-artist.[66] The whitewashed windows across the series sometimes have black strokes through them, suggestive of American abstract expressionist paintings, such as those by Cy Twombly or Franz Kline (see for example *Rue de Châteaudun* [2008] and *Rue du Théâtre* [2009]). Malagrida remarks of her photographs: 'Outside their urban context they take on the features of abstract paintings, while in reality they signal the financial crisis which struck Europe in the wake of the 2007–9 market crash.'[67] The artist thus states what we have seen earlier, that artistic responses to the financial crisis often take an abstract form. A subsequent series of photographs, *Los muros hablaron* (2011–13), showing the traces of washed-off graffiti and slogans on the walls and at the bases of pillars of banks and political institutions in Spain following the anti-austerity demonstrations of the Indignados movement, testify to her continuing interest in the fallout of the financial crisis.[68]

Malagrida recounts how the images arose from a practice of the *flâneuse*, wandering the streets of Paris – particularly around the 9th and 15th arrondissements, where she is based – during the period of economic unrest.[69] The organising principle of Malagrida's series are streets in which she finds herself, and the photographs are named after the streets on which they were taken. In this way, like other artists in this chapter, her practice draws on chance and the contingency of one's encounters when one physically puts oneself in public spaces, allowing her to read the epoch through, as it were, the writing on the wall. Focusing on Parisian shop windows, this series is partly influenced by the work of the fin-de-siècle photographer Eugène Atget (1857–1927). However, while Atget's work evokes the birth of twentieth-century consumerism, of walking around the city and looking in shop windows, *Escaparates* suggests rather the end of this epoch – not only because of the economic crisis, but also, as Malagrida suggests, because of the displacement of window shopping by online shopping mediated by computer screens.[70] In the era of Atget, Malagrida comments, the use of shop window displays changed the complexion and experience of the urban environment: Atget was interested in those windows, she says, 'comme un endroit qui fait rêver' ('as a dreamlike space').[71] While Malagrida's shop windows are not smashed by protestors like Bareyre's cash machine, nonetheless both images bespeak a cracked or faltering iconomy, a forced arrest of circulation during economic downturn. Yet Malagrida's images do not merely dream of waste and expenditure, but also open a space for contemplation, like *le boiteux*'s screen, and alternative modes of projection in the future.

Martin writes that 2008 marks the end of a 'dreamscape' which began with the emergence of derivatives in the 1970s and 1980s, and, in the wake of 2008, time is marked by precarity and the seeming cancellation of the future.[72] This became clear during the financial crisis as it came to affect ordinary people. As Elena Esposito writes:

> Businesses and families found no more money with which to finance their projects or consumption, to build the future. Society as a whole seemed to have no future available, and feared exposure to an unforeseeable and uncontrollable course of time without any tools or possibilities of initiative.[73]

As Hanna shows, the inability to 'project oneself' in the future is characteristic of the precarity of artists, yet as we saw in Chapter 4 this can also be the case for traders such as Kerviel.[74] It is thus a function of the general volatility of the contemporary financialised condition for all those who work in it. The wider stakes are political: tending to exhaust political action, the inability to project a future leads to either a horizon of insignificance in which there is no point in aiming for anything or otherwise unrealisable, utopian goals.[75] As a technology for managing the future in the present, derivatives in one sense increase the availability of the future by increasing liquidity, but they are also used to control the future, to 'de-futurize' it, thus limiting our possibilities and yet paradoxically making it more chaotic and unpredictable.[76] It is in this way that Cédric Durand argues that finance 'appropriates' our future.[77] Esposito writes that deflation and dysphoria are the affects when there is seemingly no future left, as resulted from the austerity and disinvestment following the financial crisis, while euphoria comes from the feeling of living in a future that is just beginning.[78]

The works in this chapter demonstrate Martin's point that it is the social surplus of nonknowledge which needs to be mobilised in order to reconstruct economic futures. In Hanna's, Bruneau's and Bareyre's works, this is released by inviting 'ordinary' people to reflect on their economic condition. What thinkers such as Beller, Citton, Feher and Martin try to formulate in intellectual terms, all four works in this chapter gesture towards through aesthetic forms: that is, they all refashion the derivative condition with a view to a freer conception of the future. What *Argent* and *L'Époque* in particular show is that society is rich with an overflowing abundance of people and projects that could be funded and contributions that could be better valorised. In simpler terms, the works show there are too many people who have things to offer for whom the economy is not working. It is thus that we can interpret a comparison with cinema made by a writer on derivatives (and a former trader): 'From the continuous film of time, the derivative cuts out and enframes a particular interval – an interval that presents itself as a *forthcoming.*'[79] That is, these works allow us to grasp how other possible futures could be created in the present.

Notes

1. Christophe Hanna, *Argent* (Paris: Éditions Amsterdam, 2018).
2. See for example the remarks on public readings, ibid. p. 10.
3. See for example ibid. pp. 93–4, p. 142, pp. 147–9, p. 232.
4. Ibid. p. 16.
5. Ibid. p. 51.
6. Ibid. p. 206.
7. Nathalie Wourm, *Poètes français du 21ème siècle: Entretiens* (Leiden: Brill Rodopi, 2017).
8. Martin, *Knowledge LTD*, p. 67.
9. See Hanna, *Argent*, p. 16 for the percentages.
10. Ibid. p. 67.
11. For example ibid. p. 229.
12. Ibid. p. 128.
13. Ibid. p. 72, p. 13.
14. See https://evalge.hypotheses.org/484 and https://evalge.hypotheses.org/1255 (both last accessed 16 August 2021).
15. *L'Argent* can be found in Christophe Tarkos, *Écrits poétiques* (Paris: P.O.L., 2008). For a discussion of this text, see Alain Farah, '*L'Argent* de Christophe Tarkos, un poème à gages', in Emmanuel Bouju (ed.), *L'Engagement littéraire* (Rennes: Presses Universitaires de Rennes, 2005), pp. 153–63. Doubtless another intertext, situating the reflection within a longer history, would be Zola's *L'Argent* (1891), referenced in Hanna, *Argent*, p. 72.
16. Hanna, *Argent*, p. 14. Compare pp. 54–5.
17. Ibid. p. 19.
18. Ibid. p. 19.
19. Ibid. p. 72. See also Hanna, 'La Fiction comme institutionnalisation'.
20. Hanna, *Argent*, p. 203.
21. Ibid. p. 133.
22. Discussion between Christophe Hanna and Pierre Zaoui, 'Lire l'argent?', Université Paris Diderot, 27 February 2020.
23. Hanna, *Argent*, p. 182.
24. Ibid. p. 182.
25. Christophe Hanna, *Poésie action directe* (Romainville: Éditions Al Dante, 2003), pp. 66–70, pp. 91–103. On the notion of *dispositif*, see also Hanna, *Nos dispositifs poétiques* and Olivier Quintyn, *Dispositifs/Dislocations* (Marseille: Al Dante, 2007).
26. On the politics of Hanna's theory, see Nathalie Wourm, 'Poetic Sabotage and the Control Society: Christophe Hanna, Nathalie Quintane, Jean-Marie Gleize', *Revue critique de fixxion française contemporaine*, 20 (2020), 76–86 and Gabriel Proulx, 'Critique virale et genre trafiqué dans *Valérie par Valérie* par La Rédaction', *Nottingham French Studies*, 59: 1 (2020), 51–66.
27. Michel Feher, 'Tous notables! De la recherche du profit à la quête du crédit', talk given at the *journée d'étude* 'Évaluation générale: L'Agence de Notation

28. Frederik Tygstrup, 'Speculation and the End of Fiction', *Paragrana*, 25: 2 (2016), 97–111 (p. 107, p. 109).
29. Yves Citton, '*Argent* sans prix – à propos du nouveau livre de Christophe Hanna', *AOC*, 3 December 2018, aoc.media/critique/2018/12/03/argent-prix-a-propos-nouveau-livre-de-christophe-hanna/ (last accessed 16 August 2021).
30. Ibid. On the term *ovni*, see Hanna, *Nos dispositifs poétiques*, p. 1.
31. Hanna, *Argent*, pp. 64–5.
32. The film was inspired by Charlotte Beradt, *The Third Reich of Dreams: The Nightmares of a Nation 1933–1939*, trans. Adriane Gottwald (Wellingborough: The Aquarian Press, [1966] 1985), a book which gathers dreams from 1930s Berlin.
33. Recalling Chapter 1, this could be called *prolétarisation*.
34. On consciousness as a dark room, see Patrick ffrench, *Thinking Cinema with Proust* (Oxford: Legenda, 2018), pp. 8–49.
35. Transcription from 'Douze récits de rêves de travail', alteregofilms.be/images/pdf/ALT-REVER-Dossier-reve-web-02.pdf (last accessed 16 August 2021).
36. Translation taken from DVD subtitles.
37. In the document with the transcriptions of the dreams, this dreamer is simply identified as a public sector worker.
38. Lane, *Republican Citizens, Precarious Subjects*. The locus classicus on *souffrance au travail* is Christophe Dejours, *Souffrance en France* (Paris: Seuil, 1998). See also the references in given in Chapter 4 concerning suicide.
39. Jeremy Lane and Sarah Waters, 'Work in Crisis: Film, Fiction and Theory', in Jeremy Lane and Sarah Waters (eds), 'Work in Crisis', *Modern & Contemporary France*, 26: 3 (2018), 225–32 (p. 225).
40. Presentation at Cinéma du réel festival, Sorbonne Nouvelle, 26 March 2018. Bruneau previously co-directed *Ils ne mouraient pas tous mais tous étaient frappés* (2006), which also uses testimony. On the stakes of testimony in documentary film, see Martin Goutte, 'Notes sur le(s) geste(s) du témoignage documentaire', in Véronique Campan, Marie Martin and Sylvie Rollet (eds), *Qu'est-ce qu'un geste politique au cinéma?* (Rennes: Presses Universitaires de Rennes, 2019), pp. 165–75.
41. Jappe, *Crédit à mort*, pp. 96–7. Jappe rehearses some of these arguments in his appearance (speaking French) in the Portuguese film about the financial crisis, *The Nothing Factory* (Pedro Pinho, 2017). Jappe's key statement of the critique of value is *Les Aventures de la marchandise: Pour une critique de la valeur*, new edn (Paris: La Découverte, 2017).
42. Esposito, *The Future of Futures*, p. 179.
43. The images of buildings may recall the photography of Jean-Pierre Attal.
44. *Rêver sous le capitalisme* Dossier de presse/Livret DVD, p. 16, alteregofilms.be/images/pdf/ALT-REVER-Livret-DVD-WEB.pdf (last accessed 16 August 2021).

On apparitions in cinema, see Jacques Aumont, 'Le cinéma, un art d'apparition', *Les Carnets du BAL*, 4 (2013), 86–103.
45. Angelos Koutsourakis, 'The Resurgence of Modernism and its Critique of Liberalism in the Cinema of Crisis', in Thomas Austin and Angelos Koutsourakis (eds), *Cinema of Crisis: Film and Contemporary Europe* (Edinburgh: Edinburgh University Press, 2020), pp. 60–75.
46. *Rêver sous le capitalisme* Dossier de presse, p. 10.
47. Josh Cohen, *Not Working: Why We Have to Stop* (London: Granta, 2018), p. xxxvii.
48. 'Une des origines, c'était l'envie de filmer la sortie du travail' – *L'Époque* Dossier de presse, p. 7, https://medias.unifrance.org/medias/155/245/193947/presse/l-epoque-dossier-de-presse-francais.pdf (last accessed 16 August 2021).
49. Bénédicte Prot, 'Locarno 2018: Filmmakers of the Present: Matthieu Bareyre', Cineuropa (2018), cineuropa.org/en/interview/358346/ (last accessed 16 August 2021).
50. One might compare Sylvain George's *Paris est une fête* (2017).
51. See *Rêver sous le capitalisme* Dossier de presse, p. 28 and *L'Époque* Dossier de presse, p. 12.
52. Romain Lefebvre, '*L'Époque*, Matthieu Bareyre: Le feu qui couve', *Débordements* (April 2019), debordements.fr/L-epoque-Matthieu-Bareyre (last accessed 16 August 2021).
53. Stiegler, *De la misère symbolique*.
54. *L'Époque* is Bareyre's first feature-length film, but his first film, the medium-length *Nocturnes* (2015), is similarly sensitive to the mediatisation of contemporary experience.
55. Bareyre has announced that his next film, *La Vie en Rose*, will be a 'sort of biopic' of Rose – Mathieu Mallard, 'Rencontre avec Matthieu Bareyre, partie 3' (2019), retro-hd.com/documents/interviews/227-rencontre-avec-matthieu-bareyre-partie-3-le-caillou-dans-la-chaussure.html (last accessed 16 August 2021).
56. The film can here be usefully paired with Mariana Otero's *L'Assemblée* (2017).
57. Bareyre describes something like a derivative logic when he uses the metaphor of the dance to evoke 'the general movement' of his film: 'Il s'agissait aussi de faire communiquer ce qui est d'habitude séparé, que cela circule. On n'est jamais uniquement ivre, uniquement militant, uniquement sérieux. Il n'y a pas de séparation, on n'est pas des catégories, on n'est pas des genres. [. . .] Moi j'aime bien mélanger, montrer que les choses elles sont toujours tissées ensemble. [. . .] On n'est jamais purement dans la danse, la frivolité, tout est teinté. On ne peut pas être toujours léger ou toujours lourd. La danse est traversée par la pesanteur, et inversement. C'est le mouvement général du film' ('It was also about communicating that which is normally separated, to make this circulate. You are never *only* drunk, *only* militant, *only* serious. There is no separation, we're not categories or types. [. . .] I like mixing things up, showing that things are always woven together. [. . .] You are never purely in the dance, the frivolity, everything is always tainted. You can't always be light or always heavy. The dance is traversed

by heaviness, and vice versa. This is the general movement of the film'). Romain Lefebvre and Raphaël Nieuwjaer, 'Filmer l'espace public: Conversation potentielle avec Les Scotcheuses, Mariana Otero et Matthieu Bareyre', *Débordements*, 1 (2019), 200–37.
58. Martin, *Knowledge LTD*, p. 75.
59. Ibid. p. 206.
60. On how meaning is created by statues in film, see Vinzenz Hediger, 'The Ephemeral Cathedral: Bodies of Stone and Configurations of Film', in Alessandra Violi, Barbara Grespi, Andrea Pinotti and Pietro Conti (eds), *Bodies of Stone in the Media, Visual Culture and the Arts* (Amsterdam: Amsterdam University Press, 2020), pp. 105–25.
61. On *Cash Machine*, see Szendy et al. (eds), *Le Supermarché des images*, pp. 210–11; for a discussion, see Edward Welch, 'Stars of CCTV: Technology, Visibility and Identity in the Work of Sophie Calle and Annie Ernaux', *Nottingham French Studies*, 48: 2 (2009), 55–67. On the Bresson trailer, see Szendy et al. (eds), *Le Supermarché des images*, pp. 234–5.
62. Szendy, *Le Supermarché du visible*, pp. 29–31/ *The Supermarket of the Visible*, pp. 15–16.
63. A further example is *Bricks* (2017), a documentary by the CNRS sociologist Quentin Ravelli about the collapse of the housing bubble in Spain following the 2008 crisis. The film plays visually on the various meanings of 'brick' (surplus physical bricks to be destroyed, but also as a metonymy for a corrupt housing system) to show how the crisis aftershocks tore people from their homes as had happened in the USA. See also the book that accompanies the film, published in the same series as *Argent*: Quentin Ravelli, *Les Briques Rouges: Dettes, logement et luttes sociales en Espagne* (Paris: Éditions Amsterdam, 2017).
64. The images can be seen in Anna Malagrida, *Anna Malagrida: 21 mayo–1 agosto 2010* (Madrid: Fundación Mapfre, 2010), pp. 152–73 and on the artist's website, http://annamalagrida.com/home/escaparates-2008-2009/ (last accessed 16 August 2021).
65. Malagrida, *Anna Malagrida*, p. 165.
66. Ibid. p. 131.
67. 'A Conversation with Anna Malagrida, Carte Blanche PMU 2016', *L'œil de la photographie* (2016), loeildelaphotographie.com/en/2016/07/12/article/159914256/rencontre-avec-anna-malagrida-carte-blanche-pmu-2016/ (last accessed 16 August 2021).
68. See http://annamalagrida.com/home/los-muros-hablaron-2011-2013/ (last accessed 16 August 2021).
69. Interview with the artist, Le Terminus Balard, Paris 75015, 16 November 2017.
70. Ibid.
71. Ibid.
72. Martin, *Knowledge LTD*, p. 210.
73. Esposito, *The Future of Futures*, p. 178.

74. A similar point is made in Marc Crépon, 'Precarity: The Conditions of Labor and Employment', trans. D. J. S. Cross and Tyler M. Williams, *Diacritics*, 47: 1 (2019), 80–95.
75. Revault D'Allonnes, *La Crise sans fin*, p. 131.
76. Esposito, *The Future of Futures*, p. 122, p. 181.
77. Durand, *Le Capital fictif*.
78. Esposito, *The Future of Futures*, p. 184.
79. LiPuma, *The Social Life of Financial Derivatives*, p. 38.

Conclusion: Ambivalences of the Derivative

Ten years on from the crash, Lordon cautions his activist readers against the dead end of the 'anti-political' philosophy of *vivre sans* ('living without'): that is, it is not possible to 'leave' the economy, because 'economy' means the division of labour and the social relations of our material reproduction.[1] For him, there is nothing inevitable about this division of labour being based around markets or the capitalist employment relation, and while it will take a long time to overcome these forms, it is always possible to 'faire mieux' ('do better').[2] For several of the thinkers discussed in Chapter 3, this requires grasping derivatives and financial technologies. The use of the derivative as a concept in this study is not to endorse current political economic conditions; rather, it aims to gesture to how the reimagining of the derivative carried out by French artists and intellectuals shows the potentially socially productive role of the humanities in the reconstruction of our post-crash world. Literary and film theory are appropriate modes for engaging with financial derivatives because they can fictionalise and hence remake them, as Hanna might say.[3] Literature, says Citton, does not offer 'solutions' to social and economic issues, but rather different ways of thinking about problems, and this is also true more generally of film and literary theory.[4] In this sense, they are part of what sociologists see as a wider cultural contestation of how the financial crisis and attendant concepts are 'imagined'.[5] Thinking the derivative from the point of view of texts and images may help generate agency vis-à-vis finance itself; in this sense, Beller's speculative engagement with blockchain technologies to find new ways of funding projects and creating the future – of imagining 'what could potentially be the beauty of our mutual indebtedness' – would merely be the extension of Hanna's literary experiments in *Argent*.[6]

I have argued in this book that, for several of the thinkers studied, part of the importance of the 2008 financial crisis is that it is the moment in which the contemporary configuration of media and economic processes is crystallised in a vision of derivative images. It is a moment within, as Beller shows, a much longer history of the relation between images and economy; it is also thus that the history of derivatives, as Szendy puts it, 'began a long time ago; and it is yet to come'.[7] As Szendy also says, referring back to Deleuze's famous

1986 letter to Serge Daney, a world submerged in images is one of data and control – which in turn, as we have seen, is one whose 'texture' is the derivative.[8] Resisting this control, Szendy remarks to Dork Zabunyan, is however something we do not yet know how to do.[9] Zabunyan is himself concerned with this question and approves of Szendy's work because it offers 'un réel antidote aux réflexions catastrophistes sur les effets présumés d'un visible en surrégime' ('an antidote to the pessimistic observations about the presumed effects of a visible world in overdrive').[10] The letter to Daney was of course itself a study in ambivalence at a time of increasing saturation of images in the world with the expansion of television during the 1980s.[11] Even if we do not know how to resist, for Zabunyan the value of Szendy's work is 'd'esquisser une voix [sic] de sortie critique, ou de dessiner un pas de côté qui nous laisse entrevoir la possibilité d'autre chose' ('to outline a critique that provides a way out, or to hint at an evasive manoeuvre that allows us to glimpse an alternative').[12] As I have suggested, this is what several of the works discussed in this book do. In that sense, if a prescription is needed in view of this ocean of derivative images, the strategy should be one of 'immersion' in it, as an artist or amateur, in order to transform it as the raw material for new work.[13]

Both taking risks and seeking to construct security from risk are co-constitutive human instincts – but as Anne Dufourmantelle shows, risk cannot be escaped and nor should we seek to escape it.[14] It is because of the volatility generated by the human taste for risk – and arguably even more by the desire to control it – that we arrived in a securitised world of risk management systems. In 2008, the belief that it was possible to eliminate risk through financial technology was shown to be disastrous; human beings could never be 'masters of the universe'. The derivative is a potentially generative trope for the humanities because it cuts to the heart of human ambivalence about the economic. That is, it emblematises how there may be something ineluctable in how humans exploit each other as commodities, yet it also offers itself as a tool in the possible construction of new forms of 'we' in which this tendency might be managed more equitably, or at least in a different way.[15] The derivative is equivalent to the 'peut-être' in the formulation of the psyche as 'perhaps' a market. Another way of expressing this conceptual arbitrage would be to say that derivatives and derivative images are, in Stiegler's terms, pharmacological: potentially the cure as well as the poison, if we can apply ourselves to making them so, within the context of a wider political project. Leslie Hill writes that literature is born of the incalculable and of radical indecision.[16] Criticism, however, must make decisions, even if they are always provisional, are always hedges.[17] Literary texts and films, like financial derivatives, are technologies to help us manage and live with the radical uncertainty and nonknowledge of human experience. If in the wake of the crisis finance had 'confiscated' our future, the future-generating capacity of fiction may help us remake it.[18]

Notes

1. Lordon, *Vivre sans?*, p. 43, p. 225.
2. Ibid. pp. 243–5.
3. Christophe Hanna, 'Pourquoi théorisons-nous (encore)?', in Dominiq Jenvrey, *Théorie du fictionnaire* (Paris: Questions Théoriques, 2011), pp. i–xxiv.
4. Yves Citton, *La Grande table idées*, France Culture, 28 June 2021, franceculture.fr/emissions/la-grande-table-idees/la-grande-table-idees-2nde-partie-emission-du-lundi-28-juin-2021 (last accessed 16 August 2021).
5. Komporozos-Athanasiou and Fotaki, 'The Imaginary Constitution of Financial Crises'. Lordon makes a comparable point when he argues that the struggle over what comes after capitalism will involve a 'combat d'*images*' ('a struggle of *images*') and inviting images of alternative futures will be required. Lordon, *Figures du communisme*, p. 16.
6. Beller, *The World Computer*, p. 218.
7. Szendy, 'Derivative Shakespeare', p. 73.
8. Szendy and Zabunyan, 'Ausculter les images', pp. 10–11.
9. Ibid. p. 11.
10. Ibid. p. 1.
11. Gilles Deleuze, 'Lettre à Serge Daney: Optimisme, pessimisme et voyage', in Serge Daney, *Ciné journal 1981–1986* (Paris: Cahiers du cinéma, 1986), pp. 5–13.
12. Szendy and Zabunyan, 'Ausculter les images', p. 1.
13. Dork Zabunyan, *Fictions de Trump: Puissances des images et exercices du pouvoir* (Paris: Le Point du Jour, 2020), pp. 109–13; Crowley, 'The Artist and the Amateur', pp. 131–3.
14. Dufourmantelle, *Éloge du risque*.
15. Stiegler, *De la misère symbolique*.
16. Hill, *Radical Indecision*, p. 24. See also p. 66, p. 334.
17. Ibid. pp. 53–4.
18. Dominiq Jenvrey, *Théorie du fictionnaire* (Paris: Questions Théoriques, 2011), p. 4.

Select Bibliography

Amable, Bruno, *Structural Crisis and Institutional Change in Modern Capitalism: French Capitalism in Transition* (Oxford: Oxford University Press, 2017).
Appadurai, Arjun, *Banking on Words: The Failure of Language in the Age of Derivative Finance* (Chicago: University of Chicago Press, 2015).
Apter, Emily and Martin Crowley, 'Economies of Existence', *Diacritics*, 47: 1 (2019), 3–15.
Ayache, Elie, *The Blank Swan: The End of Probability* (Chichester: Wiley, 2010).
—— 'On Black-Scholes', in Benjamin Lee and Randy Martin (eds), *Derivatives and the Wealth of Societies* (Chicago: University of Chicago Press, 2016), pp. 240–51.
Bargenda, Angela, *La Communication visuelle dans le secteur bancaire européen: L'Esthétique de la finance* (Paris: L'Harmattan, 2014).
—— 'Sense-Making in Financial Communication: Semiotic Vectors and Iconographic Strategies in Banking Advertising', *Studies in Communication Sciences*, 15 (2015), 93–102.
Beller, Jonathan, *The Cinematic Mode of Production: Attention Economy and the Society of the Spectacle* (Lebanon, NH: University Press of New England, 2006).
—— 'The Cinematic Program', *La Furia Umana*, 23 (2016), lafuriaumana.it/index.php/56-archive/lfu-23/350-jonathan-beller-the-cinematic-program (last accessed 16 August 2021).
—— 'The Derivative Condition' (2018), youtube.com/watch?v=D29DjMvMAq0 (last accessed 16 August 2021).
—— 'Economic Media: Crypto and the Myth of Total Liquidity', *Australian Humanities Review*, 66 (May 2020), 215–25.
—— *The Message is Murder: Substrates of Computational Capital* (London: Pluto Press, 2018).
—— *The World Computer: Derivative Conditions of Racial Capitalism* (Durham, NC; London: Duke University Press, 2021).
La Berge, Leigh Claire, 'The Rules of Abstraction: Methods and Discourses of Finance', *Radical History Review*, 118 (Winter 2014), 93–112.
Brunton, Finn, *Digital Cash: The Unknown History of the Anarchists, Utopians, and Technologists Who Built Cryptocurrency* (Princeton: Princeton University Press, 2019).
Bryan, Dick and Michael Rafferty, *Capitalism with Derivatives: A Political Economy of Financial Derivatives, Capital and Class* (Basingstoke: Palgrave Macmillan, 2006).
Citton, Yves, '*Argent* sans prix – à propos du nouveau livre de Christophe Hanna', *AOC*, 3 December 2018, aoc.media/critique/2018/12/03/argent-prix-a-propos-nouveau-livre-de-christophe-hanna/ (last accessed 16 August 2021).
—— *Médiarchie* (Paris: Seuil, 2017).
—— 'Postface à *Post-histoire*', in Vilém Flusser, *Post-histoire* (Paris: T&P Work UNit, 2019), pp. 183–200.

—— 'Post-scriptum sur les sociétés de recherche-création', in Erin Manning and Brian Massumi, *Pensée en acte: Vingt propositions sur la recherche-création* (Dijon: Presses du réel, 2018), pp. 97–124.

—— *Pour une écologie de l'attention* (Paris: Seuil, 2014).

—— 'Vers un horizon post-capitaliste des dérives financières?', *Multitudes*, 71 (2018), 33–44.

Committee on Oversight and Government Reform, 'The Financial Crisis and the Role of Federal Regulators', Government Publishing Office, U.S. Congress House of Representatives, 23 October 2008; transcript: https://www.gpo.gov/fdsys/pkg/CHRG-110hhrg55764/pdf/CHRG-110hhrg55764.pdf; recording: https://archive.org/details/gov.house.ogr.20081023_hrs15REF2154 (both last accessed 16 August 2021).

Constantopoulou, Christiana (ed.), *Récits de la crise: Mythes et réalités de la société contemporaine* (Paris: L'Harmattan, 2017).

Creton, Laurent, *Économie du cinéma: Perspectives stratégiques*, 6th edn (Malakoff: Armand Colin, 2020).

—— 'Godard et l'art stratégique de la redéfinition du métier', in Gilles Delavaud, Jean-Pierre Esquenazi and Marie-Françoise Grange (eds), *Godard et le métier d'artiste* (Paris: L'Harmattan, 2001), pp. 315–34.

Crosthwaite, Paul, 'Blood on the Trading Floor: Waste, Sacrifice and Death in Financial Crises', *Angelaki: Journal of the Theoretical Humanities*, 15: 2 (2010), 3–18.

Davis, Gerald F., *Managed by the Markets: How Finance Re-shaped America* (Oxford: Oxford University Press, 2009).

Dufourmantelle, Anne, *Éloge du risque* (Paris: Éditions Payot & Rivages, [2011] 2014).

Durand, Cédric, *Le Capital fictif: Comment la finance s'approprie notre avenir* (Paris: Les Prairies ordinaires, 2014); trans. by David Broder as *Fictitious Capital: How Finance is Appropriating Our Future* (London: Verso, 2017).

Esposito, Elena, *The Future of Futures: The Time of Money in Financing and Society* (Cheltenham: Edward Elgar, [2009] 2011).

Feher, Michel, *Le Temps des investis: Essai sur la nouvelle question sociale* (Paris: Éditions La Découverte, 2017); trans. by Gregory Elliott as *Rated Agency: Investee Politics in a Speculative Age* (New York: Zone Books, 2018).

Flusser, Vilém, *Post-histoire* (Paris: T&P Work UNit, 2019).

—— *Towards a Philosophy of Photography*, trans. Anthony Mathews (London: Reaktion Books, 2000).

Gabrysiak, Diane and Phil Powrie (eds), 'Money: now you see it now you don't', special issue of *Studies in French Cinema*, 15: 3 (2015), 197–206.

Gales, Michelle and Claudie Jouandon (eds), 'Crises en thème: Filmer l'économie', *La Revue Documentaires*, 25 (2014).

Godechot, Olivier, *Les Traders: Essai de sociologie des marchés financiers* (Paris: La Découverte, [2001] 2005).

Grossman, Evelyne, *La Créativité de la crise* (Paris: Les Éditions de Minuit, 2020).

Hanna, Christophe, *Argent* (Paris: Éditions Amsterdam, 2018).

—— 'La Fiction comme institutionnalisation', preface to Dominiq Jenvrey, *Le Cas Betty Hill: Une introduction à la psychologie prédictive* (Paris: Questions Théoriques, 2015), pp. i–x.

—— *Nos dispositifs poétiques* (Paris: Questions Théoriques, 2010).

—— 'Pourquoi théorisons-nous (encore)?', in Dominiq Jenvrey, *Théorie du fictionnaire* (Paris: Questions Théoriques, 2011), pp. i–xxiv.

Hill, Leslie, *Radical Indecision: Barthes, Blanchot, Derrida, and the Future of Criticism* (Notre Dame, IN: University of Notre Dame Press, 2010).

Hull, John C., *Options, Futures, and Other Derivatives*, 9th edn (Harlow: Pearson, 2015).
Jameson, Fredric, 'Culture and Finance Capital', in *The Cultural Turn: Selected Writings on the Postmodern 1983–1998* (London: Verso, 1998), pp. 136–61.
Jappe, Anselm, *Crédit à mort: La Décomposition du capitalisme et ses critiques* (Paris: Éditions Lignes, 2011); trans. by Alastair Hemmens as *The Writing on the Wall: The Decomposition of Capitalism and its Critics* (Ropley: Zero Books, 2017).
Kerviel, Jérôme, *L'Engrenage: Mémoires d'un trader* (Paris: Flammarion, 2010).
Keynes, John Maynard, *The Essential Keynes*, ed. Robert Skidelsky (London: Penguin, 2015).
King, Alasdair, 'Documenting Financial Performativity: Film Aesthetics and Financial Crisis', *Journal of Cultural Economy*, 9: 6 (2016), 555–69.
—— 'Film and the Financial City', *Studies in European Cinema*, 14: 1 (2017), 7–21.
Komporozos-Athanasiou, Aris and Marianna Fotaki, 'The Imaginary Constitution of Financial Crises', *The Sociological Review*, 68: 5 (2020), 932–47.
Lane, Jeremy, *Republican Citizens, Precarious Subjects: Representations of Work in Post-Fordist France* (Liverpool: Liverpool University Press, 2020).
Lane, Jeremy and Sarah Waters (eds), 'Work in Crisis', *Modern & Contemporary France*, 26: 3 (2018).
Larnaudie, Mathieu, *Les Effondrés* (Arles: Actes Sud, 2010).
de Larosière, Jacques et al., *The High-Level Group on Financial Supervision in the EU*, Brussels (2009), ec.europa.eu/economy_finance/publications/pages/publication14527_en.pdf (last accessed 16 August 2021).
Lee, Benjamin and Randy Martin (eds), *Derivatives and the Wealth of Societies* (Chicago: University of Chicago Press, 2016).
Lépinay, Vincent Antonin, *Codes of Finance: Engineering Derivatives in a Global Bank* (Princeton: Princeton University Press, 2011).
LiPuma, Edward, *The Social Life of Financial Derivatives: Markets, Risk, and Time* (Durham, NC; London: Duke University Press, 2017).
Lordon, Frédéric, *Les Affects de la politique* (Paris: Seuil, 2016).
—— *Capitalisme, désir et servitude: Marx et Spinoza* (Paris: La Fabrique éditions, 2010); trans. by Gabriel Ash as *Willing Slaves of Capital: Marx and Spinoza on Desire* (London: Verso, 2014).
—— *La Condition anarchique: Affects et institutions de la valeur* (Paris: Seuil, 2018).
—— *La Crise de trop: Reconstruction d'un monde failli* (Paris: Fayard, 2009).
—— *D'un retournement l'autre: Comédie sérieuse sur la crise financière: En quatre actes et en alexandrins* (Paris: Seuil, 2011).
—— *Figures du communisme* (Paris: La Fabrique éditions, 2021).
—— 'Un film d'action directe', *Le Monde diplomatique*, February 2016, p. 28.
—— *Jusqu'à quand? Pour en finir avec les crises financières* (Paris: Raisons d'agir, 2008).
—— *La Malfaçon: Monnaie européenne et souveraineté démocratique* (Paris: Les Liens qui libèrent, 2014).
—— *La Société des affects* (Paris: Seuil, 2013).
—— *Vivre sans? Institutions, police, travail, argent...* (Paris: La Fabrique éditions, 2019).
MacKenzie, Donald, *An Engine, Not a Camera: How Financial Models Shape Markets* (Cambridge, MA: MIT Press, 2006).
Malagrida, Anna, *Anna Malagrida: 21 mayo–1 agosto 2010* (Madrid: Fundación Mapfre, 2010).
Malik, Suhail, 'The Ontology of Finance: Price, Power and the Arkhéderivative', in Robin Mackay (ed.), *Collapse 8: Casino Real* (Falmouth: Urbanomic, 2014), pp. 629–811.

Mallaby, Sebastian, *The Man Who Knew: The Life & Times of Alan Greenspan* (London: Penguin, 2016).

Maris, Bernard, *Journal d'un économiste en crise* (Paris: Les Échappés-Charlie Hebdo, 2013).

Maris, Bernard and Gilles Dostaler, *Capitalisme et pulsion de mort* (Paris: Albin Michel, 2009).

Martin, Randy, *Knowledge Ltd: Toward a Social Logic of the Derivative* (Philadelphia: Temple University Press, 2015).

Meissner, Miriam, *Narrating the Global Financial Crisis: Urban Imaginaries and the Politics of Myth* (Basingstoke; New York: Palgrave Macmillan, 2017).

Mondzain, Marie-José, *Image, icône, économie: Les Sources byzantines de l'imaginaire contemporain* (Paris: Seuil, 1996).

Morin, Edgar, *Pour une crisologie* (Paris: L'Herne, 2016).

Moullet, Luc, *Le Rebelle de King Vidor* (Crisnée: Yellow Now, 2009).

Multitudes, 'Abécédaire de la crise', *Multitudes*, 37–8 (Autumn 2009), 28–67, 144–67, 208–23, 260–83.

Nau, Frédéric, 'Candide au pays des subprimes', *Images de la culture*, 26 (December 2011), 48–51.

Orléan, André, *De l'euphorie à la panique: Penser la crise financière* (Paris: Éditions Rue d'Ulm, 2009).

O'Shaughnessy, Martin, 'Beyond Language and the Subject: Machinic Enslavement in Contemporary European Cinema', *Studies in European Cinema*, 16: 3 (2019), 197–217.

—— 'Putting the Dead to Work: Making Sense of Worker Suicide in Contemporary French and Francophone Belgian Film', *Studies in French Cinema*, 19: 4 (2019), 314–34.

Poujol, Patrice, *Online Film Production in China Using Blockchain and Smart Contracts: The Development of Collaborative Platforms for Emerging Creative Talents* (Cham: Springer, 2019).

Revault D'Allonnes, Myriam, *La Crise sans fin: Essai sur l'expérience moderne du temps* (Paris: Seuil, 2012).

Rey, Jean-Michel, *Le Temps du crédit* (Paris: Desclée de Brouwer, 2002).

Roche, Marc, *Histoire secrète d'un krach qui dure* (Paris: Albin Michel, 2016).

Schleier, Merrill, *Skyscraper Cinema: Architecture and Gender in American Film* (Minneapolis: University of Minnesota Press, 2009).

Siety, Emmanuel, *Fictions d'images: Essai sur l'attribution de propriétés fictives aux images de films* (Rennes: Presses Universitaires de Rennes, 2009).

Société Réaliste, *Empire, State, Building* (Paris: Éditions Amsterdam, 2011).

Stiegler, Bernard, *Dans la disruption: Comment ne pas devenir fou?* (Paris: Les Liens qui libèrent, 2016).

—— *De la misère symbolique 1: L'Époque hyperindustrielle* (Paris: Galilée, 2004); trans. by Barnaby Norman as *Symbolic Misery, Volume 1: The Hyper-industrial Epoch* (Cambridge: Polity, 2014).

—— *L'Emploi est mort, vive le travail!* (Paris: Mille et une nuits, 2015).

—— *Qu'appelle-t-on panser?: L'Immense Régression* (Paris: Les Liens qui libèrent, 2018).

—— *La Société automatique 1. L'Avenir du travail* (Paris: Fayard, 2015); trans. by Daniel Ross as *Automatic Society, Volume 1: The Future of Work* (Cambridge: Polity, 2016).

Streeck, Wolfgang, *Buying Time: The Delayed Crisis of Democratic Capitalism*, 2nd edn, trans. Patrick Camiller and David Fernbach (London: Verso, [2014] 2017).

—— *How Will Capitalism End? Essays on a Failing System* (London: Verso, 2016).

Szendy, Peter, 'Derivative Shakespeare: *The Merchant of Venice* and Dividual Capitalism', *Diacritics*, 47: 1 (2019), 62–79.

—— *Le Supermarché du visible: Essai d'iconomie* (Paris: Les Éditions de Minuit, 2017); trans. by Jan Plug as *The Supermarket of the Visible: Toward a General Economy of Images* (New York: Fordham University Press, 2019).

—— *Tubes: La Philosophie dans le juke-box* (Paris: Les Éditions de Minuit, 2008); trans. by Will Bishop as *Hits: Philosophy in the Jukebox* (New York: Fordham University Press, 2012).

Szendy, Peter, Emmanuel Alloa and Marta Ponsa (eds), *Le Supermarché des images/The Supermarket of Images* (Paris: Gallimard/Jeu de Paume, 2020).

Szendy, Peter and Dork Zabunyan, 'Entretien: Ausculter les images', *Meeting Point*, 2 (2018), lemagazine.jeudepaume.org/2018/02/meeting-point-zabunyan-peter-szendy-fr/ (last accessed 16 August 2021).

Tooze, Adam, *Crashed: How a Decade of Financial Crises Changed the World* (London: Allen Lane, 2018).

Toscano, Alberto and Jeff Kinkle, *Cartographies of the Absolute* (Alresford: Zero Books, 2015).

Tygstrup, Fredrik, 'The Debt Chronotope', *differences: A Journal of Feminist Cultural Studies*, 31: 3 (2020), 29–47.

—— 'Speculation and the End of Fiction', *Paragrana*, 25: 2 (2016), 97–111.

Vogl, Joseph, *The Ascendancy of Finance*, trans. Simon Garnett (Cambridge, UK; Malden, MA: Polity, [2015] 2017).

—— *The Specter of Capital*, trans. Joachim Redner and Robert Savage (Stanford, CA: Stanford University Press, [2010] 2015).

Waters, Sarah, *Between Republic and Market: Globalization and Identity in Contemporary France* (London: Continuum, 2012).

—— 'Disappearing Bodies: The Workplace and Documentary Film in an Era of Pure Money', *French Cultural Studies*, 26: 3 (2015), 289–301.

—— *Suicide Voices: Labour Trauma in France* (Liverpool: Liverpool University Press, 2020).

Woll, Cornelia, *The Power of Inaction: Bank Bailouts in Comparison* (New York: Cornell University Press, 2014).

Select Filmography

L'An 2008 (Martin Le Chevallier, 2010)
Bricks (Quentin Ravelli, 2017)
Cleveland contre Wall Street (Jean-Stéphane Bron, 2010)
Clickworkers (Martin Le Chevallier, 2017)
Confessions financières (Lionel Bernardin, 2015)
L'Époque (Mathieu Bareyre, 2018)
Et que ça saute! (Jeanne Delafosse, 2013)
Film Catastrophe (Paul Grivas, 2018)
Film Socialisme (Jean-Luc Godard, 2010)
The Fountainhead (King Vidor, 1949)
The Fountainhead (Société Réaliste, 2010)
Le Grand Retournement (Gérard Mordillat, 2013)
L'Incomparable du pas comparable (Paul Grivas, 2019)
Maître du monde (Enrico Giordano, 2011)
Merci Patron! (François Ruffin, 2016)
La Mise à mort du travail (Jean-Robert Viallet, 2009)
Oncle Bernard: L'anti-leçon d'économie (Richard Brouillette, 2015)
L'Outsider (Christophe Barratier, 2016)
Rêver sous le capitalisme (Sophie Bruneau, 2017)

Index

affect, 6–7, 16, 22–30, 107, 172
Ayache, E., 8, 81–4

Bareyre, M., 11, 166–72, 175n
Bataille, G., 8, 61–2, 82, 122n
Beller, J., 8–9, 12n, 65–7, 70–7, 80, 83–4, 91n, 112, 172, 178
Bellour, R., 8, 69–70, 138
Blanchot, M., 70, 83
BNP Paribas, 6, 15–16, 30n, 74, 104
Bron, S-J., 32n, 117n
Bruneau, S., 11, 161–166, 170, 172

calque, 8, 55n, 76, 84, 114, 123n
central banks, 3, 16–17, 26, 42–3, 52, 60, 98, 105, 132, 134–5, 138
Le Chevallier, M., 67–8, 89n, 119n
Citton, Y., 8–9, 39, 63–6, 75–6, 84, 143, 160–1, 173, 178
Le Comité invisible, 28, 34n
crisis, 1–4, 6–7, 12n, 13n, 17–18, 22–4, 28–9, 37, 39–40, 45, 51–2, 54, 55n, 61–2, 67, 77, 82, 84, 109, 112, 126, 131–2, 164, 171–2, 178–9

Daney, S., 122, 179
Deleuze, G., 8, 62–5, 68, 74, 82, 126, 178

derivative images, 1, 3, 5, 7–8, 10, 12n, 21, 40, 49, 67, 68–76, 84, 102, 115, 133, 139, 143, 150, 156, 158–9, 178–9
Dufourmantelle, A., 83, 179
D'un retournement l'autre, 6–7, 15–30, 44, 112

Les Effondrés, 7, 9, 36–54, 112, 158
L'Époque, 11, 166–70, 172
Esposito, E., 172

Feher, M., 65–6, 73, 76, 159, 172
fiction, 4, 7, 21, 38, 45, 76, 114, 136, 160, 178, 180
Film Catastrophe, 10, 138, 143–50, 167
Film Socialisme, 10, 134–44, 146–9, 167
financial derivatives, 2, 5–11, 14n, 16, 18–21, 25, 41, 46, 59–67, 71–6, 81–2, 91n, 99–101, 104–5, 115, 127, 132–3, 156–7, 160–1, 168, 172, 178–9
Flusser, V., 75–6, 108, 148, 161
The Fountainhead (Société Réaliste), 10, 124–33, 139–40, 142, 150

Godard, J.-L., 10, 134–49
Le Grand Retournement, 6, 15–6, 18, 20–1, 25

Greenspan, A., 7, 36, 41–54, 60, 82, 108, 125–6
Grivas, P., 10, 143–50, 161
Grossman, E., 2, 82, 84

Hanna, C., 8, 11, 65, 76, 155–61, 169–72, 178

intermediality, 3, 5, 11, 66–70, 73, 76

Jappe, A., 164

Kerviel, J., 9, 96–115, 141, 143, 169, 172

Larnaudie, M., 7, 35–50, 52–4, 108–9, 158
Lordon, F., 3, 6–7, 15–35, 40, 44, 64–6, 78–9, 107, 109, 112, 178, 180

Macron, E., 27–9, 167
Malagrida, A., 11, 170–1
Malik, S., 85n
Mallarmé, S., 70, 83
Maris, B., 10, 135–44, 147–9, 158, 169
Martin, R., 5–6, 8, 59–65, 73, 75, 83–4, 85n, 148, 156, 168, 171–2
Marx, K., 6, 71, 77–8
Mordillat, G., 6, 16, 33n
Morin, E., 2

Nestler, G., 91n
nonknowledge, 8, 12, 59–62, 65, 73, 83, 166, 172, 179

L'Outsider, 9, 96–115

proletarianisation, 7, 50–4,

Rand, A., 10, 125–6, 128
Revault D'Allonnes, M., 2
Rêver sous le capitalisme, 11, 161–6
Rey, J.-M., 5

Sarkozy, N., 6–7, 16–17, 36, 55n
Société Générale, 9, 96–115, 116n, 119n, 121n
Société Réaliste, 10, 124–33
Spinoza, B., 6, 22–3, 29
Stiegler, B., 7, 49–54, 157, 167, 179
Szendy, P., 4, 8–9, 59, 63, 65–70, 72–3, 77–81, 84, 101, 114, 126, 128, 133, 139, 167, 178–9

Tarkos, C., 158
Tooze, A., 1, 16, 131–2
Toscano, A., 4–5, 149

Vidor, K., 10, 124–33

Zabunyan, D., 179

EU representative:
Easy Access System Europe
Mustamäe tee 50, 10621 Tallinn, Estonia
Gpsr.requests@easproject.com